Day Trips® from San Antonio and Austin

"If you're looking for a one- or two-day getaway but you're not
sure where to go, then Paris Permenter and John Bigley
may have just the ticket for you."
—*Hill Country News*

"If the idea of traveling Texas this summer appeals to you, but
you don't have a week or two to devote to wandering the farm-to-
market roads searching for interesting Lone Star
locales, there is a solution: day trips."
—*San Antonio Current*

"*Day Trips from San Antonio and Austin* will be useful
to visitors and new residents as well as folks
who have been in Central Texas for a while."
—*Austin American-Statesman*

"The value of any guidebook is its ease of use, and *Day Trips* is a
very user-friendly guide. *Day Trips* has its share of golden
nuggets. This guidebook is good for stashing in the car for those
spontaneous Sunday drives or when planning a vacation.
Next time family comes to visit, send them a copy of this book before they get here. It will make mom and dad want to spend at least
one day exploring Hill Country to find out why it was
voted best scenic drives."
—*Austin Chronicle*

"Your family loves to travel but you have limited time, energy,
and/or budget. Have we found the book
for you. *Day Trips*."
—*Austin Child*

Other books in the Shifra Stein Day Trips® Series

Shifra Stein's *Day Trips® from Baltimore*

Shifra Stein's *Day Trips® from Cincinnati*

Shifra Stein's *Day Trips® from Houston*

Shifra Stein's *Day Trips® from Kansas City*

Shrifa Stein's *Day Trips® from Nashville*

Shifra Stein's *Day Trips® from Phoenix, Tucson, and Flagstaff*

Shifra Stein's Day Trips® Series

Shifra Stein's
Day Trips®
from
San Antonio and Austin

Third Edition

Paris Permenter and John Bigley

The Globe Pequot Press

Old Saybrook, Connecticut

Cover and text design by Nancy Freeborn
Cover photograph copyright © 1996 (IMA) Kaorv Mikami/Photonica

Library of Congress Cataloging-in-Publication Data

Permenter, Paris.
  Shifra Stein's Day trips from San Antonio and Austin
        p.   cm. — (Shifra Stein's day trips America)
    Includes index.
    ISBN 0-7627-0134-X
    1. San Antonio Region (Tex.)—Tours. 2. Austin Region (Tex.)—
  Tours. I. Bigley, John. II. Stein, Shifra. III. Series.
  F394.S23P47 1997
  917.64'30463—dc21
                                                        97-4404
                                                        CIP

Manufactured in the United States of America
Third Edition/Third Printing

Contents

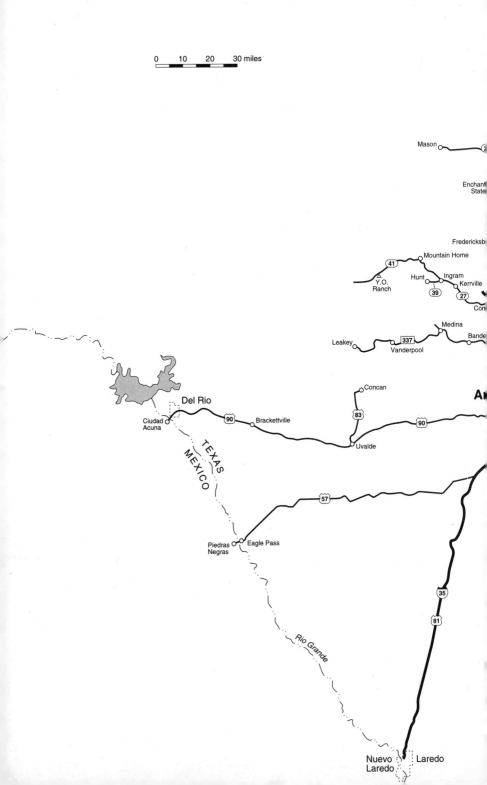

Preface

Most people have a mental image of Texas as miles of rugged, unciv-ilized land where the outlines of cattle and lonely windmills stretch above the horizon. But that's just one side of the Lone Star State, known as the "land of contrast." Texas also boasts high-tech cities, piney woods, sandy beaches, rolling hills, and fertile farmland—much of it within a two-hour drive of San Antonio and Austin.

The region covered in this book is as diverse as the more than thirty cultures who helped found the state. German, French, Mex-ican, Polish, and even Alsatian settlers brought their traditions to Texas in the 1800s. The influences of these pioneers are still ap-parent today in the varied festivals and ethnic foods that vacationers come here to enjoy.

The day trips within this book span terrain ranging from farm-land to rocky hills. This difference in topography is the result of an ancient earthquake that created the Balcones Fault, which runs north to south. The fault line, slightly west of I-35, forms the di-viding line between the eastern agricultural region and what is known as the Hill Country to the west.

Many of the attractions lie along the route taken by the 350,000 Winter Texans who flock here during the cooler months. So, whether you're heading for the Rio Grande Valley, the coast, or the Mexican border, you'll find a wealth of useful tips and information in this guide. Be sure to check the sections marked "Especially for Winter Texans." This will help you identify special services, festivals, or parks aimed at making you feel right at home.

You'll find that Texans are friendly folk who wave on country roads and nod as they pass you on the sidewalk. Talk to local citizens as you wind through the back roads for even more travel tips and a first-hand look at the varied cultures that make up the pieces of your journey.

Help Us Keep This Guide Up to Date

Every effort has been made by the authors and editors to make this guide as accurate and useful as possible. However, many things can change after a guide is published—establishments close, phone numbers change, hiking trails are rerouted, facilities come under new management, etc.

We would love to hear from you concerning your experiences with this guide and how you feel it could be make better and be kept up to date. While we may not be able to respond to all comments and suggestions, we'll take them to heart and we'll also make certain to share them with the authors. Please send your comments and suggestions to the following address:

The Globe Pequot Press
Reader Response/Editorial Department
P.O. Box 833
Old Saybrook, CT 06475

Or you may e-mail us at:

editorial@globe-pequot.com

Thanks for your input, and happy travels!

Texas Travel Tips

CARRY A ROAD MAP

Although we've included directions, it's best to carry a Texas road map as you travel. It's also advisable to carry a county map for a better look at farm-to-market (FM) and ranch roads (RR). You can get brochures on Texas attractions and a free copy of the "Texas State Travel Guide" from the Texas Department of Transportation, P.O. Box 5064, Austin, TX 78763-5064, or by calling (800) 452-9292. The guide is coded to a free Texas state map also provided by the Highway Department. These maps are also available from any of the Tourist Information Centers located on routes into Texas and at the Texas State Capitol in Austin. The Tourist Information Centers are open daily, except for Thanksgiving, Christmas, and New Year's Day.

The expansiveness of Texas sets it apart from other states. Note the scale of the map. With 266,807 square miles of land, Texas is the second largest state in the country. One inch on the state road map spans 23 miles.

Driving varies with terrain: The two-hour time limit that constitutes a "day trip" here has been stretched for the westernmost trips in this book. You won't find many towns en route from San Antonio to the Mexican border, and there's little traffic to slow your drive. To the east, population is more dense, and day trips involve quiet, slow drives along farm-to-market and ranch roads.

AVOID MID-DAY HEAT

In summer, the Texas heat is hotter than sizzling fajitas. In warm weather, it's best to drive in the early morning hours or after sunset. If you are traveling with pets, never leave them in an enclosed car; temperatures soar to ovenlike heights in just minutes.

HEED ROAD SIGNS AND WEATHER WARNINGS

Always be on the lookout for road signs, and if you see a notice, observe it. Obey flash flood warnings: A sudden rainstorm can turn a wash into a deadly torrent. Never cross a flooded roadway; it may be deeper than you think.

WATCH OUT FOR STRAY LIVESTOCK

When driving through open-ranch cattle country on farm-to-market or ranch roads, be on the lookout for livestock and deer wandering across the road, especially near dusk.

USING THIS TRAVEL GUIDE

Highway designations: Federal highways are designated US. State routes use TX for Texas. Farm-to-market roads are defined as FM, and ranch roads are labeled RR. County roads (which are not on the Texas state map) are identified as such.

Hours: In most cases, hours are omitted in the listings because they are subject to frequent changes. Instead, phone numbers appear for obtaining up-to-date information.

Restaurants: Restaurant prices are designated as $$$ (Expensive: $15 and over per person); $$ (Moderate: $5–15); and $ (Inexpensive: $5 and under).

Accommodations: Room prices are designated as $$$ (Expensive: over $100 for a standard room); $$ (Moderate: $50–100); and $ (Inexpensive: under $50).

Credit cards: The symbol ☐ denotes that credit cards are accepted.

Day Trips from
San Antonio

Welcome to San Antonio, the Alamo City and the gateway to South Texas. Boasting a semitropical climate, San Antonio is a city of lush vegetation, offering a south-of-the-border atmosphere with north-of-the-border amenities.

San Antonio lies at the juncture of the Hill Country, farmland, and brush country that stretches to the Mexican border. Because it's in the middle of such geographic diversity, San Antonio has a wealth of day trips awaiting you. You can head to the urban areas of Austin or Corpus Christi, or to small towns where it's not uncommon to hear German, Czech, Spanish, or even Alsatian spoken on the street. You also can get away from it all with a quiet walk along miles of undeveloped beach on Padre Island, or take a bird-watching cruise along the intracoastal waterway of the Rockport-Fulton area.

Many day trips include information about overnight accommodations to make your visit more relaxing and unhurried. And don't forget to leave plenty of time for watching a Texas-sized sunset or sunrise over the Gulf waters.

For brochures and maps on San Antonio area attractions, call (800) 447–3372 or (210) 270–8700, or write: San Antonio Convention and Visitors Bureau, P.O. Box 2277, San Antonio, TX 78298.

BLANCO

To reach Blanco, follow US 281 north of San Antonio past miles of cattle ranches and Hill Country vistas. Formerly a "Wild West" kind of town, the community was originally the seat of Blanco County. Although the county seat eventually moved to nearby Johnson City, where it remains today, local residents are hard at work restoring Blanco's old limestone courthouse as a museum and art gallery.

Around the courthouse square are several art galleries and antique shops aimed at weekend visitors, many of whom stop to camp at the Blanco River State Recreation Area south of town.

WHERE TO GO

Blanco State Park. South of Blanco on US 281. During the Depression, the Civilian Conservation Corps built two stone dams, a group pavilion, stone picnic tables, and an arched bridge in this 110-acre riverside park. Today the park is popular with swimmers, anglers, and campers. Fee. (830) 833-4333.

Shrine of the Blessed Virgin Mary. At Christ of the Hills Monastery. Turn left off US 281 at the Blanco River State Park, then follow County Road 102 across the river for 2 miles. Turn at the "Clear Spring Ranch" gate (County Road 103) and continue for 2.5 miles.

The Christ of the Hills Monastery houses an order of Eastern Orthodox monks and nuns who practice a religion similar to the Russian Orthodox, except that services are conducted in English.

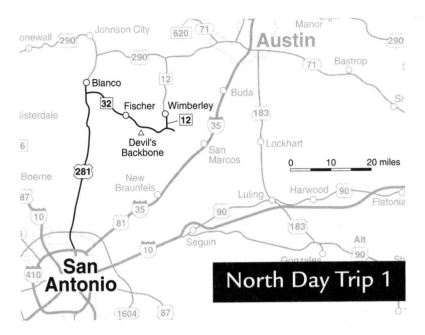

North Day Trip 1

Budget about an hour for a tour of the chapel and a look at the weeping icon. Painted in 1983 by a California monk, the icon is a representation of Mary and Jesus. After two years in its Blanco location, the icon began to weep myrrh. Drops of the oil roll from the eyes of both the mother and child. According to the inhabitants of the monastery, the painting weeps intermittently, although the oily streaks of the tears can be seen at almost any time. The myrrh is caught in cotton balls at the base of the icon, and visitors are anointed with the fragrant oil after viewing the painting.

The monastery is open to all, regardless of faith. Tours are conducted Thursday through Monday from 10:00 A.M. to 6:00: P.M. Sunday tours are given at 1:00 P.M. Appropriate dress is required; shorts are not allowed. Women are asked to cover their heads; scarves are provided. Free. (830) 833-5363.

Blanco Bowling Club. East of the square on Fourth Street. Housed in 1940s' buildings, the bowling club and the adjacent cafe have changed little with the passing years. The nine-pin game is still set up by hand as it has been for generations. The bowling club opens at 7:30 P.M. , Monday through Friday (except during football season, when everyone's at the Friday night high school game). To bowl you must be a league member. Fee. (830) 833-4416.

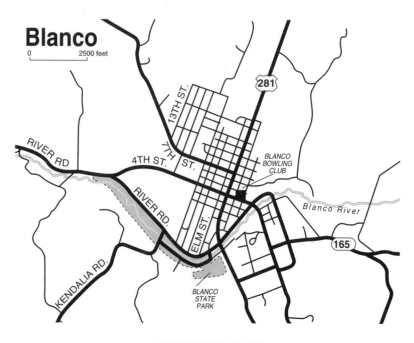

Blanco

0   2500 feet

13TH ST.

7TH ST.

RIVER RD

4TH ST.

RIVER RD.

ELM ST.

KENDALIA RD.

BLANCO BOWLING CLUB

Blanco River

281

165

BLANCO STATE PARK

WHERE TO SHOP

Rainbird Gallery. 109 Main Street. Blanco is home to many well-known artists who've relocated here from around the country. One artist, Janet Fisher, owns and operates this art gallery, an eclectic collection of Southwest, Indian, Western, and Texas art. Housed in a turn-of-the-century church building, the gallery spans over 2,400 square feet, filled with unique gift items and artwork. Navajo rugs, carved fossil rocks, wood and bronze sculptures, and silver jewelry are offered for sale along with many paintings of scenes of Texas bluebonnets, the state flower. A *kiva* room near the entrance of the gallery contains Native American artifacts, paintings, and one-of-a-kind items. The last Saturday of October, the gallery hosts an open house with visits by the artists in the collection. Closed Wednesdays and also on Sundays during winter months. (830) 833–4545.

WHERE TO EAT

Blanco Bowling Club Cafe. East of the square on Fourth Street. This is a traditional Texas diner, with linoleum floor and Formica tables, and chairs filled with locals who come here at the same time every day. Chicken-fried steak is the specialty; on Friday nights there's a catfish plate as well. Stop by in the morning for huge glazed twists and doughnuts made from scratch. Open daily for breakfast, lunch, and dinner. $; no ☐. (830) 833-4416.

FISCHER

It's just a short, winding drive through the country from Blanco to the tiny hamlet of Fischer. Retrace your drive south on US 281 for a couple of miles to the intersection of RR 32. Take a left and enjoy a quiet ride through miles of ranchland and rolling hills.

Fischer is on the left side of the road. Today not much remains of this community, just a post office, complete with an old-fashioned postmaster's cage and tiny brass mailboxes. Inside, enormous counters span the length of the dark and musty building.

DEVIL'S BACKBONE SCENIC DRIVE

The Devil's Backbone scenic drive stretches along RR 32 from Fischer to the intersection of RR 12, your turnoff for Wimberley. There aren't any steep climbs or stomach-churning lookouts; a high ridge of hills provides a gentle drive with excellent views along the way. There's very little traffic, plus a beautiful picnic spot on the left, just a few miles out of Fischer. This stretch of road is often cited as one of the most scenic drives in Texas.

WHERE TO STAY

Stage Stop Ranch. RR32. The Devil's Backbone is the home of the Stage Stop Ranch, a combination bed-and-breakfast inn and guest ranch that's nestled right on a former stagecoach trail. Here you can enjoy a stay in an elegantly furnished B&B room or in a private cabin for more privacy. Soak away your cares in a private hot tub just outside your door. $$$; ☐. (800) STAGESTOP.

WIMBERLEY

At the end of the Devil's Backbone, RR 32 intersects with RR 12. Take a left on RR 12, and then drive for 5 miles. This road drops from the steep ridge to the fertile valley that's home to the Blanco River and Cypress Creek.

Wimberley's history goes back to the 1850s when a resourceful Texas Revolution veteran named William Winters opened a mill here. As was tradition at the time, he named the new community Winters' Mill. When Winters died, John Cade bought the mill, and the town became Cade's Mill. Finally in 1870, a wealthy Llano man named Pleasant Wimberley rode into town. Tired of Indian raids on his horses in Llano, he moved in, bought the mill, and changed the town's name one last time.

The small town of Wimberley is one of those "shop 'til you drop" kinds of places. Even with only 2,500 residents, the town boasts dozens of specialty stores, art galleries and studios, and accommodations ranging from river resorts to historic bed-and-breakfasts.

Wimberley is a quiet place except when the shops open their doors on Fridays, Mondays, and weekends. The busiest time to visit is the first Saturday of the month, from April through December. This is Market Day, when over 400 vendors set up to sell antiques, collectibles, and arts and crafts. Also on the third Saturday of each month (April through December), visit the Celebration of the Arts Festival where Wimberley's best artists demonstrate their talents around the square.

Many visitors come to enjoy the town's two water sources: the Blanco River and clear, chilly Cypress Creek. Both are filled with inner-tubers and swimmers during hot summer months. The waterways provide a temporary home for campers and vacationers who stay in resorts and cabins along the shady water's edge. The most popular swimming spot on Cypress Creek is the Blue Hole Recreation Club, a privately owned park on Old Kyle Road.

WHERE TO GO

Wimberley Chamber of Commerce. Wimberley North Shopping Center, RR 12 past Cypress Creek. Stop by the chamber offices on weekdays to load up on brochures, maps, and friendly shopping tips. (512) 847-2201.

Pioneertown. 7-A Ranch Resort, 1 mile west of RR 12 on County Road 178, at the intersection of County Road 179. See a medicine show, tour a general store museum, or spend some time at the town jail in this Wild West village. There's also a child-sized train ride with a mile of tracks, an old log fort, cowboy shows, and a Western cafe. Open weekends year-round and daily during the summer months. Fee. (512) 847-2517.

Blue Hole Recreation Club. Follow Cypress Creek Road and turn left at the cemetery onto Blue Hole Road. A favorite with locals since the area's pioneer days, this traditional Texas swimming hole comes complete with swinging ropes, tall cypress trees, and the ice-cold water of Cypress Creek. You can stay for the day and picnic on the riverbanks or camp overnight (rustic or hookup). Fee. (512) 847-9127.

WHERE TO SHOP

Like nearby Blanco, Wimberley is home to many artists who've relocated to Texas's serene Hill Country. Specialty shops abound, selling everything from imports to sculpture and antiques. Arts and crafts are especially well represented. Plan to shop Friday through Monday. Some stores are open all week, but most close mid-week, especially during cooler months.

Rancho Deluxe. On the square. Bring the cowboy look to your home with this shop's Western merchandise. You'll find everything from spurs to Mexican sideboards, and from horns to handcrafted furniture. (512) 847-9570.

Sable V. On the square. Wimberley's largest fine art gallery exhibits blown glass, sculpture, paintings, ceramics, woodwork, and more. The gallery hosts three long-running shows annually: The eight-week glass show in the fall has been named the most comprehensive glass show in the South, with over sixty-five artists featured; the November wood show features over two dozen artists; and the Texas artists show, running six weeks every spring, features Texans working in every medium. (512) 847-8975.

Teeks Gallery. On the square. This shop features an eclectic blend of art, books, jewelry, and stationery. (512) 847-8868.

Wimberley Glass Works and Spoke Hill Gallery. 1½ miles east of the square on RR12. Watch demonstrations on the art of hand-blown glass and shop for one-of-a-kind creations. (512) 847-9348.

Wimberley Stained Glass Shop. On the square. Highlighted by handcrafted Tiffany lamp reproductions, this shop also features custom-leaded doors, window panels, and sun catchers. (512) 847-3930.

Billie Bob's Knob. Two miles north of Wimberley on RR 12. This is Wimberley's largest store, a twelve-room shopping extravaganza sprawled over 6,000 square feet. Antiques, designer clothing, jewelry, home furnishings, and collectibles are featured. (512) 847-3379.

WHERE TO STAY

Wimberley is filled with bed-and-breakfast accommodations that range from historic homes in town to ranches in the surrounding Hill Country to camps alongside Cypress Creek. For information on these many accommodations, give one of the reservations services a call: Bed and Breakfast of Wimberley, (800) 827-1913; Country Innkeepers, (800) 230-0805; Hill Country Accommodations, (800) 926-5028. For brochures on Wimberley's other accommodations, call the Chamber of Commerce at (512) 847-2201.

Little Arkansas Resort. 6 miles east of Wimberley at end of County Road 174. This favorite family campground has sites on the Blanco River with electricity. Enjoy an evening campfire after a day of swimming or just enjoying the country surroundings. (512) 847-2767.

JOHNSON CITY

The Lyndon B. Johnson National Historic Park takes in two areas: Johnson City and the LBJ Ranch. To reach Johnson City, follow US 281 north to Blanco (see NORTH FROM SAN ANTONIO, DAY TRIP 1 in this section for attractions along this stretch of road).

LBJ brought the attention of the world to his hometown, located 14 miles north from Blanco on US 281. The most popular stop here is the LBJ Boyhood Home, managed by the U.S. Park Service. LBJ was five years old in 1913 when his family moved from their country home near the Pedernales River to this simple frame house. The visitors center provides information on this location, nearby Johnson Settlement, and other LBJ attractions. Park admission is free of charge, a stipulation of the late president.

Johnson City hosts Historic Nugent Street Market Days on the third weekend of every month from April through October, with antiques, crafts, collectibles, and food booths.

WHERE TO GO

LBJ National Historic Park. South of US 290 at Ninth Street. Park at the new Visitors Center and go inside for brochures and a look at exhibits. From the center, you can walk to two historic areas: Johnson Settlement and the LBJ Boyhood Home.

Johnson Settlement. The settlement gives visitors a look at the beginnings of the Johnson legacy. These rustic cabins and outbuildings once belonged to LBJ's grandfather, Sam Ealy Johnson, and his brother

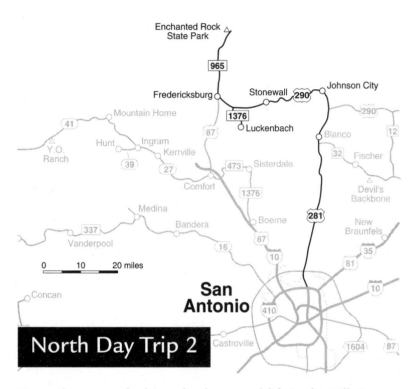

Enchanted Rock
State Park

965

Fredericksburg   Stonewall 290   Johnson City

Mountain Home   290

41   Hunt   Ingram   1376
Y.O.   Kerrville   O Luckenbach   Blanco   12
Ranch   39   27   32   Fischer
                              473   Sisterdale
                    Comfort   1376   Devil's
                                                     Backbone
             Medina
                     Bandera   Boerne   281   New
        337   Braunfels
   Vanderpool   87
                            16   35
0   10   20 miles   10
                                              81

Concan   10

                 San
              Antonio 410

North Day Trip 2   Castroville

                                    1604   87

Tom. The two cattle drivers lived a rugged life in the Hill Country
during the 1860s and '70s. An exhibit center tells this story in pictures
and artifacts. You also can tour the brothers' cabins and see costumed
docents carrying out nineteenth-century chores. Open daily. Free.

LBJ Boyhood Home. Next to the Johnson Settlement. LBJ was a
schoolboy when his family moved here in 1913. The home is still furnished with the Johnsons' belongings. Guided tours run every half
hour. Open daily. Free.

The Exotic Resort. 4 miles north of Johnson City on US 281. Unusual species (including many endangered animals) roam across the
137 acres of wooded hill country. In this park, leave the driving to
someone else and enjoy a guided ride aboard a safari truck. Professional guides conduct tours of the ranch and provide visitors with
information such as animal behavior as you feed the friendly park
residents. After the tour, you can see some wildlife up close at the
petting zoo. Kids enjoy petting child-size miniature donkeys, baby
deer, llama, baby elk, and even a kangaroo at this special area. Open
daily. Fee. (830) 868–4357.

Pedernales Falls State Park. About 8 miles east on FM 2766. A favorite summer getaway, this 4,800-acre state park is highlighted with gently cascading waterfalls. Swimming, fishing, camping, and hiking available. Open daily. Fee. (830) 868-7304.

WHERE TO SHOP

The Feed Mill. US 290. You don't need an address to find this shopping mall—just look for most unusual building in town. This complex utilizes a former feed mill and transforms it into a compendium of shopping and dining opportunities. The complex is decorated in a surrealistic style with everything from armadillos to zebras to farm tools. (830) 868-7299.

Horse Feathers Mall. US 290 and Avenue F. This mall combines antiques, woodwork, leather goods, and collectibles in both open-air and enclosed spaces. (830) 868-4147.

WHERE TO EAT

Charles' Restaurant. US 281 as you enter town. If someone decided to make a poster of a typical Texas diner, they might choose Charles'.

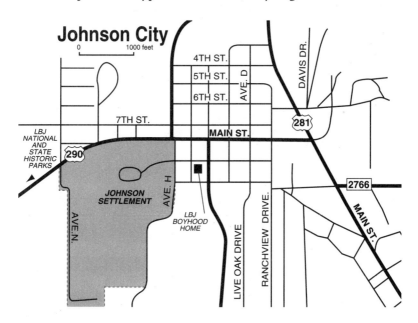

It's all here, from the Formica tables to the mirrored-glass pie display case. The chicken-fried steak holds up the Texas tradition. Open daily for breakfast, lunch, and dinner. $; ☐. (830) 868–4222.

Uncle Kunkel's Bar B Q. 208 US 281 South. For years the Kunkels did the catering for the LBJ Ranch, and today they prepare their award-winning pork ribs, brisket, and sausage for the public. Have a plate of smoked meats with side dishes of potato salad, coleslaw, or pinto beans, followed by a slice of homemade pie. $; no ☐. (830) 868–0251.

WHERE TO STAY

Bed and Breakfast of Johnson City. Choose from seven properties that range from a stone cottage to an antique-filled home. Some properties come with wood-burning stoves, kitchens, and porch swings; all feature air conditioning and sleep at least four guests. $$; ☐. (830) 868–4548.

STONEWALL

From Johnson City, head west on US 290 to the tiny community of Stonewall, the capital of the Texas peach industry. The road passes through miles of peach orchards, and during early summer, farm-fresh fruit is sold at roadside stands throughout the area. Stonewall is also the home of the LBJ National and State Historic Parks, encompassing the LBJ Ranch.

WHERE TO GO

LBJ National and State Historic Parks. Located west on US 290, these two combined parks together span approximately 700 acres. The area is composed of three main sections: the Visitors Center, the LBJ Ranch and tour, and the Sauer-Beckman Farm. The most scenic route to the LBJ Park falls along RR 1, paralleling the wide, shallow Pedernales River. (Exit US 290 a few miles east of Stonewall.)

During Johnson's life, the ranch was closed to all but official visitors. In hopes of catching a glimpse of the president, travelers often stopped along RR 1, located across the river from the "Texas White House," the nickname of the Johnsons' home. Today the parks draw visitors from around the world, who come for a look at the history behind the Hill Country, the presidency of LBJ, and a working Texas ranch.

Make your first stop the visitors center for a look at displays on LBJ's life, which include mementos of President Johnson's boyhood years. Attached to the visitors center is the Behrens Cabin, a dogtrot-style structure built by a German immigrant in the 1870s. Inside, the home is furnished with household items from over a century ago.

While you're in the visitors center, sign up for a ninety-minute guided tour of the LBJ Ranch, operated by the National Park Service. Tour buses run from 10:00 A.M. to 4:00 P.M. daily and travel across the president's ranch, making a stop at the one-room Junction School where Johnson began his education. The bus slows down for a photo of the Texas White House then continues past the president's airstrip and cattle barns. Other stops include a look at the reconstructed birthplace home as well as the family cemetery where the former president is buried.

Near the end of the tour, the bus makes an optional stop at the Sauer-Beckman Living Historical Farm. The two 1918 farm homes are furnished in period style. Children can have a great time petting the farm animals. From here, it's just a short walk back to the Visitors Center.

Although the park does not have overnight facilities, there are two picnic areas and hiking trails for day use. Open daily. Free; fee for bus tour. (830) 868-7128 ext. 231.

Grape Creek Vineyards. Four miles west of Stonewall on US 290. The fertile land of the Pedernales Valley is a natural for vineyards, and you'll find acres of beautiful grapevines at this winery that produces Cabernet Sauvignon and Chardonnay varieties. The winery is open Tuesday through Sunday from Easter through Labor Day, and Fridays and weekends in winter. Call for tour times. Free. (830) 664-2710.

LUCKENBACH

Waylon Jennings's popular country-western song made this community a Texas institution. The town consists of a shop or two and a small general store serving as a post office, dance hall, beer joint, and general gathering place.

To reach Luckenbach, leave Stonewall on US 290. Turn left on FM 1376 and continue for about 4¼ miles. Don't expect to see signs pointing to the turnoff for Luckenbach Road; they are stolen as fast as the Highway Department can get them in the ground. After the turn for Grapetown, take the next right down a narrow country road. Luckenbach is just around the bend.

This town was founded in 1852 by Jacob, William, and August Luckenbach. The brothers opened a post office at the site and called it South Grape Creek. In 1886 a man named August Engel reopened the post office and renamed it Luckenbach in honor of the early founders.

The old post office is still there, the walls covered with scrawled names penned by Luckenbach fans. The store sells souvenirs of the town daily except Wednesdays. For more information on Luckenbach happenings, call (830) 997–3224.

FREDERICKSBURG

Retrace your steps from Luckenbach and continue west on US 290 to Fredericksburg, once the edge of the frontier and home to brave German pioneers. These first inhabitants faced many hardships, including hostile Comanche Indians; now the town is a favorite with antique shoppers, history buffs, and fans of good German food.

US 290 runs through the heart of the downtown district, becoming Main Street within the city limits. Originally the street was designed to be large enough to allow a wagon and team of mules to turn around in the center of town. Today, Main Street is filled with shoppers who come to explore the stores and restaurants of downtown Fredericksburg.

Fredericksburg welcomes all visitors—just look at the street signs for proof. Starting at the Adams Street intersection, head east on Main Street and take the first letter of every intersecting street name: they spell "All Welcome." Drive west on Main Street starting after the Adams Street intersection, and the first letter of the intersecting streets spell "Come Back."

WHERE TO GO

Fredericksburg Chamber of Commerce. 106 North Adams. Stop by the chamber offices for brochures, maps, and information on a self-guided walking tour of historic downtown buildings, many of which now house shops and restaurants. The staff here also can direct you to bed-and-breakfast facilities in the area. Open Monday through Saturday. Free. (830) 997-6523.

Admiral Nimitz State Historical Park. 340 East Main Street. This historic park is composed of three sections: the former Nimitz Steamboat Hotel, the Garden of Peace, and the Pacific History Walk.

Admiral Chester Nimitz, World War II Commander-in-Chief of the Pacific (CinCPac), was Fredericksburg's most famous resident. He commanded 2.5 million troops from the time he assumed command eighteen days after the attack on Pearl Harbor until the Japanese surrendered.

The Nimitz name was well known here even years earlier. Having spent time in the merchant marines, Captain Charles H. Nimitz, the admiral's grandfather, decided to build a hotel here, adding a structure much like a ship's bridge to the front of his establishment. Built in 1852, the Nimitz Steamboat Hotel catered to guests who enjoyed a room, a meal, and the use of an outdoor bathhouse.

Today the former hotel houses a three-story museum honoring Admiral Nimitz and Fredericksburg's early residents. Many exhibits are devoted to World War II, including several that illustrate the Pacific campaign. In addition to displays that record the building's past, several early hotel rooms, the hotel kitchen, and the bathhouse have been restored.

Behind the museum lies the Garden of Peace, a gift from the people of Japan. This classic Japanese garden includes a flowing stream, a raked bed of pebbles and stones representing the sea and the Pacific islands, and a replica of the study used by Admiral Togo, Nimitz's counterpart in the Japanese forces.

Follow the signs from the Garden of Peace for one block to the Pacific History Walk. This takes you past a collection of military artifacts including a "fat man" Nagasaki-type atomic bomb case, a Japanese tank, and a restored barge like the one used by Nimitz. Open daily. Fee. (830) 997-4379.

Pioneer Museum Complex. 309 West Main Street. This collection of historic old homes includes a 1849 pioneer log home and store, the old First Methodist Church, and a smokehouse and log cabin. Also on the premises you'll see a typical nineteenth-century "Sunday house." Built in Fredericksburg, Sunday houses catered to farmers who would travel long distances to do business in town, often staying the weekend. With the advent of the automobile, such accommodations became obsolete. Today the old Sunday houses scattered throughout the town are used as bed-and-breakfasts, shops, and even private residences. They are easy to identify by their small size and the fact that most have half-story outside staircases. Open daily March through mid-December; weekends only mid-December through February. Fee. (830) 997–2835.

Bauer Toy Museum. 223 East Main Street. This museum houses over 3,000 antique toys dating from the late nineteenth century to the early mid-twentieth. Also on hand is a collection of old Texas license plates and a miniature replica of a small Texas town. Open Wednesday through Monday. Free. (No phone.)

Fort Martin Scott Historic Site. 1606 East Main Street, 2 miles east of Fredericksburg on US 290. Established in 1848, this was the first frontier military fort in Texas. Today the original stockade, a guardhouse, and visitors center with displays on local Indians are open to tour, and historic reenactments keep the history lesson lively. Ongoing archaeological research conducted here offers a glimpse into the fort's past. Reenactments involving costumed Indians, infantrymen, and civilians are scheduled at least once a month. Open Friday though Sunday. Fee. (830) 997–9895.

Vereins Kirche Museum. Market Square on Main Street across from the courthouse. You can't miss this attraction: It's housed in an exact replica of an octagonal structure erected in 1847. Back then the edifice was used as a church, as well as a school, fort, meeting hall, and storehouse. The museum is sometimes called the Coffee Mill (or Die Kaffe-Muehle) Church because of its unusual shape. Exhibits here display Fredericksburg's German heritage, plus Indian artifacts from archaeological digs. Open Monday through Saturday from March through September, and Monday through Friday the rest of the year. Fee. (830) 997–7832 or 997–2835.

Bell Mountain/Oberhellmann Vineyards. TX 16 North, 14 miles from Fredericksburg. Tour the chateau-type winery that produces Chardonnay, Reisling, Pinot Noir, and several private reserve estate varieties. Guided tours and tastings are offered every Saturday from March through mid-December. Free. (830) 685–3297.

Pedernales Vineyards. TX 16 South, 5.4 miles south of Fredericksburg. Visitors here can tour the winery and then taste the proprietors' Sauvignon Blanc and Cabernet Sauvignon. Open Monday through Saturday. Free. (830) 997-8326.

Fredericksburg Herb Farm. 402 Whitney Street. These herb gardens produce everything from teas to potpourris. Tour the grounds then visit the shop for a look at the final product. A bed-and-breakfast is also located on site. Open daily (Sunday—afternoons only). Free. (830) 997-8615.

WHERE TO SHOP

Fredericksburg's many specialty shops offer antiques, linens, Texana, art, and collectibles. Most stores are housed in historic buildings along Main Street.

Charles Beckendorf Gallery. 519 East Main Street. This enormous gallery showcases the locally known work of artist Charles Beckendorf and is a good place to pick up a print of regional scenes, from one-room schoolhouses to brilliant fall scenics. Open daily. (830) 997-5955.

Hand Carved Candles. 121 East Main Street and 155 East Main Street. Here artisans fashion unique hand-dipped and intricately carved candles. The larger of the stores, at 121 East Main Street, has rooms filled with Christmas candles and ornaments of every description. You may find yourself with the holiday spirit even when the thermometer reads 100 degrees on an August afternoon. Open daily. (830) 997-2933.

The Dulcimer Factory. 155 East Main Street and 715 South Washington Street. The Washington Street factory carries handcrafted folk instruments made from cherry, cypress, sassafras, birch, walnut, and maple woods. Free factory tours are given on weekdays; call for hours. The Main Street retail store is open daily. (830) 997-6704 for information on the factory; (830) 997-2626 for the store.

Iron Art. 605 East Main Street. Many Hill Country ranches have metal signs over the entrance, often adorned with cut-out silhouettes of deer, cattle, or horses. Welder Dale Holly creates these works of art as well as wall hangings, wind chimes, weather vanes, and planters. Many of Holly's creations feature traditional Texas symbols such as the lone star and the Texas longhorn, as well as country designs like cats and pigs. Open daily. (830) 997-8307.

WHERE TO EAT

Altdorf German Biergarten and Restaurant. 301 West Main Street. Take a break from shopping and enjoy some good German food in a pleasant outdoor setting. Sandwiches, steaks, burgers, and Mexican food are served here as well. There's also dining in an adjacent stone building erected by the city's pioneers. The restaurant is open for lunch and dinner daily; closed February. $-$$; ☐. (830) 997-7865.

    Peach Tree Tea Room. 210 South Adams Street. Enjoy a lunch of quiche, soup, or salad in this tea room whose name is synonymous with Fredericksburg. Open for lunch Monday through Saturday. $; ☐. (830) 997-9527.

WHERE TO STAY

Fredericksburg is the capital city of Texas bed-and-breakfast inns, with accommodations in everything from Sunday houses to local farmhouses to residences just off Main Street. Several reservation services provide information on properties throughout the area.

    Gastehaus Schmidt. 231 West Main Street. This service represents one hundred bed-and-breakfast accommodations, including cottages, log cabins, and a 125-year-old rock barn. All price ranges; ☐. (830) 997-5612.

    Bed and Breakfast of Fredericksburg. 619 West Main Street. This service handles over twenty-five properties ranging from private homes to cabins. All price ranges; ☐. (830) 997-4712.

    Be My Guest. 110 North Milam. Over twenty-five properties in Fredericksburg and nearby Lost Maples are handled by this service, with choices ranging from log cabins to historic homes. All price ranges; ☐. (830) 997-7227.

ESPECIALLY FOR WINTER TEXANS

If you're traveling by RV or trailer, spend some time at the 113-site Lady Bird Johnson Municipal Park, just southwest of Fredericksburg on TX 16. Campsites have electrical, water, sewer, and cable TV hookups. There's a fourteen-day limit on camping from April through September.

The park also sports a nine-hole golf course, six tennis courts, and badminton and volleyball courts. There's also a seventeen-acre lake for fishing. For more information, call (830) 997–4202, or write: Lady Bird Municipal Park, P.O. Box 111, Fredericksburg, TX 78624.

ENCHANTED ROCK STATE PARK

Whether you're a climber or just looking for a good picnic spot, drive out to Enchanted Rock State Park. Located 18 miles north of Fredericksburg on RR 965, this state park features the largest stone formation in the West. Nationally this 640-acre granite outcropping takes second only to Georgia's Stone Mountain. According to Indian legend, the rock is haunted. Sometimes, as the rock cools at night, it makes a creaking sound, which probably accounts for the story.

People of all ages in reasonably good physical condition can enjoy a climb up Enchanted Rock. The walk takes about an hour, and hikers are rewarded with a magnificent view of the Hill Country. In warm weather (from April through October), start your ascent early in the morning before the relentless sun turns the rock into a griddle.

Experienced climbers can scale the smaller formations located adjacent to the main dome. These bare rocks are steep and dotted with boulders and crevices, and their ascent requires special equipment.

Picnic facilities and a sixty-site primitive campground at the base of the rock round out the offerings here. No vehicular camping is permitted. Buy all your supplies in Fredericksburg; there are no concessions here. To prevent overcrowding, a limited number of visitors are allowed in the park during peak periods. Arrive early. Open daily. Fee. (915) 247-3903.

AUSTIN

Maybe it's the college student population that tops 50,000. Maybe it's the live music industry that has made this city a haven for fans and performers alike. Or maybe it's just geography, situated on a downtown lake and perched at the edge of a rambling Hill Country lake that offers everything from windsurfing to nude sunbathing.

Whatever the reason, there's one thing for certain: Austin is a town that doesn't want to grow up. Like a perpetual teenager, the capital of Texas is brash, sassy, and sometimes just downright silly. Sure, the city is home to both high-tech industry and countless state officials, but residents use any excuse to toss off the ties and three-piece suits. They don elaborate costumes for an annual party in Pease Park to celebrate (believe it or not) the birthday of Eeyore, the pal of Winnie the Pooh. But those costumes are just a dress rehearsal for the Halloween party that takes place on Sixth Street, complete with 20,000 to 70,000 merrymakers.

Located 80 miles north from San Antonio on I-35, the city of Austin dates back to 1838, when Mirabeau B. Lamar, president-elect of the Texas Republic, came here to hunt buffalo. He found an even greater prize: a home for the new capital. Lamar fell in love with Waterloo, a tiny settlement surrounded by rolling hills and fed by cool springs. By the next year, the government had arrived and construction on the capitol building had begun.

Today's Austin straddles both sides of the Colorado River. Once unpredictable during rainy years, the Colorado has been tamed into a series of seven lakes. Many Austinites head to just beyond the city to Lake Travis for weekend recreation. Others stay closer to home, enjoying the lakes within Austin's city limits: Lake Austin and Town Lake.

Lake Austin begins at the foot of the Hill Country and flows for 22 miles through the western part of the city. Although high-priced residential structures are scattered along the shores, much of the countryside is still preserved in public parks. Lake Austin empties into Town Lake, a narrow stretch of water that slices through the center of downtown. Beautifully planted greenbelts compose the shoreline, which also includes 15 miles of hike and bike trails. Although swimming and motorboating are prohibited, visitors can rent canoes near the lakeside Hyatt Regency Hotel. The calm waters of Town Lake draw collegiate rowing teams from around the country to train in the warm climate.

Attractions abound on both sides of the Colorado River, most just a few minutes off I–35. A bit north of the river and within five min-

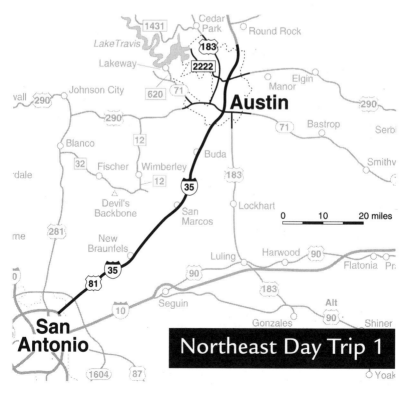

Northeast Day Trip 1

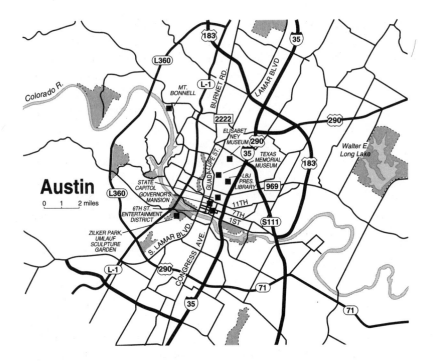

utes of the interstate are the best two shows in town: the Texas Legislature and the University of Texas. The legislature meets in the State Capitol from January through May in odd-numbered years. Even when this body is not in session, you can take a free tour of the historic building and watch the hustle and bustle of state government.

Parking in the Capitol and downtown area comes at a premium. The best way to explore is aboard a 'Dillo, the trolley service that starts at the Coliseum's free parking lot at the intersection of West Riverside Drive at Bouldin Avenue. These green trolleys travel up and down the streets from the river to the university.

From the Capitol, it's a ten-minute walk north on Congress Avenue to Martin Luther King Boulevard and the southern edge of the University of Texas campus. This sprawling institution boasts students and faculty from around the world and some of the finest educational facilities in the country. The centerpiece of the university is the Main Tower, illuminated by orange lights whenever the University of Texas Longhorns win. The tower stands in the open mall, which includes the large Student Union building where students and the general public can grab a low-priced lunch.

Guadalupe (pronounced in Austin as "GWAD-a-loop") Street divides the educational campus from a commercial strip called "The Drag," the stretch of Guadalupe that runs from Martin Luther King Boulevard to 26th Street. The area is always crowded and fun, filled with shops and eateries that cater to every student need. The People's Renaissance Market, just across the street from the Student Union, is an open-air bazaar where crafters sell their wares. It's especially popular with Austinites for Christmas shopping.

Most of the University of Texas grounds are closed to motorized traffic, but you can park at the LBJ Presidential Library, located on the north side of campus. Before touring the Presidential Library, walk to the fountain for an unparalleled view of both the university and downtown Austin.

As your day draws to a close, head back to Town Lake. During summer months, people flock to the shoreline near the Congress Avenue Bridge at Town Lake to witness the nightly departure of bats from the Bat Colony. Austin boasts the largest urban population of bats in the nation and every night 1.5 million of these winged mammals make their exodus at sunset. Take watch on the banks of Town Lake near the Congress Avenue bridge to see the Mexican free-tail bats. A free bat viewing area with an informational kiosk is located in the parking lot of the Austin American-Statesman at 305 South Congress Avenue or stand on the bridge itself or along the hike-and-bike trail.

Finally, spend your evening on Sixth Street, Austin's entertainment district that runs from Congress Avenue east to I-35. It's lined with restaurants, bars, and clubs featuring nightly music performed by Austin musicians. Friday and Saturday evenings are crowded. Be forewarned: Many clubs don't crank up the music until the wee hours.

WHERE TO GO

Visitor Information Center. 300 Bouldin Avenue. Stop here for attractions, trolley and bus routes, and dining information. Open daily and Sunday afternoons. Free. (512) 478-0098.

State Capitol. 11th Street and Congress Avenue. You might think that Texas's motto is "The bigger, the better," especially after a visit to the State Capitol. Taller than its national counterpart, the pink granite building houses the governor's office, the Texas Legislature, and several other executive state agencies. Recently the building has undergone a major facelift and is now worth a visit even for those who had toured the structure previously. Guided tours depart from the first floor rotunda daily. Free. (512) 463–0063.

Capital Complex Visitors Center. East 11th and Brazos. Learn more about the capital complex in this visitors center and museum housed in the 1857 General Land Office, the oldest government office building in the state. Once the workplace of short story writer O. Henry, this building is now filled with exhibits and displays to introduce visitors to the workings of state government. Open Tuesday through Saturday. Free. (512) 305–8400.

Governor's Mansion. 1010 Colorado Street. For over 130 years, Texas governors have enjoyed the opulence of this grand home. Visitors are taken past the main staircase, through the formal parlor, and finally into the dining room. Tours (scheduled every twenty minutes) are conducted Monday through Friday from 10:00 A.M. to noon. Call to check the status of tours; the home is sometimes closed because of incoming dignitaries. Free. (512) 463–5516.

Lyndon Baines Johnson Presidential Library. 2313 Red River Street. (From I-35, exit west at 26th Street.) Located on the campus of the University of Texas, this facility serves as a reminder of the Hill Country's most famous resident, Lyndon Baines Johnson. The library is filled with over 35 million historic documents, housed in archival boxes and available for scholarly research. The first two floors offer films on Johnson's life and career, as well as exhibits featuring jeweled gifts from foreign dignitaries and simpler handmade tokens from appreciative Americans. Visitors also can take in special displays of political, civil rights, and educational memorabilia. The top floor holds a reproduction of LBJ's White House Oval Office furnished as it was during his term. Open daily. Free. (512) 482–5279.

Zilker Park. From I-35, take the Riverside Drive exit west and continue to Barton Springs Road. Follow Barton Springs Road to the park. Located just south of Town Lake, this city park is a favorite with joggers, picnickers, swimmers, soccer teams, and kite flyers. Here lies the beautiful spring-fed Barton Springs pool, where you can take a dip in the sixty-eight-degree, crystal-clear waters all year. Things to see include a miniature train for the kids, dinosaur tracks, a Japanese garden, a rose garden, and a nature center. Free; fee for pool and train. (512) 472-4914.

Town Lake Cruises. Depart from dock of Hyatt Regency Hotel at 208 Barton Springs Road. Enjoy a ninety-minute excursion on Town Lake aboard the *Lone Star Riverboat* paddle wheeler. Public cruises March through late October; call for schedule. Fee. (512) 327-1388.

Umlauf Sculpture Garden and Museum. 605 Robert E. Lee Road. Take a peaceful walk through this garden featuring the works of Charles Umlauf, former professor emeritus at the University of Texas. Located near Barton Springs Road, the garden displays about sixty sculptures, and the museum exhibits about an equal number of smaller pieces. A video provides a look at the life of the sculptor. Open Thursday through Sunday. Fee. (512) 445-5582.

Elisabet Ney Museum. 304 East 44th Street. German immigrant Elisabet Ney was considered Texas's first sculptress, and this stone building served as her studio and home. It's filled with her statues, working drawings, and personal belongings. Ney's work also can be seen in the entrance of the State Capitol. Open Wednesday through Sunday. Free. (512) 458-2255.

Austin Museum of Art at Laguna Gloria. 3809 West 35th Street. This Mediterranean-style villa, located on Lake Austin, was built in 1916. Today the elegant structure is home to a museum that hosts changing exhibits of twentieth-century art. Open Tuesday through Sunday. Fee; free on Thursday. (512) 458-8191.

National Wildflower Research Center. 4801 LaCrosse Avenue. (Loop 1 south to .8 mile south of Slaughter Lane.) This unique institution is the only one in the nation devoted to the conservation and promotion of native plants and flowers. The center was the dream of Lady Bird Johnson, wife of the late president. Mrs. Johnson is also responsible for the beautiful bluebonnet and wildflower plantings along the interstate highways in Texas.

The center, located on a forty-two-acre site in an $8 million facility, includes a children's discovery room, gallery, gift shop, and the Wildflower Cafe. Visitors can take a self-guided educational tour of the grounds; groups of ten or more may arrange for a guide. The center acts as an information clearinghouse, distributing numerous fact sheets on the more than one hundred native species. Annual events include landscaping seminars and workshops. The center is open Tuesday through Sunday. Free (the center suggests a per car donation). (512) 292-4100.

Jourdan-Bachman Pioneer Farm. East of town at 11418 Sprinkle Road. Here children can watch daily chores of the period being carried out with authentic tools. The farm hosts special events such as "A Taste of Texas Past," with old-time cooking methods and recipes. Call for seasonal hours. Fee. (512) 837-1215.

Austin Nature Center. 301 Nature Center Drive west of Zilker Park. The Hill Country's smallest residents, from field mice to raccoons, are featured at this popular ecological stop. All animals here have been injured and can no longer live in the wild. Along with exhibits on local wildlife, the center sponsors special workshops and festivities throughout the year like "Hummingbird Day" and "Safari Day." Open daily. Free. (512) 327-8181.

Texas Memorial Museum. 2400 Trinity Street. This university museum has exhibits on everything Texan, from dinosaur bones found in the Lone Star State to historic displays on the Indians who lived on this land. Open daily. Free. (512) 471-1604.

Celis Brewery. 2431 Forbes Drive (2 miles east of I-35). Take a tour of this microbrewery Tuesday through Saturday at 2:00 P.M. or 4:00 P.M. You'll see several varieties of beer under preparation. The founder of the company came to Austin from Belgium, from whence he also imported the beer-making equipment. Free. (512) 835-0884.

Archer M. Huntington Gallery. 21st and Guadalupe Streets in the Humanities Research Center. Boasting the extensive Michener collection, this University of Texas museum is considered one of the top ten university art galleries in the country. Have a look at the fifteenth-century Gutenburg Bible on the first floor and Greek and Roman antiquities on the second. Open daily (afternoons only on Sunday). Free. (512) 471-7324.

Treaty Oak. 503 Baylor Street. This 600-year old oak captured the nation's attention in 1989 when it was poisoned. Once called the finest example of a tree in North America, today one-third of the original tree is gone.

Hike and Bike Trails. Few metropolitan areas boast more fitness-conscious folks than Austin. Residents and visitors alike enjoy over 25 miles of trails, including many around Town Lake. Pick up a free trail guide at the Parks and Recreation Department, 200 South Lamar Boulevard, (512) 499-6700.

Sixth Street. This entertainment district is one of the first introductions many visitors get to Austin, but it's a destination just as popular with residents. Friday and Saturday nights are often standing room only in an entertainment district that's sometimes compared to New Orleans's Bourbon Street. Here blues rather than jazz is king, and it's found in little clubs like Joe's Generic Bar, Maggie Mae's, and the 311 Club. They're all well received by music fans in this city that gave Janis Joplin her start years ago as well as favorites like Willie Nelson, Stevie Ray Vaughn, and the Fabulous Thunderbirds.

Austin Zoo. 10807 Rawhide Trail. Bring along the kids to this privately owned zoo located near Oak Hill to enjoy pony rides, train rides, a petting zoo, and plenty of exotic creatures. Young visitors can purchase animal food to feed some of the inhabitants by hand. Open daily. Fee. (800) 291-1490 or (512) 288-1490.

Mount Bonnell. 3800 Mount Bonnell Road. Climb up for a look across Lake Austin and the outlying Hill Country from atop one of the city's best lookouts. The view is located 1 mile past the west end of West 35th Street. Closes at 10:00 P.M. daily. Free.

WHERE TO SHOP

Callahan's General Store. 501 US 183. Like a true general store, this sprawling store has just about everything a person could want. Western wear, saddles, boots, household items, and, yes, even chicks and ducks make up the extensive inventory. Open Monday through Saturday. (512) 385-3452.

Bookpeople. 603 North Lamar Boulevard. This megastore calls itself the largest bookstore in the United States, spanning four floors with more than 300,000 titles, 2,000 magazines and newspapers, and plenty of space just to hang out and browse. An espresso bar fills the first floor with the scent of fresh brew. Open daily. (512) 472-5050.

Central Market. 4001 North Lamar Boulevard. More than just a grocery store, this market is an international smorgasbord of produce, wines, meats, fish, and seasonings from around the globe. Regularly scheduled cooking classes offer visitors the chance to learn techniques from the pros. Open daily. (512) 206-1000.

Clarksville Pottery. 4001 North Lamar Boulevard. Shop for handmade stoneware, from bowls to goblets to decorative ware at this fine crafts gallery. Another location in the Arboretum Market is convenient for shoppers in Northwest Austin. Open daily. (512) 454-9079.

Kerbey Lane and Jefferson Square. West 35th Street at Kerbey Lane. This shopping enclave is a favorite for those looking for unique gift items, collectibles, and fashions. Located off Austin's medical district, the shops line Kerbey Lane and the open air Jefferson Square center. Most shops open Monday through Saturday.

Pecan Street Emporium. 1122 West 6th Street. Fine European imports, from Swiss music boxes to German nutcrackers, fill this charming gift shop. This shop claims to have Austin's largest selection of German collectibles, and you'll also find year-round Christmas decorations as well as plenty of small gift purchases. Open daily. (512) 477-4900.

Renaissance Market. 23rd and Guadalupe Streets. Tucked right off the Drag in the University of Texas area, this open-air market is filled with the work of Austin artisans who sell handmade jewelry, woodcrafts, tie-die shirts, glasswork, toys, pottery, and more one-of-a kind items. This market claims to be Texas's only continuously operating open-air arts and crafts market. The number of artists varies by season, reaching a crescendo in the weeks before the holidays and a low point during the Christmas break when UT students are few and far between. Open daily. No phone.

South Congress Avenue. Austin's best imports, antiques, and funky purchases can be acquired on South Congress Avenue, just south of Town Lake. This eclectic district is definitely for those looking for something a little different, whether that means a mariachi costume or wood carvings, handcarved furniture or 1970s disco polyester getups. Most shops open Monday to Saturday and Sunday afternoons.

Travelfest. 1214 West 6th Street. This store combines travel books, travel gadgets, and a travel agency under one roof. Separate rooms are dedicated to different parts of the globe with videos, guides, and maps to plan any trip. Travel magazines and gadgets designed to do everything from purify water to hide money are located in the front of the store, alongside a full service travel agency. Open daily. (512) 469-7906.

WHERE TO EAT

Austin is filled with restaurants of every description, ranging from vegetarian to Vietnamese. For a list of Austin eateries, stop by the

Austin Visitors Center at 300 Bouldin Avenue, located between Palmer Auditorium and City Auditorium. The center is open seven days a week.

Sixth Street has many restaurants and bars featuring live music, especially blues. Most of the dining establishments are casual.

Trudy's Texas Star. 409 West 30th Street. This popular university-area restaurant feeds you Tex-Mex for breakfast, lunch, and dinner. The green chicken (meaning the sauce, not the chicken) enchiladas are the best in town. Open daily. $–$$; ☐. (512) 495–1867.

Iron Works Barbecue. 100 Red River Street. This former foundry is still decorated with branding irons. Diners flock here to enjoy plates of juicy barbecue. If you have a big appetite, order the ribs. Open weekdays only. $–$$; ☐. (512) 478–4855.

Threadgill's. 6416 North Lamar Boulevard. Janis Joplin used to sing in this restaurant back in the early '60s. Today the place is best known for its home-style cooking, including jumbo chicken-fried steaks, fried chicken, and vegetables like Grandma used to make. Open for breakfast, lunch, and dinner. $–$$; ☐. (512) 451–5440.

Chuy's. 1728 Barton Springs Road. Chuy's takes great pride in being one of the strangest restaurants in town. With the name, you might expect Chinese food, but you'll get Tex-Mex in a funky decor featuring multitudes of those Elvis-on-black-velvet paintings. The food is great, but watch out for the spiciest dishes—they're ultra hot, even for seasoned Tex-Mex lovers. $; ☐. (512) 474–4452.

Scholz Garten. 1607 San Jacinto. Dine on burgers or chicken-fried steaks in the beer garden of this restaurant that dates back to 1866. A popular hangout for legislative types. Open Monday through Saturday. $–$$; ☐. (512) 477–4171.

Katz's. 618 West 6th Street. Since 1979, this deli has been an Austrian tradition, upholding the boast, "We never klose." Around the clock you can enjoy bagels and lox, chicken soup with matzoh balls, homemade blintzes, or Reuben sandwiches. Upstairs, the Top of the Marc hops with music and dancing nightly. $–$$; ☐. (512) 472–2037.

Dan McKlusky's. 301 East 6th Street. Steak lovers have long flocked to this downtown eatery for steaks, seafood, lamb, quail, and more. All served with a generous house salad and your preference of baked or fried potatoes, rice pilaf or the fresh vegetable of the day. Open for lunch weekdays; dinner nightly. $$$; ☐. (512) 473–8924.

Hut's Hamburgers. 807 West 6th Street. This lively diner serves up some of Austin's most popular burgers just as it has since 1939. Choose from over twenty types of burgers or enjoy chicken-fried steak, salads, and a daily special. One of the specialties of the house is an order of Texas-sized onion rings. Open for lunch and dinner daily. $; ☐.

WHERE TO STAY

Hyatt Regency Austin. 208 Barton Springs Road. This 448-room hotel has a signature Hyatt lobby, with glass elevators, a flowing stream, and a beautiful view of Town Lake. $$$; ⚓. (512) 477-1234.

Four Seasons Hotel. 98 San Jacinto Boulevard. Located on the northern edge of Town Lake, this hotel offers a Southwestern atmosphere and a great view of the lake. Its back terrace is very popular with Austinites during the summer months, affording patrons one of the best looks at the city's famed Town Lake bat colony. $$$; ☐.(800) 332-3442 or (512) 478-4500.

Driskill Hotel. 112 East Sixth Street. Built in 1886 by cattle baron Jesse Driskill, this is Austin's oldest hotel. Its 177 rooms and beautiful lobby recall an elegant age in the city's history. The hotel sits within easy walking distance of the State Capitol and the Sixth Street entertainment district. Two restaurants and bars offer food and refreshments to guests preferring to "stay in." $$$; ☐. (800) 252-9367 or (512) 474-5911.

Southard House. 908 Blanco Road. Located downtown, this bed-and-breakfast inn features five rooms with private baths, some with clawfoot tubs and fireplaces. $$; ☐. (512) 474-4731.

Ziller House. 800 Edgecliff Terrace. This downtown bed-and-breakfast is one of the city's most popular retreats with celebrity guests. Walter Cronkite, Meg Ryan, Dennis Quaid, Clint Eastwood, and many other stellar names select this getaway located on a rock bluff overlooking Town Lake. There are four guest rooms, all with private bath, and each has a cabinet containing a microwave, coffee maker, refrigerator and utensils, in case you don't want to eat out. $$$; ☐. (800) 949-5446 or (512) 462-0100.

Lake Austin Spa Resort. 1705 South Quinlan Park Road. Perched on a quiet shore of Lake Austin in the rolling hills, the resort is casual elegance at its best. You'll find plenty of activity here in the form of aerobics classes on a suspended wood floor, tennis, dancing, mountain biking, and even sculling on the lake's calm waters. Activity goes hand-in-hand with relaxation, and here that means stress reduction sessions. For the ultimate in relaxation, enjoy a massage, facial, manicure, aloe vera body masque, invigorating sea salt scrub, or aromatherapy scalp conditioning. $$$; ☐. (800) 847-5637 or (512) 266-2444.

San Marcos · Buda

SAN MARCOS

San Marcos is located 51 miles northeast of San Antonio on I-35. It's a drive that's always busy, especially on Friday and Sunday afternoons. Like neighboring New Braunfels, San Marcos is best known for its pure spring waters. The San Marcos River, which has been used by humans for over 13,000 years, flows through town, providing the city with beautiful swimming and snorkeling spots and an amusement park.

Permanent settlement of the area began in 1845. Today San Marcos is a popular tourist town and the home of Southwest Texas State University. On the third weekend of every month, the downtown courthouse lawn plays host to Market Days. Shop for arts and crafts, antiques, and specialty food and gift items at this old-fashioned outdoor market.

WHERE TO GO

Tourist Information Center. Exit 206 (Aquarena Springs Drive.) from I-35 on the northwest side of town. Stop here for brochures on area attractions and accommodations, as well as free maps. Open daily. Free. (888) 200-5620 or (512) 353-3435.

Aquarena Springs Resort. Take Aquarena Springs exit from I-35 and follow signs west of the highway. This resort dates back to 1928, when A. B. Rogers purchased 125 acres at the headwaters of the San Marcos River to create a grand hotel. He added glass-bottomed boats

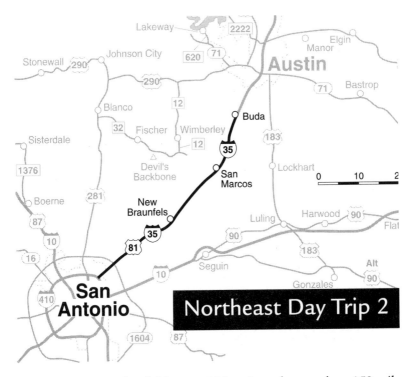

Northeast Day Trip 2

to cruise Spring Lake, fed by over 200 springs that produce 150 million gallons daily. This 98 percent pure water is home to many fish (including some white albino catfish) and various types of plant life. Today visitors can still enjoy a cruise on the glass-bottomed boats and see the site of an underwater archaeological dig that unearthed the remains of Clovis Man, one of the hunter-gatherers who lived on the San Marcos River over 13,000 years ago.

Formerly a family amusement park, today Aquarena Springs Resort focuses on ecotourism, with exhibits and activities aimed at introducing visitors of all ages to the natural history and natural attractions of this region. This family park features glass-bottom boat rides, an endangered species exhibit, the San Xaiver Spanish Mission, an 1890s' general store, historic homes from San Marcos's earliest days, and plenty of educational fun. The park offers special guided trips that feature the park's historic attractions as well as other excursions focusing on endangered species, archaeological sites, bird watching, and the flora and fauna of the area.

Open daily, although hours change seasonally. Fee. (800) 999-9767 or (512) 396-8900.

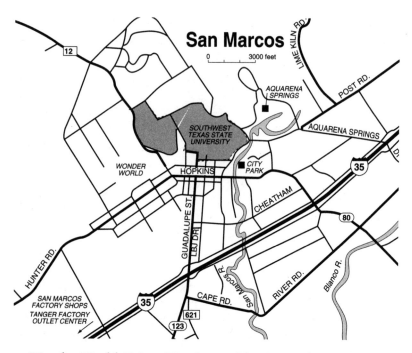

Wonder World. Exit at Wonder World Drive on the south side of San Marcos and follow signs for about a mile. A guided tour lasting nearly two hours covers the entire park, including the 7.5-acre Texas Wildlife Park, Texas's largest petting zoo. A miniature train chugs through the animal enclosure, stopping to allow riders to pet and feed white-tailed deer, wild turkeys, and many exotic species.

The next stop on the tour is Wonder Cave, created during a 3.5-minute earthquake 30 million years ago. The same earthquake produced the Balcones Fault, an 1,800-mile line separating the western Hill Country from the flat eastern farmland. Within the cave is the actual crack in the two land masses, containing huge boulders lodged in the fissure. At the end of the cave tour, take the elevator ride to the top of the 110-foot Tejas Tower, which offers a spectacular view of the Balcones Fault and the contrasting terrain it produced.

The last stop is the Anti-Gravity House, a structure employing optical illusions and a slanted floor to create the feeling that you're leaning backwards. In this house, water appears to run "uphill," creating yet another illusion. Fee. (800) 782-7653, ext. CAVE, or (512) 392-3760 for group and tour reservations.

City Park. Across from Southwest Texas State University. Concessioners here rent inner tubes so that you can float down the San Marcos Loop. The floating excursion, in 72-degree water, takes about an hour and a half. Snorkeling is popular here as well, and you might see a fresh-water prawn (which can reach 12 inches in length), the rare San Marcos salamander, or one of fifty-two kinds of fish.

Millie Seaton Collection of Dolls and Toys. 1104 West Hopkins. For thirty years, Millie Seaton has collected dolls from around the world. The number of dolls grew and grew—until finally the avid collector bought a three-story Victorian home just to house the 4,000 dolls! Tours are given between 8:00 A.M. and 5:00 P.M. by appointment only. Call to set up a time with Millie or one of her docents for a guided walk through this cherished collection. Fee. (512) 396-1305.

WHERE TO SHOP

San Marcos Factory Shops. Exit 200 from I-35 on the south side of San Marcos. This open-air mall features over one hundred shops that sell direct from the factory. Luggage, shoes, leather goods, outdoor gear, china, kitchen goods, and other specialties are offered for sale. Chartered buses from as far as Dallas and Houston stop here regularly. Open daily. (800) 628-9465.

Tanger Factory Outlet Center. Exit 200 from I-35 south of San Marcos. Over thirty shops feature name-brand designers and manufacturers in this open-air mall. Housewares, footwear, home furnishings, leather goods, perfumes, and books are offered. Open daily. (512) 396-7444.

Centerpoint Station. Exit 200 from I-35 south of San Marcos. This charming shop, built like an old-fashioned general store, is filled with Texas and country collectibles, T-shirts, gourmet gift foods, cookbooks, and more. Up front, a counter serves sandwiches, malts, and ice cream. (512) 392-1103.

WHERE TO STAY

Aquarena Springs Inn. Located on the grounds of Aquarena Springs Resort, this hotel opened in 1928 as the Spring Lake Hotel. Today the refurbished inn offers many rooms with beautiful views of

Spring Lake. The lake is no longer used for swimming because the aquatic life is so dense (some plants can grow up to 6 inches a day and must be "mowed" frequently). However, there is a large pool and a full-service restaurant. $$; ☐. (512) 396–8901.

Crystal River Inn. 326 West Hopkins Street. The Crystal River Inn offers visitors elegant Victorian accommodations in rooms named for Texas rivers. Owners Cathy and Mike Dillon provide guests with a selection of special packages, including tubing on the San Marcos, sunset cruises at Aquarena Springs, and popular murder mystery weekends where costumed guests work to solve a mystery using clues based on actual events in San Marcos history. $$–$$$; ☐. (512) 396–3739.

BUDA

From San Marcos, it's an easy fifteen-minute drive north on I–35 to Buda, a former railroad town located on Loop 4 (Main Street) west of the highway.

Buda is one of the most mispronounced communities in Texas (and with names like Gruene, Leakey, and Boerne around, that's saying a lot). To sound like a local, just say "b-YOU-da." The name has caused more than one foreign visitor to come here expecting an old-world Hungarian settlement. Though possibly a reference to Budapest, it's more likely of Spanish origin. According to legend, several widows cooked in the local hotel restaurant that was popular with employees of the International–Great Northern Railroad. The Spanish word for "widow" is *viuda*. Since the "v" is pronounced as a "b" in Spanish, Buda may be a phonetic spelling for *viuda*.

Buda is still a railroad town, with double tracks running parallel to Main Street.

WHERE TO SHOP

Many Buda stores are closed Monday through Wednesday, although some are open by appointment. Most shops are located in a 2-block stretch of Main Street.

BJ's Treasure Trove. 214 North Main. This eclectic shop features collectibles from around the world, as well as antiques, crafts, and gifts. Open Wednesday and Saturday only or by appointment. (512)

295–2437 or 295–7070.

Don's Den. Main Street. This antique's shop has a little of everything, but it specializes in toys, electric trains, and metal cars. Open Wednesday through Sunday. (512) 295-5211.

Memory Lane Antiques. Main Street. This two-story shop has a good selection of quilts, collectibles, and refinished furniture. Open daily. (512) 312–1559.

Texas Hatters. Exit 220 on east side of I–35. This store's founder, the late Manny Gammage, was "Texas's Hatmaker to the Stars." His hats topped the heads of Roy Rogers, Willie Nelson, Ronald Reagan, Burt Reynolds, and many other celebrities whose pictures decorate the shop walls. Besides the obligatory cowboy hats, this store also sells hand-blocked high-rollers, Panamas, and derbies. Open Tuesday through Saturday. (512) 295–HATS.

NORTHEAST DAY TRIP 3

New Braunfels · Gruene

NEW BRAUNFELS

If you're looking for a romantic getaway in a historic inn or a weekend of outdoor fun, New Braunfels is the place. Just half an hour northeast of San Antonio on I-35, this town of 30,700 offers something for every interest, from antiques and water sports to German culture.

In the 1840s, a group of German businessmen bought some land in Texas, planning to parcel off the acreage to German immigrants. Led by Prince Carl of Germany's Solms-Braunfels region, the group came to Texas to check on their new purchase. They discovered that it was over 300 miles from the Texas coast, far from supplies in San Antonio and located in the midst of Comanche Indian territory. Prince Carl sent a letter warning other settlers not to come, but it was too late—almost 400 already had set sail for Texas. The prince saved the day by buying another parcel of land, this in the central part of the state. Called "The Fountains" by the Indians, it offered plentiful springs and agricultural opportunities. The Germans soon divided the land into farms, irrigating with springwater. The settlement they founded was named "New Braunfels" in honor of their homeland.

New Braunfels has never forgotten these ties to the old country. Even today German is spoken in many local homes. Every November the town puts on its *lederhosen* for Wurstfest, one of the largest German celebrations in the country.

The German settlers were a practical lot, and they saved old items of every description. Everything from handmade cradles to used bot-

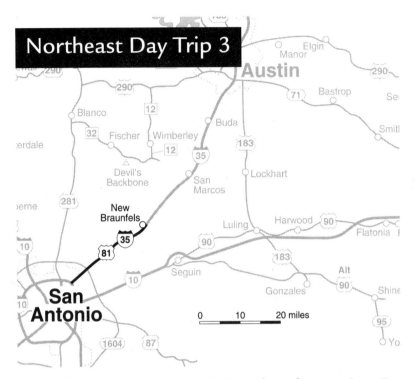

tles and jars were kept and passed down through generations. Because of this, New Braunfels touts itself as "The Antique Capital of Texas."

The early settlers of New Braunfels also were attracted by the Comal and Guadalupe Rivers. Today swimmers, rafters, inner-tubers, and campers are drawn to these shady banks. The 2-mile-long Comal holds the distinction as the world's shortest river. Its crystal-clear waters begin with the springs in downtown Landa Park, eventually merging with the Guadalupe River, home to many local outfitters. Located on the scenic drive called River Road, the outfitters provide equipment and transportation for inner-tubers and rafters of all skill levels who like nothing better on a hot Texas day than to float down the cypress-shaded waters.

WHERE TO GO

Chamber of Commerce. 390 South Seguin Avenue. Drop by for maps, brochures, shopping information, and friendly hometown advice about the area. Open daily. (800) 572–2626.

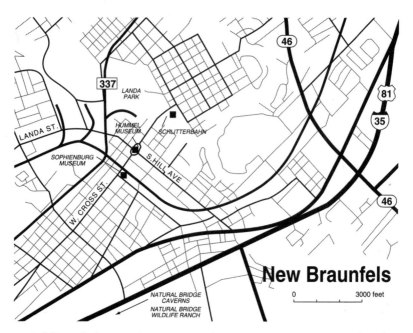

Schlitterbahn. 305 West Austin Street. From I–35, take the Boerne exit (Loop 337) to Common Street, then turn left and continue to Liberty Street. This water park ranks first in Texas and is tops in the United States among seasonal water parks. With sixty-five acres, this is the largest water theme park in the state.

Schlitterbahn, which means "slippery road" in German, is also the largest tubing park in the world, with nine tube chutes, two uphill water coasters, seventeen water slides, five playgrounds, and more. The Comal River supplies 24,000 gallons a minute of cool spring-water and also provides the only natural river rapids found in a water theme park.

Among the most colorful rides are the Soda Straws, huge Plexiglas-enclosed slides that take riders from the top of a 27-foot concrete soda to a pool below. In 1986 the cola glasses were filled with 2,000 gallons of soda and Blue Bell ice cream to create the world's largest Coke float. There's a steep 60-foot Schlittercoaster and the mile-long Raging River tube chute for daredevils, and a 50,000-gallon hot tub with a swim-up bar and the gentle wave pool for the less adventurous.

Two new attractions here are the Boogie Bahn, a moving mountain of water for surfing, and the Dragon Blaster, the world's first uphill water coaster. The latter shoots inner-tube riders uphill for a roller-coaster-type ride through hills, dips, and curves. Plan to spend a whole day here, and bring a picnic if you like. Open May through September. Fee. (830) 625-2351.

Hummel Museum. 199 Main Plaza. This 15,000-square-foot collection chronicles the life of German nun Sister Maria Innocentia Hummel through her sketches, paintings, and personal diaries. It's filled with 350 original paintings and early sketches that spawned the popular Hummel figurines, plates, and other collectibles. Sister Maria Innocentia first began producing these works during World War II. Today the figurines and plates, which portray young children, are sought by collectors from around the world. Occasionally the museum brings craftspeople from Germany to demonstrate the production of today's Hummel items. Collectors will find a Hummel bonanza in the adjacent gift shop. Open daily (afternoon only on Sunday). Fee. (800) 456-4866.

Sophienburg Museum. 401 West Coll Street. For a look at the hard-working people who settled this rugged area, spend an hour or two at the Sophienburg. Named for the wife of settlement leader Prince Carl, the museum's displays include a reproduction of an early New Braunfels home, a doctor's office (complete with medical tools), a blacksmith's shop, and carriages used by early residents. Open daily, but call for hours. Fee. (830) 629-1572.

Lindheimer Home. 491 Comal Avenue. Located on the banks of the Comal River, this home belonged to Ferdinand Lindheimer, a botanist who lent his name to over thirty Texas plant species. Now restored, it contains early memorabilia from Lindheimer's career as both botanist and newspaper publisher. A backyard garden is filled with examples of his native flora discoveries. Hours are seasonal; call before you go. Fee. (830) 608-1512.

Museum of Texas Handmade Furniture. 1370 Church Hill Drive, in Conservation Plaza. This nineteenth-century home contains cedar, oak, and cypress furniture handcrafted by early German settlers. Open Tuesday through Sunday from Memorial Day through Labor Day, and on weekend afternoons the rest of the year. Fee. (830) 629-6504.

Natural Bridge Caverns. On RR 3009, southwest of New Braunfels. Named for the rock arch over the entrance, this cave is one of the most spectacular in the area. The guided tour is well lit; the slope of the trail may be taxing for some. Open daily year-round; phone for tour times. Fee. (830) 651-6101.

Natural Bridge Wildlife Ranch. Next to the caverns. From I-35 south of New Braunfels, take RR 3009 west. From TX 46 west of town, you also can take a left on RR 1863 for a slightly longer but very scenic route. The drive through the ranch takes you past zebras, gazelles, antelopes, and ostriches, and feeding is allowed. The entrance area includes a petting zoo with pygmy goats. Open daily. Fee. (830) 438-7400.

Landa Park. Landa and San Antonio Streets. Named for Joseph Landa, New Braunfels's first millionaire, this downtown park includes a miniature train, a glass-bottomed boat cruise, a golf course, and a 1½-acre spring-fed swimming pool. This is the headwaters of the Comal River, where springs gush 8 million gallons of pure water every hour. Picnicking is welcome in the park, but no camping. Free. (830) 608-2160.

Canyon Lake. FM 306, northwest of town. With 80 miles of protected shoreline, Canyon Lake is very popular with campers, cyclists, scuba divers, and boaters. The lake has seven parks with boat ramps and picnic facilities. (800) 528-2104.

River Road. This winding drive stretches northwest of the city for 18 miles from Loop 337 at the city limits to the Canyon Lake Dam. It's lined with river outfitters and beautiful spots to pull over and look at the rapids, which delight rafters, canoeists, and inner-tubers.

Alamo Classic Car Museum. I-35 at Exits 180 and 182 on the northbound access road. Car buffs will find over 150 vehicles on display in this privately owned collection. Texas's largest auto museum, spanning 35,000 square feet, features everything from Edsels to DeLoreans and antique cars to fire trucks. Open daily. Fee. (830) 606-4311.

Rockin' R River Rides. 1405 Gruene Road. You can take a river ride here anytime between March and October. Excursions range from family tubing trips to whitewater thrillers. This company also operates a campground, Camp Hueco Springs, on River Road. (800) 55-FLOAT or (830) 629-9999.

The Children's Museum. Off I-35 at exit 187. Bring the kids to enjoy hands-on fun at this interactive museum that features a television studio. Open Tuesday to Sunday (Sunday afternoon only). Fee. (830) 620-0939.

WHERE TO SHOP

Downtowner I Antique Mall. 223 West San Antonio Street, off the Plaza. This antique mall, spanning over 17,000 square feet, is filled with everything from Raggedy Ann dolls to old matchbooks. Closed Tuesday. (830) 629-3947.

    New Braunfels Factory Stores. Exits 187 and 189 off I-35. What started out as a factory store for West Point Pepperell has become a destination for busloads of shoppers from Houston and Dallas. The stores, which often sell new product lines, are owned by the factories, but unlike some factory outlets this mall does not feature seconds or discounted merchandise. Open daily. (830) 620-6806.

WHERE TO EAT

Oma's Haus. Take Seguin exit 1890 off I-35 and drive east to 541 TX 46 South. This restaurant serves a wide selection of German dishes in a family atmosphere. The menu includes chicken and pork *schnitzel,* and a specialty of the house called Oma's Pride, a spinach-filled pastry shell. For the less adventurous, chicken-fried steak and chicken breast also are offered. Open for lunch and dinner daily. $$; ☐. (830) 625-3280.

    Naegelin's Bakery. 129 South Seguin Avenue. Naegelin's has operated on the same spot since 1868. The original building is gone now, replaced by the current structure in 1942. The store's specialty is apple strudel, a 2-foot long creation that is certain to make any pastry lover's mouth water. During the holidays, some of Naegelin's best sellers are *springerle,* a licorice cookie, and *lebkucken,* a frosted gingerbread cookie. Open Monday through Saturday. (830) 625-5722.

    New Braunfels Smokehouse. TX 46 and US 81. If you get the chance to attend Wurstfest, you'll undoubtedly sample the product of this smokehouse. For this fall event, New Braunfels Smokehouse produces between 40,000 and 60,000 pounds of sausage. That sausage is the specialty of the house, but the restaurant has a little of everything, including smoked ham and barbecue brisket. A large gift shop up front offers Texas specialty foods and cookbooks. The company's mail order business ships over 600,000 catalogs to sausage lovers around the country.

WHERE TO STAY

New Braunfels has plenty of accommodations for everyone. Check with the Chamber of Commerce (800) 572-2626.

Prince Solms Inn. 295 East San Antonio Street. Built in 1900, this quiet bed-and-breakfast has two suites and a guest parlor downstairs; upstairs there are eight guest rooms. All rooms are furnished with period antiques. $$; ☐. (830) 625-9169.

Faust Hotel. 240 South Seguin Avenue. A New Braunfels tradition, this 1929 four-story, renovated hotel features a bar that's popular with locals and visitors. The lobby is appointed with beautiful antique furnishings. $$; ☐. (830) 625-7791.

ESPECIALLY FOR WINTER TEXANS

Heidelberg Lodges. 1020 North Houston Avenue. Located near the headwaters of the Comal River, this scenic family resort is popular in the summer with swimmers, snorkelers, and scuba divers. During off-season it's home to Winter Texans, who are welcomed with potluck dinners and get-togethers. Accommodations include A-frame cottages and motel units. Call for long-term winter rates. $$; ☐. (830) 625-9967.

GRUENE

Although it has the feel of a separate community, Gruene actually sits within the northern New Braunfels city limits. Exit I-35 on FM 306 and head west for 1.5 miles to Hunter Road. Turn left and continue to Gruene. Like Waxahachie and Refugio, the pronunciation of Gruene is one of those things that sets a real Texan apart. To sound like a local, just say "Green" when referring to this weekend destination.

In the days when cotton was king, Gruene was a roaring town on the banks of the Guadalupe River. Started in the 1870s by H. D. Gruene, the community featured a swinging dance hall and a cotton gin. Prosperity reigned until the boll weevil came to Texas, with the Great Depression right on its heels. Gruene's foreman hanged himself from the water tower, and H. D.'s plans for the town withered like the cotton in the fields. Gruene became a ghost town.

One hundred years after its founding, investors began restoring Gruene's historic buildings and, little by little, businesses began moving into the once-deserted structures. Now Gruene is favored by antique shoppers, barbecue and country music lovers, and those looking to step back into a simpler time. On weekdays you may find Gruene's streets quiet, but expect crowds every weekend.

There's free parking across from the Gruene Mansion Inn, former home of H. D. Gruene. Today the mansion is a private residence owned by the proprietors of an adjacent bed-and-breakfast.

Gruene is compact, with everything within easy walking distance. If you'd like more information on the community's history, pick up a free copy of "A Pedestrian Guide for Gruene Guests" at local shops.

Over one hundred arts and crafts vendors sell their wares during Market Days. This event is held February through November on the third Saturday and Sunday of the month, and a Christmas market takes place on the first weekend in December.

WHERE TO GO

Texas Wines. 1612 Hunter Road. This shop serves as a tasting room and a distributor for many Texas wine makers. Free. (830) 620–4503.

Gruene Hall. 1281 Gruene Road. The oldest dance hall in Texas is as lively today as it was a century ago. Dances and concerts are regularly held here (even though the hall still offers only natural air conditioning), and it is also open to tour. Burlap bags draped from the ceiling dampen the sound, and 1930s advertisements decorate the walls. The hall opens at 11:00 A.M. most days. On weekdays, there's usually no cover charge for evening performances; weekend cover charges vary with the performer. Call for a schedule of events. (830) 606–1281.

WHERE TO SHOP

Gruene General Store. 1610 Hunter Road. This shop brings back memories of small-town life during Gruene's heyday as a cotton center. This was the first mercantile store, built in 1878 to serve the families that worked on the cotton farms. It also served as a stagecoach stop and a post office. Today instead of farm implements and dry goods, however, this 1990s general store sells cookbooks, fudge, and Texas-themed clothing. Belly up for a soda from the old-fashioned fountain and have a taste of homemade fudge. (830) 629-6021.

Gruene River Raft Company. 1404 Gruene Road. See the Guadalupe at your own pace—during a leisurely inner-tube ride or on an exciting whitewater raft journey—with this outfitter. (830) 625-2800 or 625-2873.

Lone Star Country Goods. 1613 Hunter Road. Bring the cowboy look to your home with the accessories in this shop. Lamps, dinnerware, and folk art are offered for sale. (830) 609-1613.

Bushwhackers. 1633 Hunter Road. Handmade swings hang beneath this store's shady oak trees. Crafters here produce outdoor furniture of all types as well as custom-made cypress and mesquite furniture. Open daily. (800) 676-4534 or (830) 620-4534.

Texas Homegrown. 1641 Hunter Road. Like the name suggests, the merchandise here is Texas-themed and features everything from bluebonnet earrings to coyote T-shirts. Open daily February through December; closed January. (830) 629-3176.

Gruene Antique Company. 1607 Hunter Road. Built in 1904, this was once a mercantile store. Today it's divided into several vendor areas and filled with antiques. Open daily. (830) 629-7781.

Buck Pottery. 1296 Gruene Road. Here you can watch crafters make pottery in the back room. This shop sells dinnerware, gift items, and outdoor pots, all made with unleaded glazes. Open daily. (830) 629-7975.

Gruene Haus. 1297 Gruene Road. Built in the 1880s, this shop was the former home of H. D. Gruene's foreman. Linens, lace runners, silk bluebonnets, gifts for cat lovers, and decorative accessories are offered for sale. Open daily. (830) 629-5990.

WHERE TO EAT

Guadalupe Smoked Meats. 1299 Gruene Road. Outstanding barbecue, potato salad, and beans are popular choices at this restaurant housed in the old Martin Brothers Store. The owners also operate a mail-order business for people who can't find barbecue like this at home. Open daily for lunch and dinner. $$; ☐. (830) 629-6121.

Gristmill Restaurant and Bar. 1287 Gruene Road. Housed in the ruins of a 120-year-old cotton gin, this restaurant serves chicken, chicken-fried steak, catfish, burgers, and other Texas favorites. You can eat inside or outside on the deck overlooking the Guadalupe River. Open daily. $$; ☐. (830) 625-0684.

WHERE TO STAY

Gruene Mansion Inn. 1275 Gruene Road. Guests at this inn stay in restored 1870s cottages on a bluff overlooking the Guadalupe River. Eight lovely rooms are decorated with period antiques. A two-night rental is required on weekends. $$; no ☐. (830) 629-2641.

Luling · Harwood
Flatonia · Praha
Schulenburg

LULING

You can leave San Antonio on either I-10 or US 90, traveling east past Seguin on your way to Luling. (For Seguin attractions, see EAST FROM SAN ANTONIO, DAY TRIP 2.)

Luling is best known as an oil town. Oil was discovered here in 1922, and fields pumping this "black gold" can be seen throughout the Luling area. Even before that time the town had a reputation as "the toughest town in Texas," frequented by gunfighters like John Wesley Hardin and Ben Thompson. Luling was also a cattle center and the end of a railroad line to Chihuahua, Mexico.

When oil was discovered, the economy of the town shifted to this profitable industry. Today 184 wells pump within the city limits. As part of a beautification effort, the Chamber of Commerce commissioned an artist to transform several of the pumpjacks into moving sculptures in the shapes of cartoon characters. There's even a Santa Claus and a butterfly to brighten up the streets.

WHERE TO GO

Palmetto State Park. 6 miles southeast of town on US 183, along the banks of the San Marcos River. Palmetto State Park is a topographical anomaly amidst gently rolling farm and ranchland. According to scientists, the river shifted course thousands of years ago, leaving a huge deposit of silt. This sediment absorbed rain and

East Day Trip 1

ground water, nurturing a marshy swamp estimated to be over 18,000 years old. Now part of Palmetto State Park, the swamp is filled with palmettos as well as moss-draped trees, 4-foot-tall irises, and many bird species. Nature trails wind throughout the area.

The park has full hookups and tent sites. There's also picnicking, but during the warmer months bring along mosquito repellent. Open daily. Fee. (830) 672-3266.

Francis-Ainsworth House. 200 block of South Pecan Street. Enjoy a tour of this 1894 home. Managed by the Daughters of the Republic of Texas, the residence is filled with period antiques. Open Thursday and Saturday afternoons. Free. (830) 875-3214.

Central Texas Oil Patch Museum & Luling Chamber of Commerce Visitors' Center. 421 Davis Street. Luling's oil businesses, starting with Rafael Rios No. 1 (an oil field 12 miles long and 2 miles wide), are explored in this museum. Call for hours. Free. (830) 875-3214.

WHERE TO EAT

Luling City Market. 633 Davis Street. This is small-town barbecue the way it ought to be: served up in a no-frills meat market, with ambience replaced by local atmosphere. The Luling City Market turns out smoked brisket, sausage, and ribs. $; no ☐. (830) 875-9019.

HARWOOD

WHERE TO GO

Noah's Land. TX 304, 5.5 miles north of I-10, outside of Harwood. This drive-through exotic wildlife park boasts 500 animals. The 400-acre park is divided into ten sanctuaries, covering animals of the plains and the mountains. On your trip through the park, you can feed axis deer, Corsican sheep, red kangaroos, emus, camels, rhinos, and local favorites like Texas longhorns. A large petting area is home to Angora and pygmy goats, Sicilian donkeys, and more. An aviary contains exotic chickens, peacocks, and pheasants. Open daily except Christmas. Fee. (800) 725-NOAH.

FLATONIA

Return to US 90 and continue east to the small town of Flatonia. This community was settled by English, German, Bohemian, and Czech immigrants, many of whom came to the United States in the 1850s and 1860s to avoid Austro-Hungarian oppression.

WHERE TO GO

E. A. Arnim Archives and Museum. US 90, downtown. This local history museum contains exhibits on Flatonia's early days and its settlement by many cultural groups. Open Sunday afternoon. Free. (512) 865-2451.

PRAHA

Three miles east of Flatonia on US 90 is Praha (the Slovakian spelling for "Prague"). Like its European counterpart, Praha holds a predominantly Czech population, descendants of immigrants who came here in 1855.

The main structure in Praha is the Assumption of the Blessed Virgin Mary Church, often called St. Mary's. Built in 1895, it is one of a half dozen painted churches in the area. Although few examples remain today, it was not unusual for nineteenth-century rural churches to boast painted interiors. Guided tours from nearby Schulenburg visit all the churches, but you can see most of the structures on a self-guided trip. A free brochure and map is available from the Schulenburg Chamber of Commerce (409) 743-4514.

St. Mary's has a beautifully painted vaulted ceiling, the work of Swiss-born artist Gottfried Flury. Never retouched, the 1895 murals on the tongue-and-groove ceiling depict golden angels high over a pastoral setting. This Praha church, as well as ones in High Hill and Ammannsville, are listed in the National Register of Historic Places. The churches are open Monday through Saturday 8:00 A.M. to 5:00 P.M., although it is not guaranteed that the doors will be unlocked at all times. Free. (No phone.)

SCHULENBURG

Continue east on US 90 to the agricultural community of Schulenburg (meaning "school town" in German). Carnation Milk Company's first plant was built in Schulenburg in 1929, and even today dairy products generate a major source of income for the area. Schulenburg is known as the "Home of the Painted Churches," although the elaborately painted structures are actually located in nearby small communities (Dubina, Ammannsville, Swiss Alp, High Hill, and Praha). These beautifully painted buildings are reminders of the area's rural traditions and ethnic background.

In Ammannsville, the St. John the Baptist Church includes stained-glass windows illustrating the Czech heritage of the parish. High Hill's St. Mary's Church boasts marbleized columns, religious statuary, and a history of a European-style seating arrangement with women on the left and men on the right. The murals in Dubina's Sts. Cyril and Methodius Church were covered over during a 1952 remodeling. In 1981 the paintings, depicting winged angels and elaborate stencil patterns, were renovated by a local parishioner.

WHERE TO GO

Painted Churches Tour. With a two- to three-week notice, the Schulenburg Chamber of Commerce provides guides for groups of ten or more. You can always enjoy a self-guided tour; maps of the church locations are available at the Schulenburg site at 101-B Kessler Avenue (Highway 77). Fee for guided tour. (409) 743-4514.

WHERE TO EAT

Oakridge Smokehouse Restaurant. I-10 and TX 77. Hungry I-10 travelers between San Antonio and Houston know all about Oakridge Smokehouse. In business nearly half a century, this family-owned company churns out barbecue and sausage to please travelers and mail-order customers. The comfortable restaurant is popular with families, not just for its extensive menu, but also for its large gift shop up front. $-$$; □. (409) 743-3372.

SEGUIN

You can reach Seguin (pronounced "se-GEEN") via either US 90 or I-10 east of San Antonio. It's a 36-mile trip to this town on the Guadalupe River named for Lieutenant Colonel Juan Seguin, a hero of the Texas Revolution. Prior to the Mexican invasion of 1837, Seguin was ordered by his superiors to destroy San Antonio. He refused, thus saving the city.

Many towns boast nicknames, from Austin's "River City" to San Antonio's "Alamo City." Seguin, though, has one of the most unusual: "The Mother of Concrete Cities." A Seguin chemist held several concrete production patents, which accounts for the use of the material in over ninety area buildings by the end of the nineteenth century.

The most beautiful area of Seguin is Starcke Park. It offers picnic tables under huge pecan, oak, and cypress trees, and a winding drive along the Guadalupe River. The tree Seguin is best known for is the pecan. The town even calls itself the home of the "World's Largest Pecan," a statue located on the courthouse lawn at Court Street.

WHERE TO GO

Chamber of Commerce. 427 North Austin Street. Stop by the chamber office for brochures and maps. Open weekdays. (800) 580-7322 or (830) 379-6382.

Sebastopol State Historical Park. 704 Zorn Street. This is one of the best examples of the early use of concrete in the Southwest.

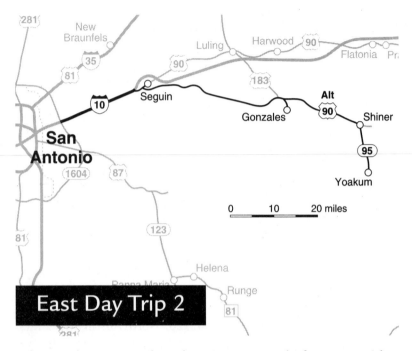

East Day Trip 2

Sebastopol was once a large home, constructed of concrete with a plaster overlay. Today it is open for tours and contains exhibits illustrating the construction of this historic building and its restoration in 1988. Tours are conducted weekends; call the Chamber of Commerce to set up group tours at other times. Fee. (830) 379–4833.

True Women Tours. Fans of Janice Woods Wendle's *True Women* can take a guided tour of the sites mentioned in this bestseller and seen in the television miniseries. Call the Seguin Chamber of Commerce for tour times; a map for a self-guided drive is also available at the chamber office. Fee for guided tour. (800) 580–7322.

Starcke Park. South side of town, off TX 123. Make time for this pleasant park, where visitors can enjoy golf, tennis, and baseball as well as many riverside picnic spots. Free. (830) 401–2480.

Seguin's Lakes. Seguin is surrounded by four lakes on the Guadalupe River that offer bass, crappie, and catfish fishing, including lighted docks for night fishing. RV facilities are available as weil. The lakes include Lake Dunlap—I-10 to TX 46 exit west of Seguin, then 8 miles on TX 46; Lake McQueeney—I-10 to FM 78 exit, FM 78 west for 3 miles to FM 725, then turn right and continue for

1 mile; Lake Placid—I-10 to FM 464 exit, stay on access road; and Meadow Lake—I-10 to TX 123 bypass, then south for 4 miles.

Los Nogales Museum. 415 South River, just south of the courthouse. Los Nogales, which means "walnuts" in Spanish, houses local artifacts. The small brick adobe building was constructed in 1849. Next door, **The Doll House** is filled with period children's toys you can see through the windows. This white miniature home was built between 1908 and 1910 by local cabinetmaker Louis Dietz as a playhouse for his niece. Later he used it to promote his business. For tour information, call the Chamber of Commerce at (800) 580-7322.

Texas Theatre. 427 North Austin Street. This 1931 theater has been used for scenes in two movies: *Raggedy Man* and *The Great Waldo Pepper*. It still sports its original marquee and recalls the old days of small-town Texas theaters.

WHERE TO STAY

Weinert House Bed and Breakfast. 1207 North Austin Street. Kick back and enjoy small-town life amid 1890s elegance in this historic Victorian home. Four guest quarters are decorated with period an-

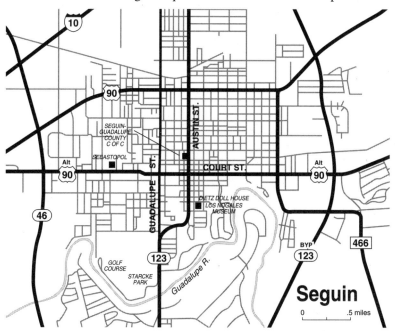

tiques. The Senator's suite includes a fireplace and screened sunporch. $$; no ☐. (830) 372-0422.

GONZALES

Take alternate US 90 (US 90A) east to Gonzales, one of Texas's most interesting historic cities. For many years this was the westernmost settlement in the state.

Plagued by constant Indian attacks, Gonzales's citizens received a small brass cannon for protection by the Mexican government in 1831. Four years later, when relations between Texas and Mexico soured, over 150 Mexican soldiers staged a battle to retrieve the weapon. The soldiers were faced with 18 Gonzaleans, who stalled the army while local citizens rolled out the small field-piece and prepared for action. Meanwhile, other townsfolk sewed the first battle flag of Texas, which pictured a cannon beneath the words "Come and Take It," a motto by which Gonzales is still known. The Texans fired the first shot and the Mexican troops retreated. Although the confrontation was brief, this act began the Texas Revolution.

The site of this historic first conflict is marked by a monument located 7 miles southwest of Gonzales on TX 97. The first shots were fired one-half mile north of the present monument.

WHERE TO GO

Chamber of Commerce. 414 St. Lawrence Street. Located in the Old Jail Museum, this office has brochures on local attractions and events. Open weekdays. (830) 672-6532.

Old Jail Museum. 414 St. Lawrence Street. This unusual museum is housed in the old Gonzales jail, built in 1887 and used until 1975. Downstairs you can tour the room where female prisoners and mentally ill persons once were incarcerated together. Exhibits include jail weapons created from spoons and bedsprings.

The walls of the second floor are chiseled with graffiti of past residents. The large room is rimmed with iron cells, all overlooking a reproduction of the old gallows that carried off its last hanging in 1921. According to legend, this prisoner continually watched the clocks on the adjacent courthouse, counting the hours he had left to live. He swore that he was innocent, and said that if he were hanged the clocks would never keep accurate time again. Although the four clock faces have been changed since that time, none of them has ever kept the same time again.

The museum is open daily (afternoons only on Sunday). Free. (830) 672-6532 (Chamber of Commerce).

Memorial Museum. 414 Smith Street, between St. Lawrence and St. Louis Streets. This museum is dedicated to the history of Gonzales. Exhibits on the town's early days include the "Come and Take It" cannon. Open Tuesday through Sunday. Free. (830) 672-6350.

Gonzales Pioneer Village. One-half-mile north of town on US 183. This living history center takes visitors back to Gonzales's frontier days. The village is composed of log cabins, a cypress-constructed home, a grand Victorian home, a smokehouse, a blacksmith shop, and a church. The village also stages reenactments, including the "Come and Take It" celebration in October. Open weekends; group tours by appointment Fee. (830) 672-2157.

SHINER

Continue east on US 90A for 18 miles to Shiner, best known as the home of Shiner beer, a Texas favorite produced by the tiny Spoetzl Brewery since 1909.

WHERE TO GO

Spoetzl Brewery. 603 Brewery Street, off TX 95 North. This tiny but historic brewery was founded in 1909 by Kosmos Spoetzl, a Bavarian brewmaster. Here several Shiner beers are produced in one of the smallest commercial brew kettles in the country. Across the street, a museum and gift shop overflow with Shiner memorabilia, antiques, and photos of Spoetzl's early days. Free brewery tours on weekdays at 11:00 A.M. and 1:30 P.M. Hospitality room open following tour. Free. (512) 594-3852.

City Hall. US 90A, downtown. This two-story building houses the fire department, police department, and city offices. Enter on the left side for city brochures and a free map. (512) 594-4180.

Wolters Memorial Museum. 306 South Avenue I off TX 95 South. This museum is filled with home implements, weapons, fossils, and even a country store representing the community's early days. Open weekdays and the second and fourth Sunday afternoons. Free. (512) 594-3774.

WHERE TO STAY

The Old Kasper House. 219 Avenue C. This bed-and-breakfast is located in the former home of a cotton ginner and his wife from Austria and Czechoslovakia who was best known as a relative of Gregor Mendel, discoverer of genetic information (remember those Mendel pea models in Biology I?). Today the two-story home is a great small-town getaway, offering seven rooms with private baths and a cottage. Behind the bed-and-breakfast there's an RV park with eight full-service hookups. $-$$; □. (512) 594-4336.

YOAKUM

From Shiner, drive south on TX 95 for 8 miles to US 77A. Turn right and continue for 2 miles. Yoakum was the starting point of many cattle drives along the Chisholm Trail, and in 1887 it became the junction for the San Antonio and Aransas Pass Railroad. When the railroad came to town, meat packinghouses followed. In 1919 the first tannery opened, producing leather kneepads for cotton pickers. Soon more leather businesses arrived, and eventually Yoakum earned its title as "The Leather Capital of the World."

Today twelve leather companies produce belts, saddles, bullwhips, gunslings, and wallets. Although the companies do not sell directly from their factories, the Leather Capital Store operates as a showroom and factory outlet for many Yoakum manufacturers. Tours of the leather companies are offered during the annual Land of Leather Days festival, the last weekend in February.

WHERE TO GO

Yoakum Heritage Museum. 312 Simpson Street. This two-story museum is filled with Yoakum memorabilia, from railroad paraphernalia to household items. The most interesting exhibit area is the Leather Room, with its displays on the leather factories. Open afternoons daily. Free. (512) 293-7022.

WHERE TO SHOP

The Leather Capital Store. 123 West Grand Street. This shop is a leather museum and store rolled into one. Its display windows are painted with silhouettes of Texas history scenes. Inside, thousands of belts, purses, and boots—even gunslings and holsters—are offered for sale. Upstairs the facade of a Wild West village brightens a floor filled with saddles and Southwestern and Western art. Deer shoulder blades etched with Indian scenes are produced by owner Leo Smith, who for many years worked as a commercial illustrator for one of the leather companies. Open Monday through Saturday. (512) 293-7274.

Return home from Yoakum by retracing your steps or by heading north on TX 95 to Flatonia. From here, go west on either I-10 or US 90. Attractions on this stretch are covered in EAST FROM SAN ANTONIO, DAY TRIP 1.

PANNA MARIA

To reach Panna Maria, leave San Antonio southeast on US 87. At the intersection of TX 123, drive south past the tiny Polish communities of Kosciusko and Cestohowa. At the intersection of FM 81, turn left for the 1-mile drive to Panna Maria.

If you weren't aware of its interesting history, you might just call this another pint-sized Texas town, perched on a shady hilltop with a nice breeze and a beautiful view. But there's a lot more to Panna Maria, which means "Virgin Mary" in Polish, than meets the eye. This quiet community holds the title of the first Polish settlement in America, and it still maintains a place in the history of Poland, well known among the people of the old country.

This small town was founded in 1854 by one hundred Polish families led by Father Leopold Moczygemba. After a nine-week voyage to Galveston, the settlers rented Mexican carts to transport their farm tools and bedding as well as the cross from their parish church. They made the difficult journey to central Texas on foot, finally stopping at the hillside that overlooks the San Antonio River and Cibolo Creek. The day was December 24, 1854, and the pioneers offered a midnight mass beneath one of the large hilltop oaks. They settled here.

The year that followed was a grueling one, a time when the pioneers learned the harshness of their new home. A cold winter was followed by a hot, dry summer filled with snakes and insects. Most of the settlers did succeed with their new venture and were soon joined by more Polish immigrants.

Southeast Day Trip 1

WHERE TO GO

Church of the Immaculate Conception. TX 81, in town. Within two years of settling in Panna Maria, the pioneers built the Church of the Immaculate Conception, the first Polish church in America. The original church was destroyed by fire and replaced in 1878 by the present structure, which serves as the center of worship for Panna Maria's citizens.

The church is home to a replica of the mosaic of Our Lady of Czestochowa, or the Black Madonna. The original Black Madonna is enshrined at the Monastery of Jasna Gora in Czestochowa, Poland, a city about 65 miles east of the area from which the first Panna Maria pioneers originated. According to tradition, the Madonna was painted by St. Luke and then found in the Holy Land in A.D. 326 by Saint Helena, mother of Constantine the Great.

This replica, a gift to the United States from Poland, was presented to the town by President Johnson in 1966. It rests on display at the front of the church along with hand-carved chairs and a gold chalice that belonged to Pope John Paul II. These priceless treasures were presented to the people of Panna Maria in 1987.

The church is open daily. For a small donation, you can purchase a brochure outlining the history of the Black Madonna and Panna Maria's early settlers. Free. (No phone.)

HELENA

From Panna Maria, continue on FM 81 for 5 miles to the tiny community of Helena. This was once a thriving town on the San Antonio River, founded in 1852 by Thomas Ruckman and Louis Owings (the latter became first governor of the Arizona territory). Owings named the town after his wife, Helen.

During the Civil War, much of the Confederate cotton passed through the town. At the time, Helena even had its own Confederate post office, which issued Helena stamps. Today they're a rare find, worth several thousand dollars. Helena's existence as a thriving burg came to a halt in 1886 when the railroad bypassed the town. Soon the county seat moved to Karnes City, and the town all but rolled up the sidewalks.

WHERE TO GO

Karnes County Museum. FM 81. This museum is actually a collection of historic buildings from the area, including a post office, jail, farmhouse, and barn. A museum traces the history of Karnes County, including its busy days during the Civil War. The grounds, shaded by large mesquite trees, also provide a picnic area. Open Tuesday through Saturday. Free. (210) 780–3210.

RUNGE

From Helena, continue on TX 81 for 9 miles to Runge, population 1,139. This community was founded by settlers from Panna Maria, who located it on the Texas and New Orleans Railroad line. Today it's a quiet farming community.

WHERE TO GO

Runge Museum. 106 North Helena. A few years ago this museum burned, but the collection, like the town of Runge itself, has perse-

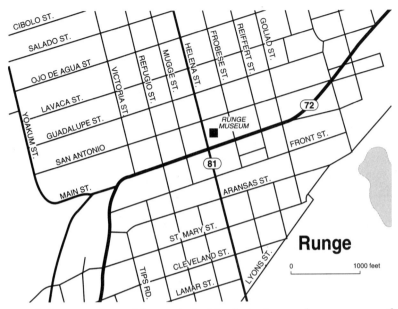

vered. Community residents pitched in their time and put a new roof on a historic structure that had served as a general store. Today this small museum contains exhibits on life in Runge during the 1880s. Set up like an old general store, it's filled with historic photos and items from Runge's past, including old-fashioned irons and household goods. Call for hours. Free. (210) 239–4289.

GOLIAD

To reach Goliad, continue southeast from Panna Maria on FM 81 past the communities of Helena and Runge, both of which were once thriving towns. Take TX 239 south at Charco to the intersection of US 59, and then head east to the historic city of Goliad.

Like the Alamo and the Battle of San Jacinto, Goliad holds a special place in Texas history. Founded by the Spanish, Goliad is the third oldest city in Texas. To protect their passage to the Gulf, the Spaniards moved their Espíritu Santo mission and its royal protector, Presidio La Bahia (Fort of the Bay), to this location in 1749. At that time the community was named Santa Dorotea. Years later, the town's name was changed to Goliad, an anagram of the spoken letters "Hidalgo" (the "h" is silent in Spanish). Hidalgo was a priest who became a hero during the Mexican Revolution.

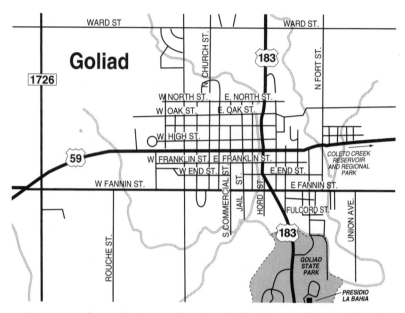

Few towns have their own flag, but Goliad boasts its own historic, if somewhat gruesome, banner. On October 9, 1835, the Texas colonists made a move in their battle for independence. The settlers took over the Presidio and raised the "Bloody Arm Flag," picturing a severed arm holding a sword.

The next year the Texans, led by Colonel James W. Fannin, Jr., surrendered at the Battle of Coleto about 9 miles east of town. Approximately 390 soldiers were marched back to the Presidio. After a week of imprisonment all but 20 soldiers (who were spared as physicians or mechanics) were placed before a firing squad. Over two dozen men escaped during the massacre, but 342 were killed, the largest loss of life during the fight for independence. "Remember Goliad" soon became a cry alongside "Remember the Alamo."

Today the Presidio and the Mission Espíritu Santo are restored and open to the public. You also can visit Colonel Fannin's grave and see the monument that marks the resting place of the Texas soldiers.

WHERE TO GO

Goliad State Historical Park. On US 183, one-quarter-mile south of town. The highlight of this 178-acre park is the Mission Espíritu Santo. The restored mission offers spinning, weaving, and pottery-making demonstrations, primarily on weekends. Park activities feature hiking, picnicking, fishing, and boating. Screened shelters as well as tent and RV camping sites are available year-round. Fee. (512) 645-3405.

Presidio La Bahia. US 183, south of the San Antonio River. The Presidio holds many titles: It is the oldest fort in the West, one of few sites west of the Mississippi that was active in the American Revolution, the only fully restored Spanish *presidio*, and the only Texas Revolution site with its original appearance intact. The stone garrison is impressive and worth a stop. While you're here, visit the fort chapel, built in the Spanish colonial style. Open daily. Fee. (512) 645-3752.

General Zaragoza Birthplace. Across from Presidio La Bahia. This modest structure was the first home of Mexican General Ignacio Zaragoza. Under Zaragoza's command, the Mexican army defeated the French at the Battle of Puebla, a date now celebrated as "Cinco de Mayo" or "Fifth of May" throughout Texas and Mexico. Today the building is filled with exhibits that depict the general's role in Mexican history. Open Friday and Saturday. Free. (512) 645-3405.

Grave of Colonel Fannin and Troops. Just east of Presidio La Bahia. A large memorial marks the site of the massacre that occurred here on March 27, 1836. Free. (No phone.)

Market House Museum. 205 South Market. This museum contains exhibits on local history. The building also houses the Goliad Chamber of Commerce, where you can pick up brochures and area maps. Open weekdays. Free. (512) 645-3563.

Coleto Creek Reservoir and Regional Park. 10 miles northeast of Goliad on US 59. This 3,100-acre reservoir is a South Texas mecca for boaters, fishers, and campers. A park store is handy for picnickers. Winter Texans can enjoy an extended stay at these campgrounds. Fee. (512) 575-6366.

WHERE TO EAT

La Bahia Restaurant. US 183, south of Presidio La Bahia. Like its name suggests, this restaurant serves Mexican food, from fajitas to tacos, as well as a good selection of steaks and seafood. $-$$; ⚓. (512) 645-3651.

Empresario Restaurant. On the courthouse square. Grab a deli sandwich followed by a slice of homemade pie at this eatery that's a favorite with locals. Open for lunch daily. $-$$; ⚓. (512) 645-2347.

Fannin · Victoria

FANNIN

Follow SOUTHEAST FROM SAN ANTONIO, DAY TRIP 1 through Goliad and then turn north on US 59 in Goliad. Follow US 59 to Fannin, a town of only ninety-four residents.

Named for James W. Fannin, Jr., a hero of the Texas Revolution, the town is home to the Fannin Battleground State Historic Site, a site of interest to those tracing the history of the revolution in towns such as Goliad and Gonzales.

WHERE TO GO

Fannin Battleground State Historic Site. 1 mile south of town on Park Road 27. At this site, Colonel James W. Fannin, Jr. surrendered to the Mexican army after the Battle of Coleto Creek. The Mexican commander offered a clemency petition; General Santa Anna over-ruled the offer and ordered Fannin and his 342 men to be executed in Goliad. Today the men are remembered with a monument that re-calls the actions of March 27, 1836. Picnic and restroom facilities available at the day-use park. Open daily. Fee. (512) 645–2020.

VICTORIA

Termed "the crossroads of Texas," Victoria is located equal distances from San Antonio, Austin, Houston, and Corpus Christi. Named for the first president of Mexico, the city was founded by forty-one

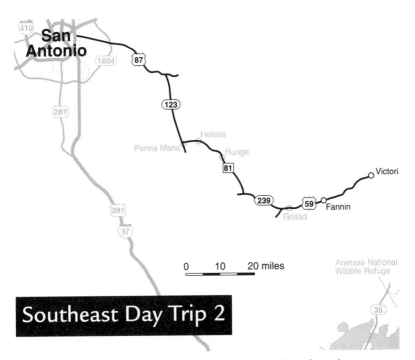

Southeast Day Trip 2

Spanish families. Later the town became one of the first three towns incorporated by the Republic of Texas.

WHERE TO GO

Coleto Creek Reservoir and Park. 15 miles west of Victoria off TX 59 south. Swim, picnic, or camp at this year-around park. Sites with electricity are available; the park includes restrooms with showers, laundry facilities, barbecue pits, volleyball courts, and more. Fee. (512) 575-6366.

McNamara Historical Museum. 502 North Liberty Street. Learn more about the history of this region at this 1876 Victorian home. Open Tuesday through Sunday afternoons. Free. (512) 575-8227.

The Texas Zoo. 110 Memorial Drive. Over 200 native Texas species of mammals, birds, reptiles, fish, and amphibians are included at this unique zoo. Endangered Texas species are highlighted. Texas species are also showcased in a native plants and wildflower garden. In 1984, the mission of the zoo was recognized by the state legislature and they proclaimed this "The National Zoo of Texas." Open daily. Fee. (512) 573-7681.

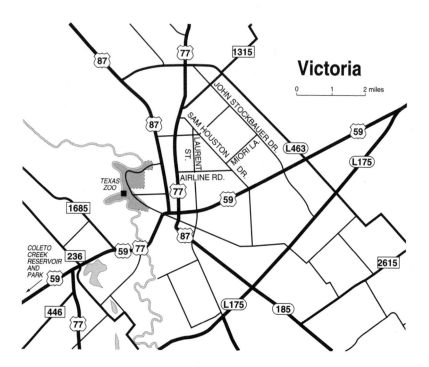

WHERE TO EAT

The Lost Cajun. 700 Coleto Park Road. Roll up your sleeves and get ready for some spicy Cajun food and all the fixin's at this restaurant. Open for dinner only Tuesday through Friday; lunch and dinner weekends. $–$$

SOUTH DAY TRIP 1

Aransas Pass · Port Aransas
Rockport-Fulton

Birders come from around the world to test their skill at spotting some of the nearly 500 species recorded in this area.

ARANSAS PASS

To reach Aransas Pass, take I-37 south from San Antonio for 145 miles to Corpus Christi. (For attractions in Corpus Christi, see SOUTH FROM SAN ANTONIO, DAY TRIP 2.) Cross the Harbor Bridge and follow US 181 north to TX 35. Continue to the intersection of TX 361, then turn right to Aransas Pass.

Aransas Pass is more a genuine fishing village and less a tourist destination than many other coastal communities. Most of its 7,000 residents are employed in the fishing industry. Make your first stop the Chamber of Commerce at 452 Cleveland Boulevard. This office can direct you to the Conn Brown Harbor for a look at the enormous shrimp fleet. The Seamen's Memorial Tower, a monument to the fishermen lost at sea, marks the entrance to the working harbor.

PORT ARANSAS

To reach Port Aransas, follow TX 361 from Aransas Pass across the Redfish Bay Causeway to Harbor Island. Look north to see a restored, privately owned lighthouse, one of the few functioning lighthouses on the coast.

Port Aransas, or just "Port A" to most Texans, is perched on the northern tip of Mustang Island. Life in the coastal community centers around the Gulf, with its crying gulls, rolling surf, and miles of pancake-colored sand. When the spring break crowds depart, it's a town that appeals to birders and anglers as much as to bikini-clad sunbathers.

Although Port A is now one of the state's most popular coastal destinations, its history as a hideaway dates back far before the days of sunscreen and surfboards. Some of the island's first residents were the fierce Karankawa Indians, a cannibalistic tribe that greeted later visitors, from pirates to Spanish missionaries. Buccaneer Jean Lafitte reputedly camped on the shores of Mustang Island, building

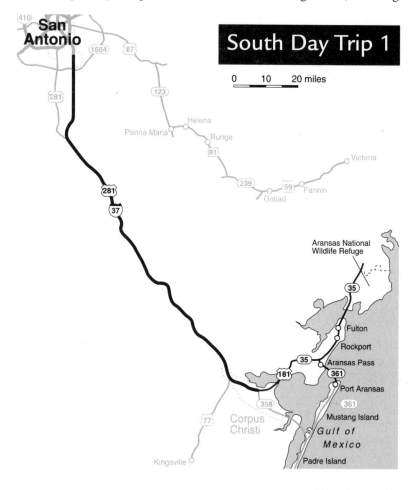

South Day Trip 1

0   10   20 miles

bonfires to lure ships seeking a pass onto the beach to be looted and plundered. Wild horses, evolved from the steeds of Spanish explorers, gave Mustang Island its name.

Just as it was over 200 years ago, the most common way to reach Port A is by water. As noted previously, you follow TX 361 from Aransas Pass across the Redfish Bay Causeway to Harbor Island. Five free ferries run twenty-four hours daily from Harbor Island across the Corpus Christi Ship Channel to Port Aransas. Tune your radio to 5:30 A.M. for ferry traffic conditions during the morning, lunch hour, and late afternoon rush times.

Port Aransas is a small town filled with year-round seaside attractions. During spring break, Port A greets over 150,000 college students (and an increasing number of families as well) from throughout the Midwest and Southwest. The crowds are very manageable the rest of the year, however. During the winter months, most visitors are anglers and Winter Texans.

A fishing cruise is great for a look at the Gulf. Trips include bait and tackle, and cost about $50 a day. Contact the Tourist & Convention Bureau at (800) 45–COAST or (512) 749–5919 for more information.

After a day of surf hopping and sand-castle building, head to the town of Port Aransas itself. Shopping for shirts, shells, or elegant jewelry is a prime activity. So is dining. You can buy shrimp and fresh fish and prepare it in a condo kitchen or visit one of the island's many restaurants.

WHERE TO GO

University of Texas Marine Science Institute. On Ship Channel. Students of oceanography, ecology, marine chemistry, and botany train at this branch of the University of Texas, located on eighty-two beachfront acres. The visitors center is open to the public, featuring exhibits and films on Texas Gulf life. Open weekdays. Free. (512) 749–6720.

Gulf Beach. The best way to learn about the beach life is to become part of it. And that's just what most visitors do. Armed with sunscreen, beach umbrellas, and folding chairs, they line the Gulf beach where swimmers and surfers frequent the shallow, warm waters and beachcombers search for fragile sand dollars, pieces of coral, and unbroken shells. Drivers on the public beach are restricted to a marked lane, and parking requires an annual permit, available for $6.00 from the Chamber of Commerce or at many Port Aransas businesses. There is free boardwalk access to the beach from many of the condominiums as well.

Mustang Island State Park. Park Road 53, southwest of Port Aransas. The facilities at this scenic beach include freshwater showers, picnic tables, and tent and RV camping. The area is protected from vehicular traffic. Open daily. Fee. (512) 749-5246.

San Jose Island. Woody's Boat Basin. Both Port Aransas and Mustang Island State Park beaches are popular with vacationers, but if you're looking for a real getaway, head to nearby San Jose Island. You'll feel like pirate Jean Lafitte, whose camp was found on the island in 1834. Large iron rings, thought to have been used to tie up small boats his group used to row ashore, were discovered at the site. Even today, the island is accessible only by boat, and there are no public facilities.

San Jose is a quiet getaway for fishing, beachcombing, swimming, or shelling. Ferries leave throughout the day from Woody's Boat Basin, so you can stay as long as you like. Open daily. Fee. (512) 749-5252.

Fishing Cruises. Few coastal cities offer more fishing cruises than Port Aransas. In varying seasons, the Gulf is home to mackerel, ling, pompano, marlin, barracuda, grouper, and amberjack. In the calmer bay waters, look for redfish, speckled trout, drum, and flounder.

Large group trips, taking as many as one hundred passengers, provide bait and tackle, and cost about $50 a day. A fishing license is not required for the deep-sea excursions since you will be fishing in out-of-state waters. These big cruises are great for families and budget travelers; serious fishers looking for big game fish such as marlin and shark should book charter excursions for personalized service.

If you do take a fishing cruise, be aware that Gulf waters can be very choppy. Except for the bay cruises, most boats travel 15 to 20 miles from shore. Seas are usually calmest in the summer, but even then 4- to 6-foot waves are possible. Seasickness has spoiled more than one vacationer's cruise, so be sure to purchase motion sickness medication or obtain a skin patch from your doctor before your trip.

For information on Port Aransas's many charters, contact the Tourist Convention Bureau at (800) 45-COAST or (512) 749-5919.

M/V *Wharf Cat.* Fisherman's Wharf. This 75-foot heated and air-conditioned catamaran departs from Fisherman's Wharf every Monday and Tuesday during the winter months for a look at the magnificent whooping cranes. (On other days, the cruise departs from nearby Rockport.) The cruise leaves Port Aransas for the Aransas National Wildlife Refuge, the winter home of the 5-foot tall whooping cranes. Binoculars and scopes are provided, along with checklists of frequently spotted birds. Fee. (800) 782-BIRD or (512) 749-5760.

***Island Queen* Cruises.** Woody's Boat Basin. This converted ferry-boat offers bay fishing for speckled trout and redfish. Your ticket includes rod, reel, and tackle. You'll need a Texas fishing license. Call for seasonal schedule. Fee. (512) 749-5252.

***The Duke* Cruises.** Woody's Boat Basin. This boat cruises the channel and often dolphins frolic alongside. A net collects marine life for visitors to view. Fee. (512) 749-5252.

WHERE TO EAT

The Crazy Cajun. 315 Alister Street. This Cajun seafood restaurant's house specialty is a steaming concoction of shrimp, sausage, potatoes, stone crab claws, and crawfish in season. The bowl is dumped onto your butcher-paper tablecloth. The atmosphere is casual and fun, and there's live entertainment many nights. Open for lunch and dinner on weekends, dinner only on weekdays; closed Mondays after Labor Day. $$; ☐. (512) 749-5069.

Seafood and Spaghetti Works. 710 Alister Street. This excellent restaurant is housed in a geodesic dome. Spaghetti primavera, shrimp and pepper pasta (a spicy dish that could be called Italian Tex-Mex if there were such a thing), filet mignon, and Cajun-style blackened redfish are popular choices. Save room for the butterfinger cheesecake. Open for dinner only. $$; ☐. (512) 749-5666.

Trout Street Bar and Grill. 104 West Cotter. Enjoy the "catch of the day" and other seafood favorites at this new restaurant. Burgers and steaks served along with oysters, shrimp, and local catch. $$; ☐. (512) 749-7800.

WHERE TO STAY

You won't find full-service hotels in Port Aransas, but the town does offer everything from luxury condominium complexes to mom-and-pop motels aimed at vacationing fishers. Many condominiums include full kitchens and appliances, and boardwalk access to the beach.

Sand Castle Condominiums. Sand Castle Drive. This six-story condominium complex is located near the beach. Every room offers a great view and comes with a fully equipped kitchen. (If you can afford it, get a room with a private balcony.) When you've had enough saltwater swimming, take a dip in the large free-form pool in the center of the complex. Minimum stay and deposit required. $$$; □. (800) 727-6201.

Tarpon Inn. 200 East Cotter Street. The most historic hotel on the island (and listed on the National Register of Historic Places) is the Tarpon Inn, which dates back to 1923. The lobby walls are papered with thousands of tarpon scales, each autographed by the lucky angler. There's even one signed by Franklin Roosevelt. Within the last few years, the hotel has been renovated, but it still has a breezy atmosphere with rockers on the verandas. Each of the twenty-three rooms is decorated and furnished with antiques. $$; □. (800) 365-6784.

ESPECIALLY FOR WINTER TEXANS

Port Aransas offers many activities for Winter Texans, from aerobic classes to potluck dinners. Condominiums offer special monthly off-season rates. For a calendar of events or information on rentals, call (800) 452-6278.

ROCKPORT-FULTON

To reach the Rockport-Fulton area, return to Aransas Pass and take TX 35 north for 11 miles. The adjoining fishing villages of Rockport and Fulton lie along scenic Aransas Bay and are havens for snowbirds of all varieties, from 5-foot-tall whooping cranes to those in 30-foot-long Winnebagos. Both flock to this part of the Texas coast in late October and remain until the end of March. Rockport residents

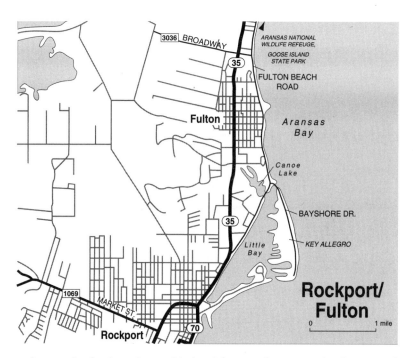

welcome the feathered snowbirds with several protected refuges, and the RVers can take their choice of many well-manicured campgrounds, complete with a friendly small-town atmosphere.

Make your first stop the Rockport-Fulton Area Chamber of Commerce at 404 Broadway. Here you can load up on free brochures and maps, as well as advice from "charmers"—volunteers representing "The Charm of the Texas Coast." The chamber also has a handy checklist of fifty-one things to do in the Rockport-Fulton area. A popular activity is a gallery walk of the town's many art galleries; another good outing is a cassette-tape tour of the region's historical attractions.

Rockport and neighboring Fulton have quickly caught the attention of the birding world. In the 1940s a feisty and dedicated local amateur bird-watcher named Connie Hagar identified hundreds of species. Her research brought Rockport-Fulton to the attention of the National Wildlife Service and other organizations, who eventually recorded nearly 500 species in the area. Today Rockport-Fulton is renowned as one of the finest birding spots in the world.

The Connie Hagar Sanctuary, downtown along TX 35 at Little Bay, is a good place to spot pelicans and many shorebirds. Whooping cranes winter at the Aransas National Wildlife Refuge northeast of town, and the drive to the refuge passes many marshes and coastal plains filled with birds.

Numerous birds fly through the area during fall and winter migration. Every September, Rockport-Fulton hosts the Hummer/Bird Celebration to mark the passage of thousands of hummingbirds who stop through Rockport-Fulton on their way south to Central and South America. Bird lovers from around the country come to watch this feeding frenzy where up to 150 hummingbirds often swarm the same feeder. The annual spring migration each May also brings hundreds of colorful songbirds to the area.

Bird-watching opportunities are available year-round. Contact the Rockport-Fulton Area Chamber of Commerce to order a copy of the "Birder's Guide." It illustrates the most common species found here, such as pelicans, cranes, storks, and laughing gulls. It also features driving tours to sixteen birding sites.

Except for year-round boat tours and special bus tours during the Hummer/Bird Celebration, you must depend on self-guided drives to good birding sites. The chamber can give you directions to the best locations outside of town as well as information about recent spottings.

WHERE TO GO

Texas Maritime Museum. 1202 Navigation Circle, on downtown waterfront. This two-story museum chronicles Texas maritime activities, starting with Spanish shipwrecks off the coast and continuing through today's offshore oil industry. Special exhibits are devoted to shipbuilding, Texans of the sea, and the U.S. Army Corps of Engineers. Open Wednesday through Sunday. Fee. (512) 729–1271.

Rockport Center for the Arts. Across the street from Texas Maritime Museum. This restored 1890 house is now the home of the Rockport Art Association and a good place to buy a painting of a Texas beach scene by a local artist. Look for changing exhibits every month. Open Tuesday through Saturday, and Sunday afternoons. Free. (512) 729–5519.

Rockport Beach Park. Downtown, just off TX 35. This is a very popular spot, especially during warm weather. The 1-mile beach offers swimming, picnicking, a children's playground, boating, fishing, and crabbing off an 800-foot pier, as well as paddleboat and jet ski rentals. There's also a bird-watching platform overlooking an island said to be the home of one of the best colonies of birds in the state. Open daily. Fee.

Fulton Mansion State Historic Structure. 3 miles north of Rockport off TX 35, corner of Henderson Street and Fulton Beach Road. Built in 1876 by Colonel George Fulton, this grand four-story home overlooks Aransas Bay. It features interesting architecture and surprising modern conveniences. Built at a cost of $100,000, the house included central forced-air heating. A central cast-iron furnace in the basement provided heat through a series of flues to false, decorative fireplaces in the main rooms. Hot and cold running water was achieved with a tank located in the tower attic. A gas plant located at the back of the house provided fuel for gas chandeliers.

Visitors are asked to wear flat, soft-soled shoes because of delicate Axminster and Brussels carpets purchased from New York. Tours of the home's twenty-nine rooms are conducted Wednesday through Sunday. Fee. (512) 729-0386.

Capt. Ted's *Skimmer.* Adjacent to the Sandollar Pavilion on Fulton Beach Road. This custom-built tour boat carries birders into shallow waters where many other vessels cannot travel. From November through March, *Skimmer* passengers can view whooping cranes. From April through May, the cruise ventures to nearby islands, including one containing the largest reddish egret rookery in the world. Reservations required. Fee. Call (800) 338-4551, or write: Star Route 1, P.O. Box 225J, Rockport, TX 78382.

***Pisces* Cruises.** Depart from Rockport Harbor. From November through March, this 58-foot vessel conducts whooping crane tours twice daily. The remainder of the year, the *Pisces* operates as a party fishing boat, offering daily morning and evening four-hour cruises in Aransas Bay. Fee. (800) 245-9324 or (512) 729-7525.

Demo Bird Gardens and Fresh Water Pond. Picnic area on east side of TX 35. Stop by this demonstration garden for a look at plants that attract hummingbirds and butterflies. Firecracker bush, Cape honeysuckle, Mexican Turk's Cap, and lantana are a few of the native plants that help keep Rockport buzzing with winged visitors. Free.

Goose Island State Park. TX 35 and Park Road 13, 21 miles northeast of Rockport. This 314-acre park is the home of "Big

Tree," the State Championship Coastal Live Oak. The park is also home to a variety of waterfowl and shore birds. Fishers try for speckled trout, redfish, drum, flounder, and sheepshead. Fee. (512) 729-2858.

Aransas National Wildlife Refuge. Forty-five minutes northeast of Rockport. Take TX 35 north to FM 774, turn right, and continue to the intersection of FM 2040. Turn right and stay on FM 2040 to the refuge. This 54,829-acre refuge is the prime wintering ground for the endangered whooping crane, plus hundreds of other bird species. The refuge includes several hiking trails and a paved, 15-mile loop drive that offer a chance to see some of eighty mammal species indigenous to the region: opossum, shrew, bat, armadillo, raccoon, coati, ringtail, mink, weasel, nutria, skunk, bobcat, white-tailed deer, coyote, and even wild boar.

The observation tower is located on the loop drive. From its heights you can view the elegant whooping cranes, whose numbers once dwindled to only sixteen. Thanks to conservation programs, the present population has increased tenfold. The visitors center includes films and exhibits on the annual migration of these 5-foot-tall birds. Across the road, have a look at native alligators resting in a swampy, fenced enclosure. Open daily. Fee. (512) 286-3559.

WHERE TO EAT

The Boiling Pot. Fulton Beach Road. Don a bib, grab a Mamba beer from one of the thirty-one Baskin-Robbins-like selections, and sit down. This roadside shack is always noisy and crowded and fun. The Cajun Combo features blue crab, shrimp, andouille sausage, new potatoes, and corn, all boiled up in a spicy pot and dumped from a metal container onto the paper-covered table. You crack the crab claws with a wooden mallet, and dip the succulent flesh in melted butter. Fingers, not forks, are the rule here; dainty eaters need not apply. This is a Texas experience to savor. Open for dinner only from Monday through Thursday; lunch and dinner Friday through Sunday. $-$$; □. (512) 729-6972.

The Sandollar Pavilion. 109 North Fulton Beach Road. This restaurant swears the food here is so fresh that "it slept in the ocean last night." Built over the water, the dining room has a beautiful view of Aransas Bay. Call for hours. Open for breakfast, lunch, and dinner, but closed between meals on some days. $$; ☐. (512) 729-8909.

WHERE TO STAY

Rockport has a huge selection of accommodations, ranging from fishing cottages to elegantly furnished condominiums. Because of the large number of Winter Texans who call Rockport home during the cooler months, there are many RV and trailer parks and condominiums that lease by the day, week, or month. For a brochure listing all of Rockport-Fulton's varied lodgings, call the Chamber of Commerce office at (800) 242-0071.

Key Allegro Rentals. 1800 Bayshore Drive, just over Key Allegro Bridge on Fulton Beach Road. Key Allegro is a small island linked to Rockport by an arched bridge. The lovely drive here is your first hint at the elegant accommodations awaiting visitors in this area. Nicely appointed condominium units and upscale homes located on the water's edge afford beautiful views of Rockport's fishing vessels heading out for the day's catch. Rental homes and condominiums are available by the day or week. $$-$$$; ☐. (512) 729-2333 or 729-6588.

Laguna Reef Condos and Hotel. 1021 Water Street. This waterfront hotel and condominium resort has an unbeatable view of the bay, especially for early risers who want to watch the gorgeous sunrise. Each fully furnished unit has a private balcony, kitchen, and dining/living room. After a day of sightseeing, take a walk along the complex's beach or down the long fishing pier. The units rent by the day, week, or month. $$; ☐. (800) 248-1057 or (512) 729-1742.

Kontiki Beach Motel and Condominiums. Fulton Beach Road. The motel offers spacious accommodations that feature a living and dining area, fully equipped kitchen, and separate bedroom, available by the day, week, or month. Guests also can rent nicely furnished condominiums. All take in a view of the water. Prices vary; ☐. (800) 242-3407.

ESPECIALLY FOR WINTER TEXANS

Rockport hosts many special events for Winter Texans, from fishing to horseshoe tournaments. The town sponsors several Winter Texan arts and crafts shows as well as concerts played by talented seasonal residents.

The Paws and Taws Center on Fulton Beach Road is the site of many gatherings for the winter visitors who stay in Rockport and Fulton. With a hardwood floor, a stage, and kitchen facilities, the center holds weekly square dances, bingo games, AARP meetings, and "state days," with parties for visitors from specific states. Chartered bus trips also depart from the center and offer shopping at the border, a tour of German eateries in New Braunfels, outlet shopping in San Marcos, and several other tours.

Fulton sponsors an annual "Welcome Winter Texans" free fish fry in early December. The Rockport area includes many excellent RV parks, with busy clubhouse activities. For more information, contact the Rockport-Fulton Area Chamber of Commerce at (800) 242-0071.

CORPUS CHRISTI

To reach Corpus Christi, follow I–37 south for 145 miles from San Antonio. Along the drive, the terrain changes from the rolling hills and shady oaks of the Hill Country to the grassy flatlands of the coastal plains.

This city of 275,000 residents is a popular year-around destination. During the summer months, the nearby beaches of Padre and Mustang Islands appeal to surfers, families, and sun worshippers. During the winter, this coastal city fills with Winter Texans.

The waters of Corpus Christi Bay are calm, protected from the Gulf of Mexico by the barrier islands of Padre and Mustang, which served as pirate hideouts even after the area was charted in 1519 by Spanish explorer Alonzo Alvarez de Pineda. He bestowed the bay with its name, which means "body of Christ."

Today Corpus Christi is a thriving city, consistently ranking as America's sixth busiest port. The bayfront is a combination fishing village and tourist spot, and the downtown piers are lined with picturesque shrimp boats. High-rise luxury hotels, specialty shops, and seafood restaurants overlook the bay. The heart of Corpus Christi is Shoreline Boulevard, with its proud palms and spectacular views of the water. The handsome boulevard begins as Ocean Drive at the gates of the U.S. Naval Air Station and winds north past grand mansions perched on the bluffs overlooking the bay.

Because of the warm weather and a fairly consistent breeze of about 12 miles per hour, Corpus Christi is known as the unofficial

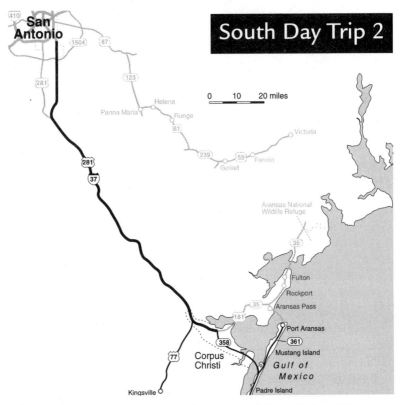

South Day Trip 2

windsurfing capital of the United States. Site of the U.S. Open Windsurfing Regatta, it's not unusual to see the bay dotted with the colorful sails. Ocean Drive's Oleander Park is the only city-sanctioned sailboard park in the world. If you want to give the sport a try, several operators along South Padre Island Drive offer instruction and rentals.

The north section of Shoreline Boulevard contains the huge piers known as Coopers Street L-Head, Lawrence Street T-Head, and Peoples Street T-Head. Each pier bustles with life, from the predawn hours when the shrimp boats leave until midnight; the night cruises offer fishers a chance at trophy tarpon, kingfish, or marlin. Peoples Street T-Head is also home of the Flagship, an 85-foot paddle wheeler that offers guided bay tours. The northern end of Shoreline Boulevard also holds the Art Museum of South Texas, the World of Discovery: Corpus Christi Museum of Science and History, and the Ships of Christopher Columbus. At the end of the drive is the Harbor Bridge. Built in 1959 to link the city with the small towns that line the Texas coast, it leads across the ship channel to the Texas State Aquarium.

WHERE TO GO

Texas State Aquarium. 2710 Shoreline Drive, across ship channel from the downtown area. The Texas State Aquarium focuses on the sea life of both the Gulf and the Caribbean Sea, the first such facility in the nation. The Gulf of Mexico Exhibit Building, a $31.5 million facility, houses 250 species, including grouper, eels, and sharks.

High-tech displays feature the use of a video monitor to help you guide the image of an underwater robotic arm. Touch-screen monitors offer a chance for visitors to try their hand at environmental decision making. When you're finished here, walk outside for a look at the ship channel, the Harbor Bridge, and an unbeatable view of the city. Open daily. Fee. (800) 477–GULF.

Dolphin Connection. Beneath US 181 bridge to Portland, just before Nueces Bay Causeway. Two Dolphin Connection boats take visi-

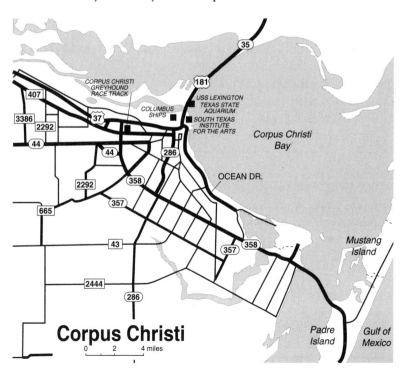

tors into the bay to feed and interact with dolphins. Owners Erv and Sonja Strong know the wild mammals by name and are glad to explain their habits, family connections, and lifestyle. You can hand feed and pet these remarkable creatures during the hour-long excursion. Open daily from March through October or November, when the dolphins leave for the winter. Fee. For reservations, call (512) 882–4126, or write: 215 Bridgeport Avenue, Suite 4, Corpus Christi, TX 78402.

International Kite Museum. 3200 Surfside Boulevard, Best Western Sandy Shores (across Harbor Bridge from downtown). Over eighty exhibits trace the history of the kite and even its use as a military spy tool. Open daily. Free. (512) 883–7456.

Corpus Christi Greyhound Race Track. 5302 Leopard Street. Take your chances here with a bet on these fast-as-lightning greyhounds. The atmosphere is very family oriented, although you must be twenty-one to gamble. The $21 million facility includes a snack bar. The basic entrance fee covers outdoor grandstand seating. During warmer months it's wise to spend a couple of extra bucks for air-conditioned reserved seating, which can be booked six days prior to the race. Call for race times. Open daily. Fee. (800) 580–RACE.

South Texas Institute for the Arts. 1902 North Shoreline Boulevard, Bayfront Arts and Science Park. Famous for its stark white architecture, this museum is filled with changing fine art exhibits of traditional and contemporary works. Open Tuesday through Sunday. Fee. (512) 884–3844.

Watergardens. Bayfront Arts and Science Park. Here a human-made stream tumbles from the entrance of the art museum down to a sunken circle of flags and fountains. This is a nice place to take a box lunch. Open daily. Free. (No phone.)

World of Discovery: Corpus Christi Museum of Science and History. 1900 North Chaparral, Bayfront Arts and Science Park. This museum is filled with natural history exhibits, including displays recalling the many Spanish shipwrecks found off the Gulf coast. Children can climb aboard a recreation of a fifteenth-century vessel for a peek at the cramped quarters endured by early explorers. Open daily. Fee. (512) 883–2862.

Ships of Christopher Columbus. At the World of Discovery: Corpus Christi Museum of Science and History. These life-sized recreations of the Columbus fleet were built by the Spanish government at the cost of over $7 million to commemorate the 500th anniversary of the explorer's voyage. You can board the *Pinta* and the *Santa Maria*; onshore exhibits explain more about sea travel and the Spanish voyages. Open daily. Fee. (512) 886–4492.

Flagship. Peoples Street T-Head. Several daily tours take visitors for a look at the shipyards and the bay. Sunset cruises are particularly scenic, when the lights of downtown reflect in the calm bay waters. Open daily. Fee. (512) 643–7128 or 884–1693.

Corpus Christi Botanical Gardens. Take South Staples Drive toward Kingsville, past Oso Creek; signs mark entrance. These gardens feature native South Texas plants and winding trails through subtropical foliage. Open Tuesday through Sunday. Fee. (512) 852–2100.

U.S.S. Lexington. This aircraft carrier is berthed just offshore from the Texas State Aquarium, and visitors have permission to come aboard. Sunk four times in World War II, the ship returned to fight again. Today this carrier, with a main deck larger than three football fields, is a museum open daily for tours. Texas's first flight simulator takes up to sixteen passengers on a three- to five-minute flight. Hydraulically powered, the "cabin" uses a combination of sight, sound, and movement to give passengers the sensation of riding in either an attack airplane or a helicopter. Fee. (800) LADY–LEX.

WHERE TO EAT

Landry's Dockside. Peoples Street T-Head. This restaurant is a restored two-story barge that sports a casual, fun atmosphere. Murals of fish span the walls, and huge picture windows offer a great view. The specialty of the house is Gulf seafood, including shrimp, oysters, and scallops. Open for lunch and dinner daily. $$; ⚓. (512) 882–6666.

The Lighthouse Restaurant and Oyster Bar. Lawrence Street T-Head. This popular restaurant is shaped like a small lighthouse. From inside, diners have a great view of sailboats on the bay and the Corpus Christi skyline. Seafood and steaks are the specialty here. Open daily for lunch and dinner. $$; ☐. (512) 883–3982.

Water Street Seafood Company and Water Street Oyster Bar. 309 North Water Street, Water Street Market. Located just a block from Shoreline Boulevard, this casual restaurant features Cajun-inspired seafood as well as the usual Gulf coast fare. Open daily for lunch and dinner. $$–$$$; ☐. (512) 881–9448.

WHERE TO STAY

Omni Bayfront. 900 North Shoreline Boulevard. This elegant 474-room hotel overlooks the bay and includes a health club, swimming pool, and rooftop dining room. Many of Corpus Christi's main attractions lie within walking distance. $$$; ☐. (800) 843-6664 or (512) 887-1600.

   Embassy Suites Hotel. 4337 South Padre Island Drive. This all-suite hotel is located on the north side of town, fifteen minutes from Shoreline Boulevard and Padre Island. The huge open lobby and atrium include a heated pool, hot tub, and sauna, as well as a dining area that serves a free all-you-can-eat breakfast plus evening cocktails. $$; ☐. (800) 678-7533 or (512) 853-7899.

PADRE AND MUSTANG ISLANDS

To reach the islands, head out on South Padre Island Drive, also called TX 358. The road is lined with shell shops, windsurfing rentals, bait stands, and car washes. In the shallow waters along the drive, many fishers stand waist deep in salt water alongside tall herons and pelicans looking for a meal.

   When you cross the Intracoastal Waterway via the enormous JFK Causeway Bridge, you leave the mainland for Padre Island. This 110-mile-long barrier island protects much of the Texas coast from hurricanes and tropical storms. Generally, the northern stretch of island paralleling the area from Corpus Christi to Port Mansfield is called Padre Island; from that point to the tip of Texas, the land mass is named South Padre Island.

   Padre and Mustang Islands feature beaches dotted with rolling dunes, clean sand, and flocks of gulls. The surf is usually gentle and shallow enough to walk for hundreds of yards before reaching chest-deep water. Occasionally undertow is a problem, but on most summer days the waves are gentle and rolling, and the water is warm.

   To reach the Padre Island beaches, continue straight on South Padre Island Drive (Park Road 22). Visitors find several parks here from which to choose, each with its own special charm. One of these, the Padre Balli Park, is named for the priest who managed a ranch on the island in the early nineteenth century. It offers a 1,200-foot fishing pier. The Padre Island National Seashore has a snack bar, and showers are available at Malaquite Beach. Although vehicles are allowed on most Padre beaches, Malaquite is one where vehicles are not permitted.

Beyond Malaquite lies 66 miles of protected beach in Padre Island National Seashore, accessible only by four-wheel drive vehicles. Little Shell and Big Shell beaches are located in this area, both named because of the wealth of seashells found on their pristine sands.

Although much of Padre Island is undeveloped, you'll find many commercial establishments on neighboring Mustang Island. To reach this barrier island, turn left off South Padre Island Drive from Corpus Christi onto Park Road 53. Only 18 miles long, Mustang Island is far smaller than its neighbor to the south, but it shares many of the same attractions. One of the best stops is Mustang Island State Park, where showers, restrooms, and camping are available. Cars, however, are prohibited on the beach. (For more information on Mustang Island, read SOUTH FROM SAN ANTONIO, DAY TRIP 1.)

Whether you choose Mustang or Padre, follow a few rules of safety. Portuguese man-of-war jellyfish are commonly seen on the beaches. Resist the urge to touch these iridescent purple creatures—their tentacles produce a nasty sting. If you are stung, locals claim the best relief is a paste of meat tenderizer and water applied to the bite. A far less dangerous, but very annoying, aspect of the Gulf beaches are tar balls. These black clumps, formed by natural seepage and offshore oil spills, wash up on the beach and stick to your skin and your shoes. Many hotels have a tar removal station near the door to help you remove the sticky substance.

WHERE TO GO

Mustang Island State Park. Park Road 53. Mustang Island State Park is clean and enjoyable, perfect for a weekend of RV or tent camping or just a few hours of beachcombing. Freshwater showers are available. Covered picnic tables help keep your gear out of the sand. Open daily. Fee. (512) 749-5246.

WHERE TO STAY

Holiday Inn North Padre Island. 15202 Windward Drive. Here you can walk from the hotel directly to the beach. When you've had

enough salt water, have a dip in the hotel swimming pool. $$; ☐.
(800) HOLIDAY or (512) 949-8041.

Island House. 15340 Leeward Drive, Padre Island. This beachfront
condominium resort has well-furnished units, many with beautiful
views of the Gulf. Each includes a furnished kitchen, a dining/living
room, and two bedrooms. Spend the extra money for an oceanfront
condo, with sliding glass doors in the living room and the master bed-
room, and fall asleep to the sound of waves. $$$; ☐. (800) 333-8806.

KINGSVILLE

Perhaps no other destination quite epitomizes "Texas size" like the
King Ranch. Larger than the state of Rhode Island, the King Ranch
sprawls across 825,000 acres and, even more importantly, stands as a
symbol of Texas ingenuity. The ranch has long been known for its
role in the American ranching industry and is still a worldwide
leader. Many of the practices used industry-wide started here.

The ranch is located on the outskirts of Kingsville. To reach this
community and extend your day trip from Corpus Christi, take US
77 south of Corpus Christi to Kingsville, about a forty-five minute
drive. The Kingsville Visitor Center is located at the intersection of
US 77 and Corral Drive and makes a good stop to pick up area
brochures and maps.

Just a few blocks away, the historic downtown is included in the
National Register of Historic Places. Kleberg Avenue and King Street
are lined with antique shops and specialty stores that invite travelers
to spend a fun afternoon shopping in a small town atmosphere.

But the prime attraction in this community is the King Ranch, located 39 miles south of Corpus Christi. Visitors can enjoy a guided
tour of the ranch in air-conditioned buses. Don't expect reenactments of typical ranch activities here, though—this is the real thing.
Cowboys, more often seen riding pick-up trucks than horses, work
more than 60,000 head of cattle on this ranch.

King Ranch traces its history to 1853 when it was founded by Captain Richard King, a self-made man who left home at an early age
and made his fortune on Rio Grande riverboats. The ranch, still one
of the largest in the world, developed th Santa Gertrudis and King
Ranch Santa Cruz breeds of cattle as well as the first registered
American quarter horse.

Many fall and winter visitors also come to enjoy a look at the feathered residents and migratory birds. A stop on the Coastal Birding Trail, the ranch is home to more than 300 feathered species. Species such as green jays, pygmy owls, and common paurauque are spotted on different areas of the ranch.

WHERE TO GO

Conner Museum. Santa Gertrudis Street on the campus of Texas A & M University. Highlighting the natural and social history of South Texas, the museum includes exhibits on ranching, South Texas ecosystems, and area fossil and minerals. Open Monday through Saturday. Free. (512) 595-2819.

King Ranch Visitor Center. Highway 141 West. The visitors center serves as a gathering place for tours of the King Ranch. With a continuously running film about the history of the ranch, guests receive an overview of the operation. Visitors also sign up for guided 1.5 hour tours (call for tour times). The guided bus tours begin at the site where Captain King first camped in 1852 and continue to see both the history and the modern workings of the ranch. Special interest tours of cattle operations, feedlot, and other aspects of the ranch are available by appointment. Nature tours, including special programs for birders, are scheduled several times annually. Open daily (afternoons only on Sundays). Free (except for tours). (512) 592-8055.

King Ranch Museum. 405 North 6th Street. Beyond the ranch in the town of Kingsville, the King legacy is also apparent. The King Ranch Museum provides visitors with a look at the history of the ranch, including a stunning photographic essay of life on King Ranch in the 1940s. A collection of saddles, antique carriages, and antique cars rounds out the exhibits. Open afternoons daily. Fee. (512) 595-1881.

WHERE TO SHOP

King Ranch Saddle Shop. 201 East Kleberg Avenue. Just down the street from the King Ranch Museum, the Saddle Shop carries on the tradition of saddlemaking that began after the Civil War when Captain King started his own saddle shop. Today the King Ranch Saddle

Shop produces fine purses, belts, and, of course, saddles in downtown Kingsville's John B. Ragland Mercantile Company Building. Open Monday through Saturday. (800) 282–KING.

Sellers Market. 205 East Kleberg. Handmade arts and crafts fill this marketplace. Open Tuesday through Saturday. (512) 595–4992.

WHERE TO EAT

Wild Olive Cafe. 205 East Kleberg. Located in the Sellers Market, this volunteer-operated cafe offers a taste of Kingsville with homemade lunches served by volunteers every Tuesday, Wednesday, and Thursday. $; no □. (512) 595–4992.

WHERE TO STAY

Holiday Inn Kingsville. 3430 South Highway 77. Located just minutes from downtown, this family-style hotel includes restaurant and outdoor pool. $$; □. (512) 595–5753.

SOUTHWEST DAY TRIP 1

Laredo
Nuevo Laredo, Mexico

LAREDO

The 153-mile drive from San Antonio to Laredo via I-35 is a fast one. Although a few small towns appear on this stretch, much of the area remains ranch land.

This city of 166,000 has long been known as the South Texas party spot. It's a popular weekend trip with college students, shoppers, and anyone in search of fun. Built on the banks of the Rio Grande, Laredo dates back to 1755. Founded by an officer of the Royal Army of Spain, it was one of the first cities established in this part of the country.

Following the war with Mexico, many Laredo residents packed up and headed across the border to start their own city in Mexico. They named the fledgling community "Nuevo Laredo" or "New Laredo." Healthy trade between the United States and Mexico along with the fact that many families straddle both sides of the border have linked the cities. Thus the nickname "Los Dos Laredos"—The Two Laredos.

To reach Laredo's downtown district, take the last exit off I-35 and drive along a narrow, one-way avenue called Zaragoza Street. With its old buildings, constant traffic, and stately palms, the venue has a definite Mexican feel. On the right is the enormous St. Augustine Church, founded in 1778. The church overlooks the St. Agustin Plaza, a popular place just to sit and watch the flurry of activity near the bridge. This plaza, with its peaceful gazebo and gas-powered lamps, was the site of one of the West's bloodiest shootouts. In 1886 the *Botas* (boots) and *Huaraches* (sandals), two rival political groups, battled here, leaving over eighty dead when the smoke cleared.

WHERE TO GO

Museum of the Republic of the Rio Grande. 1003 Zaragoza Street, adjacent to the La Posada hotel. Six flags have flown over most of Texas, but Laredo has seen seven, thanks to the short-lived Republic of the Rio Grande. This museum is housed in a one-story

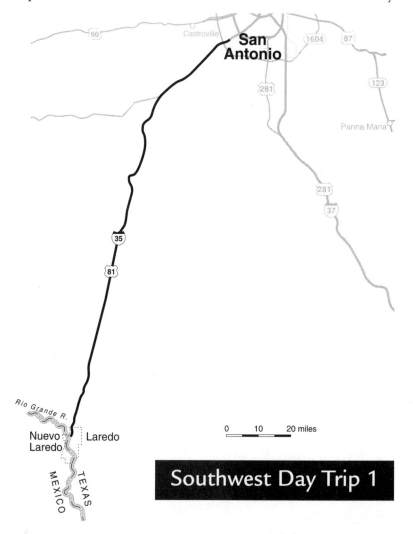

Southwest Day Trip 1

adobe structure that was once the capitol building of the latter republic, a country formed when Northern Mexico seceded from Mexico in 1839. The new state existed until 1841. The museum contains guns, saddles, and household belongings from that brief period. Open Tuesday through Sunday. Free. (956) 727–3480.

Laredo Children's Museum. West end of Washington Street. Kids enjoy touching and manipulating the exhibits at this hands-on museum. Children can even stand inside a bubble in one exhibit. Fee. (956) 725–2299.

Walking Tour of Laredo. The streets of Laredo are lined with historic structures, including many old churches and homes built in the Mexican vernacular and Victorian styles. Walking tours are provided by the Webb County Heritage Foundation at 500 Flores Avenue. Free. (956) 727–0977.

WHERE TO SHOP

San Bernardo Avenue. If you don't want to drive into Mexico, you'll find many large importers on this shopping strip. Wrought-iron furniture, clay products, and vases are popular buys.

Zaragoza Street Wholesalers. When Mexicans come into Texas to shop, many make this strip their first stop. Shops here sell the same merchandise, from handbags to headsets, found at many department stores, but at bargain prices.

Vegas's Imports. 4002 San Bernardo. Mexican home furnishings for every room of the house are sold in this well-stocked store, and much of the furniture is hand carved. (956) 724-8251.

WHERE TO EAT AND STAY

La Posada. 1000 Zaragoza Street. This 224-room hotel is the closest accommodation to the International Bridge leading from Laredo into Mexico. Two Spanish-style courtyards feature tall palms, blooming bougainvillaea, and refreshing pools, one with a swim-up bar. A relaxed lobby restaurant specializes in Mexican dishes. The Tack Room Bar and Grill is a casual restaurant featuring nightly entertainment and steak and seafood. Restaurant prices vary from $-$$$; rooms $$-$$$; □. (800) 444-2099 or (956) 722-1701.

NUEVO LAREDO, MEXICO

Visitors can cross the border into Mexico by car or on foot (the more popular choice). There's no problem driving across at either International Bridge No. 1, also known as the Old Bridge, or International Bridge No. 2, the I-35 bridge.

Nuevo Laredo, with over 500,000 inhabitants, is far larger than its American sister. The city engages in an enormous import-export business and holds the title as the largest port of entry on the Mexico-U.S. border. A seemingly endless procession of trucks crosses the I-35 bridge all day and night.

Before leaving Laredo, drivers should invest in short-term Mexican auto insurance. Two companies carrying this coverage are Sanborn's U.S.-Mexico Insurance Service at 2212 Santa Ursula (956) 723-3657 and Camper Center Mexican Insurance Agency at 2319 San Bernardo (956) 722-0141. Be sure to read "Entering Mexico," Appendix A, for details on Mexican insurance, proof of citizenship, and prohibited goods.

Most vacationers make the five-minute walk across International Bridge No. 1 to get a better view of the Rio Grande below. You can park your car at the Riverdrive Mall (1600 Water Street) and walk to the Old Bridge. After paying a toll at the entrance to the bridge, you can walk into Mexico. In the middle of the bridge is a plaque that marks the border between the two countries.

Cross over the bridge to the shopping district and Avenida Guerrero, where street vendors hawk everything from chewing gum and paper flowers to tablecloths and strands of garlic. In the downtown area, every road parallel to Guerrero is an avenue or *avenida*; one running perpendicular to the avenues (and parallel to the river) is a street or *calle*.

To call Nuevo Laredo telephone numbers from the United States, first dial the international code (011), then the country code (52), followed by the phone number.

WHERE TO GO

Turf Club. Calle Bravo and Avenida Ocampo, a few blocks from Nuevo Mercado. This air-conditioned club has live off-track betting, plus a restaurant and bar on the premises. Open daily. (87) 12-0494.

WHERE TO SHOP

Nuevo Mercado. Avenida Guerrero, four blocks from the International Bridge. The *mercado*, or market, is the one place that all tourists visit. Here you find many American faces, English-speaking shopkeepers, and a very friendly atmosphere.

Built around two open courtyards filled with umbrella-shaded tables, the two-story market sells just about every imaginable Mexican-made product. Frozen margaritas and Corona beer are in evidence everywhere, offering a chance to cool down after several hours in the stores. Most shops have no air conditioning, even though summer days often top 100 degrees. Open daily.

Marti's. Avenida Guerrero, three blocks past the International Bridge. This upscale, air-conditioned shop is the nicest store in Nuevo Laredo and the priciest. You don't get a chance to bargain here, so be content with the fact that you're buying the finest jewelry, furnishings, and clothing that Nuevo Laredo has to offer. This place is a favorite with both wealthy Mexicans and South Texas shoppers looking for something above the usual *mercado* fare. Open daily. (87) 12-3337.

Deutsch y Deutsch. Guerrero 300. Located next to Marti's, this American-owned shop offers merchandise from throughout Mexico.

For over sixty-five years the Deutsch family has traveled the country searching out quality gift items such as aluminum serving ware from Mexico City and wooden flowers from Puerto Vallarta. Open Tuesday through Saturday. (87) 12–2066.

El Cid Glass Factory. Avenida Reforma 3861. This glass factory is one of Nuevo Laredo's shopping treasures. Located over a mile beyond the *mercado,* you'll want to take a taxi here and then allow plenty of time to shop for blue-, green-, and red-rimmed glasses, bowls, Christmas ornaments, and more. This is Nuevo Laredo's only glass factory, operated by Romualdo Canales for over twenty years. Open daily. (87) 15–8679.

WHERE TO EAT

El Dorado (formerly the Cadillac Bar). Calle Belden and Avenida Ocampo, about two blocks from Nuevo Mercado. For some travelers, the El Dorado is reason enough to come to Nuevo Laredo. The favorite watering hole for many South Texans, it's the home of the Ramos Gin Fizz, a concoction of gin, lemon juice, and powdered sugar. The menu includes frog legs and red snapper. $$; ☐. (87) 12–0015.

Victoria 30-20. Calle Victoria, near Nuevo Mercado. This remodeled home-turned-restaurant is now adorned with thick, aqua-tinted windows, a pastel interior, and a forest of plants. Sip a beverage from a hand-blown glass and dine in air-conditioned comfort in one of Nuevo Laredo's most beautiful restaurants, specializing in Tex-Mex favorites such as *cabrito* (barbecued goat). $$; ☐. (87) 13–3020.

La Principal. Avenida Guerrero 624. Just a few blocks beyond the mercado, this restaurant is a favorite with Nuevo Laredo residents. It specializes in *cabrito,* with Mexican dishes such as *mollejas* (sweetbreads) and *sesos* (brains) served with *borracho* beans. Watch the chefs smoke the *cabrito* in the glassed-in kitchen, then enjoy the diner atmosphere of this authentic Mexican restaurant. $; ☐. (87) 12–1301.

EAGLE PASS

It's 142 miles southwest on US 57 from San Antonio to Eagle Pass and its sister city, Piedras Negras. These destinations are popular for a weekend of shopping, partying, and south-of-the-border fun.

The drive to Eagle Pass goes quickly, following I–35 south to Highway 57, which leads through miles of fertile farmland before it hits the mesquite-filled country near the border. You'll find basic services in Devine, but gas stations are few and far between from this farming community until you reach the border.

Eagle Pass, a city of over 25,000 residents, was founded after the Texas Revolution when Mexico prohibited all trade with Texas. Smugglers began a new route to the north. The Texas militia set up an observation camp at a crossing called Paso del Aguila (Eagle Pass), named for the birds nesting in the area. Soon settlers began coming to the area. In 1849 the U.S. Infantry built Fort Duncan to defend the new territory from Indian attack. The fort later was used during the Civil War and manned by Confederate soldiers.

Like other border towns, Eagle Pass is bilingual. Many Mexican citizens cross the border to shop at the large Mall de las Aguilas and in the downtown dress and specialty shops. For Americans, much of Eagle Pass's appeal lies in its proximity to Mexico. Many visitors spend the cooler hours shopping in Piedras Negras, then return to Eagle Pass for a swim and an evening meal.

WHERE TO GO

Fort Duncan Park. From Main Street (US 57), turn south on South Adams Street. Here you can take a self-guided tour of eleven original structures, including barracks and the headquarters building that's home to the Fort Duncan Museum. The museum presents displays on the early history of the old Indian fort and Confederate outpost. The fort saw its final action from 1890 to 1916, when National Guard units were attached to the command following disturbances in Mexico. Open Monday through Friday afternoon or by appointment. Free. (830) 773-2748.

WHERE TO EAT

Kettle Restaurant. 2525 Main Street (US 57) in front of La Quinta Inn. This chain restaurant is open twenty-four hours a day for breakfast, lunch, and dinner. $$; ☐. (830) 773-7263.

Charcoal Grill. Mall de las Aguilas, 455 South Bibb (off US 57). This family-style restaurant specializes in charcoal-grilled steaks and burgers, all brought to your table with a bowl of sliced jalapeños. $$; □. (830) 773-8023.

WHERE TO STAY

La Quinta Motor Inn. 2525 Main Street (US 57). This comfortable family motel, offering a palm-shaded swimming pool, sits just five minutes from the border. $$; □. (800) 531-5900.

PIEDRAS NEGRAS, MEXICO

From Eagle Pass, you can walk or drive across the International Bridge to Piedras Negras, named for the "black rock" (anthracite coal) found in the area after flooding on the Rio Grande. This city of over 100,000 residents is a gateway to interior Mexico for many tourists, who follow Mexico Highway 57 to Saltillo.

Drivers must purchase short-term Mexican auto insurance before entering the country. (American insurance policies are generally not valid in Mexico, where automobile mishaps are a criminal rather than a civil offense.) Coverage is available from Capitol Insurance at 1115 Main Street in Eagle Pass (830) 773-2341. (See Appendix A, "Entering Mexico," for more information.) Across the border, it's best to use secured parking, available for a small fee on the Plaza Principal, the Main Square, and at several restaurants and motels in town.

In Piedras Negras, as in other border towns, you may drink the water in the better hotels and restaurants. In other establishments, order bottled water or bring your own.

Piedras Negras's Main Square is filled with park benches, stately shade trees, and vendors selling food and drink. It's a nice place to sit for a while and watch the fascinating activity that is Old Mexico. From the Main Square, follow Zaragoza Street to the Mercado Municipal Zaragoza, the primary tourist market about three blocks away. The walk takes you past Mexican music stores, several bars, *zapaterias* (shoe stores), and *roperias* (dress shops).

The Mexican peso was reevaluated in 1993 when three decimal places were dropped. Formerly you may have seen a $150,000 price tag on a dress. Today that price would be marked N$150 (150 *nuevo* or "new" pesos). Although the exchange rate fluctuates, one U.S. dollar is generally worth about three *nuevo* pesos. Within the market, goods are marked in both dollars and pesos. The prices are open to *negociación*, a traditional way to purchase items in Mexico. T-shirts, Mexican dresses, serapes, blankets, chess sets, and men's Mexican wedding shirts are all very popular choices in the mercado. (See Appendix B, "Shopping in Mexico," for pointers.)

To dial a number in Piedras Negras from the United States, first dial the international code (011), then the country code (52), then the telephone number.

WHERE TO STAY

La Quinta Motor Inn. Avenue East Carranza 1205. This family motel, located a few miles from the market area, includes a restaurant and bar. All forty-two rooms are air conditioned and include cable TV and telephones. $; ☐. (878) 2-7479.

Casa Blanca. Avenue Lazaro Cardenas (south Mexico Highway 57). This white motel is located about fifteen minutes from the market area. All rooms are air conditioned and include a television and telephone. The motel also has a beautiful swimming pool and courtyard. $$; ☐. (878) 3-0646.

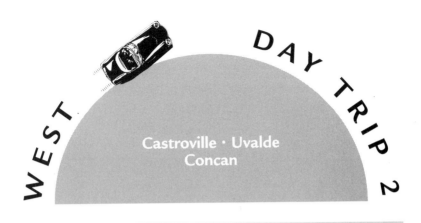

CASTROVILLE

Castroville is only 20 miles west of San Antonio on US 90, but it's another world in terms of mood and atmosphere. This small town serves up a mixture of many cultures: French, German, English, Alsatian, and Spanish. It's best known for its Alsatian roots and sometimes is called "The Little Alsace of Texas."

The community was founded by Frenchman Henri Castro, who contracted with the Republic of Texas to bring settlers from Europe. These pioneers came from the French province of Alsace in 1844, bringing with them the Alsatian language, a Germanic dialect. Today only the older residents of Castroville carry on this mother tongue.

Although the language has dropped out of everyday use, many other Alsatian customs and traditions have survived. The city still sports European-style homes with nonsymmetrical, sloping roofs. The Alsatian Dancers of Texas perform folk dancing at many festivals, including San Antonio's Texas Folklife Festival in August and during the town's St. Louis Day celebration. (See "Festivals and Celebrations" at the back of this book.)

Castroville is usually busy on weekends, as San Antonio residents come to shop the town's numerous antique stores, dine in the Alsatian restaurants, and tour the historical sites.

WHERE TO GO

Landmark Inn State Historical Park. 402 Florence Street. The Texas Parks and Wildlife Department operates the historic Land-

West Day Trip 2

mark Inn and museum. The inn was first a home and general store before becoming the Vance Hotel. Robert E. Lee and Bigfoot Wallace, a famous Texas Ranger, were said to have stayed here on the banks of the Medina River.

During World War II the hotel was renamed the Landmark Inn. Aside from accommodations (see "Where to Stay"), the inn contains displays illustrating Henri Castro's early efforts to recruit settlers as well as exhibits covering early Castroville life. Also recommended is a self-guided tour of the beautifully manicured inn grounds. Open daily. Free. (830) 931-2133.

Castroville Walking Tour. Pick up a free map from the Chamber of Commerce to see sixty-five points of interest, from Civil War–era homes to an 1845 church. (830) 538-3142.

Castroville Regional Park. South off US 90. Camp along the banks of the Medina River or enjoy swimming, picnicking, or walking in this park. Fee for camping hookups. (830) 538-2224.

WHERE TO SHOP

Alice's Antiques. 1213 Fiorella. Shop for furniture, china, kitchen collectibles, and jewelry in this antique store. Open daily. (830) 538-9318.

WHERE TO EAT

Alsatian Restaurant. 403 Angelo Street. Housed in a historic nine-teenth-century cottage typical of the provincial homes of Castroville, this restaurant specializes in Alsatian and German food, including spicy Alsatian sausage, crusty French bread, homemade noodles, and red sauerkraut. Steaks and seafood also are served. If it's a nice day, don't miss the chance to dine outside in the open-air biergarten. Open daily for lunch; dinner Thursday through Sunday. $$; □. (830) 931-3260.

Haby's Alsatian Bakery. 207 US 290 East. With Castroville's rich Alsatian and German heritage, you know the town has to have a great bakery. Well, here it is. Try to choose from apple strudel, molasses cookies, and fresh baked breads. Open Monday through Saturday. $; no □. (830) 931-2118.

WHERE TO STAY

Landmark Inn. 402 Florence Street. Guests at this historic inn can stay in one of eight beautifully appointed rooms as well as in a separate cottage that may have once served as the only bath-house between San Antonio and Eagle Pass. Most rooms come with private baths; none have telephones. Make your reservations early, especially for weekends. Guests accepted Wednesday through Sunday. $; no □. (830) 931-2133 or for reservations (512) 389-8900.

UVALDE

To reach Uvalde, continue west on US 90 through the communities of Hondo, Sabinal, and Knippa. Uvalde is located on the Leona River in the last outreaches of the Hill Country.

Spanish settlers came to this area in 1674. A century later they attempted to construct missions to convert the Lipan-Apache Indians, the foremost of the Apache groups in Texas. This plan was soon abandoned because of repeated Indian attacks on the mission. The Apaches were defeated in 1709 by Spanish military leader Juan del Uvalde in what's now known as Uvalde Canyon.

WHERE TO GO

Garner Museum. 333 North Park Street. This was once the home of Uvalde's most famous citizen: John Nance Garner, vice president of the United States during Franklin Roosevelt's first and second presidential terms. The museum is filled with reminders of Garner's political career. Open Monday through Saturday; extended hours during summer months. Fee. (830) 278-5018.

CONCAN

Word has it that this town is named for "coon can," a Mexican gambling game. Today it's a safe gamble for outdoor recreation from swimming to camping.

WHERE TO GO

Garner State Park. 31 miles north of Uvalde on US 83. Named for John Nance Garner, this beautiful state park is located on the chilly, spring-fed waters of the Frio River (frio means "cold" in Spanish). There are campsites, screened shelters, cabins with double beds, an eighteen-hole miniature golf course, and a 1-mile hiking trail built by the Civilian Conservation Corps during the 1930s. The highlight of the park is the river, filled with swimmers, inner-tubers, and paddleboats during the warmer months. Open daily. Fee. (830) 232-6132.

DAY TRIP 3

Brackettville · Del Rio
Ciudad Acuña, Mexico
Seminole Canyon
State Historical Park

This weekend trip has a lot to offer, from shoot-'em-up fun at Alamo Village to an afternoon dip in Del Rio's San Felipe Springs. Hop across the border for some bargain shopping, a margarita, and a Mexican dinner in Ciudad Acuña. The next day, take your choice of Del Rio's historic sites, a cruise on Lake Amistad, or a look at prehistoric drawings in Seminole Canyon.

BRACKETTVILLE

It's a quick 120 miles down US 90 from San Antonio to Brackettville. (For attractions along this highway, see WEST FROM SAN ANTONIO, DAY TRIP 2.)

Brackettville is the home of Fort Clark, built by the U.S. Cavalry in 1852 to protect the frontier from hostile Indians. Several important soldiers were stationed here over the years, including General George S. Patton. During World War II, Fort Clark served as a German POW camp. At the conclusion of that war, the fort was deactivated. Although Fort Clark's military days may be over, today the compound has taken on a new role as a resort, its stone barracks converted to modern motel rooms. There's also an RV park nearby.

WHERE TO GO

Old Guardhouse Jail Cavalry Museum. US 90, in Fort Clark Springs. Famous generals who served at Fort Clark are featured in this museum, along with the many troops who passed through the post. Open weekend afternoons. Free. (830) 563–9150.

105

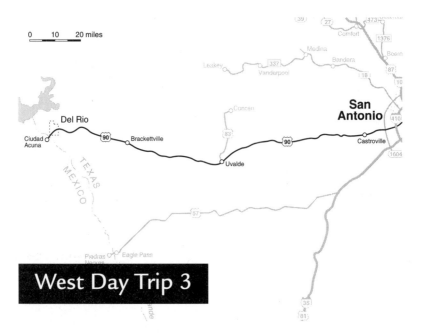

West Day Trip 3

Alamo Village. North of Brackettville; turn off US 90 on FM 674 and continue for 7 miles. This family amusement theme park, located on a 30-square-mile ranch, is often used as a movie set. It features a replica of the Alamo, built in the mid-1950s for the filming of *The Alamo*, starring John Wayne. Since that time, many movies, commercials, documentaries, and TV shows have been shot here.

While there are no amusement rides, visitors can tour the John Wayne Museum, filled with pictures and posters from his many films, as well as an Old West jail (complete with cells), a blacksmith's shop, a chapel, and a bank that's been the scene of many movie holdups. During summer months, gunslingers bite the dust four times a day at showdowns staged in front of the cantina. Open daily except the Christmas holidays. Fee. (830) 563–2580.

WHERE TO STAY

Fort Clark Springs Motel and RV Park. US 90, in Fort Clark Springs. The stone barracks of this 1872 fort have been renovated into modern motel rooms. Guests have access to a pool, plus nine- and eighteen-hole golf courses. $$; ☐. (830) 563–2493.

DEL RIO

Located 32 miles west on US 90 from Brackettville, Del Rio is the most popular border town within reach of San Antonio. It's a year-round paradise for fishers, hunters, boaters, and archaeology buffs. Many Texas border towns serve primarily as overnight stops after a day in Mexico, but Del Rio is its own main attraction. Museums, historic sites, fishing, camping, bird-watching, and boating all await within thirty minutes of downtown.

Another feature that separates Del Rio from other border cities is its abundance of water. The town is literally an oasis in the semiarid climate at the edge of the Chihuahuan Desert. Tall palm trees, lush lawns, and golf courses dotted with water hazards are seen throughout the city. The San Felipe Springs pump 90 million gallons of water daily. The crystal-clear water has drawn inhabitants to this region for 10,000 years, from prehistoric Indians who lived in the canyons west of here to Spanish missionaries who named the area "San Felipe del Rio" in 1635.

Today the San Felipe Springs provide water for the city of Del Rio, offering a cool swim on a hot summer day. At the San Felipe Amphitheater, the water is diverted through a stone moat separating the audience from a stage used for concerts and special events.

Del Rio lies 12 miles from the Amistad Dam and Lake Amistad, both the result of a cooperative effort between Mexico and the United States.

WHERE TO GO

Val Verde Winery. 100 Qualia Drive. Italian immigrant Frank Qualia established this winery in 1883, drawn to the area by its flowing springs and fertile land. The oldest winery in Texas, this enterprise is now operated by third-generation vintner Thomas Qualia. Val Verde produces many wines, including award-winning Don Luis Tawny Port. Tours and tastings are available on a drop-in basis. Open daily except Sundays. Free. (830) 775-9714.

Whitehead Memorial Museum. 1308 South Main Street. This museum is best known for its replica of the Jersey Lilly, Judge Roy Bean's saloon and courtroom. (The original Jersey Lilly remains in Langtry, about 60 miles west of Del Rio.) Judge Bean and his son

Sam are buried behind the replica of the saloon, their graves marked with simple headstones. The museum boasts over twenty exhibit sites including an 1870s' store, a windmill, a log cabin, a caboose, and the Cadena Nativity, a cultural folk art exhibit. Open Tuesday through Saturday and Sunday afternoon. Fee. (830) 774-7568.

Lake Amistad. West of Del Rio on US 90. The construction of Lake Amistad (derived from the Spanish word for "friendship") was a cooperative project between the United States and Mexico. The 67,000-acre lake was completed in 1969 as a way to control flooding, provide irrigation for South Texas farms and ranches, and offer water recreation. Surrounded by 1,000 miles of shoreline, the reservoir contains twenty-nine species of fish including striper, bass, crappie, perch, catfish, gar, and sunfish. You must have separate fishing licenses for the U.S. and Mexican areas of the lake. Both Texas and Mexico fishing licenses are sold in the marinas and in many Del Rio stores.

The 6-mile-long Amistad Dam is responsible for the creation of the enormous lake. The observation deck affords a look at the 86-mile-long reservoir. Atop the dam stand two bronze eagles, each 7 feet tall, symbolizing the two participating countries and marking the international border.

Tlaloc, the Rain God. Mexican shore of Lake Amistad, near Amistad Dam. This 23-foot stone statue is a replica of one carved by the Teotihuacán people, years before Aztec rule in Mexico. Tlaloc is believed to bring rain. Some swear the statue works, pointing to the higher-than-normal rainfalls in the years following the dam's construction.

Lake Amistad Resort and Marina. US 90, Diablo East Recreation Area. Concessioners at the marina rent small powerboats and large houseboats sleeping up to ten people. You can cruise to the main part of Lake Amistad or up the Devil's River to some clear, spring-fed swimming holes. Open daily. Fee. (830) 774-4157.

Lake Amistad Tours. The historic pictographs of the lower Pecos are featured on this boat tour. Coast Guard–approved 30-foot boats are used, and tours are led by photographer Jim Zintgraff. His work is now the only record of many pictographs that were lost when Lake Amistad was formed. Fee. For reservations, call (830) 775-7100, or write: HCR #3, Box 44, Del Rio, TX 78840.

WHERE TO EAT

Wright's Steak House. US 90, 3 miles west of the intersection of US 277. This casual steakhouse features all the usual cuts plus choices like Texas-sized chicken-fried steak. Save room for home-baked cheesecake, then work off that big dinner on the dance floor. Live entertainment appears every Friday and Saturday night. Closed Monday. Dinner only Tuesday through Saturday; lunch and dinner Sunday. $$; ☐. (830) 775-2621.

Memo's. 804 East Losoya. There's nothing fancy here, just lots of good Tex-Mex food. Located along San Felipe Creek, it features live music most days. $; ☐. (830) 774-2280.

Cripple Creek Saloon. US 90 West. Modeled after the original Cripple Creek Saloon in Colorado, this restaurant specializes in prime rib, but also serves up a mean sirloin, filet mignon, and rib eye. Seafood, from lobster to Coho salmon to swordfish, rounds out the menu. $$–$$$; ☐. (830) 775-0153.

WHERE TO STAY

Del Rio offers a wide array of accommodations: Mom-and-pop motels, popular chains, fishing resorts and bed-and-breakfasts. For a complete listing, call the Del Rio Chamber of Commerce (800) 889-8149 or (830) 775-3551, or write: 1915 Avenue F, Del Rio, TX 78840.

Ramada Inn. 2101 Avenue F. This popular ninety-six room motel is conveniently located on the main thoroughfare through town, offering guests a pool, hot tub, workout room, restaurant, and bar. $$; ☐. (800) 272-6232 or (830) 775-1511.

The 1890 House. 609 Griner Street. Named for its year of construction, this bed-and-breakfast is located in the heart of Del Rio. Boasting a Victorian elegance, guests at this B & B enjoy plenty of modern comforts including private baths with Jacuzzis. $$–$$$; ☐. (800) 282-1360.

La Mansión Del Rio. 123 Hudson Street. This nineteenth-century mansion is tucked beneath stately palms and pecan trees. Guests can stroll to Texas's oldest winery or enjoy a leisurely day in one of four suites that feature fireplace foyers, hand-painted tiled floors, and an atmosphere that recalls the days of South Texas haciendas. $$; ☐. (830) 768-1100.

ESPECIALLY FOR WINTER TEXANS

Del Rio has a very active winter-visitors community. The Chamber of Commerce hosts a Winter Texan Welcome Party, an arts and crafts fair, and an appreciation party during the season.

The Welcome Party is held on the first weekend in December and includes a traditional Texas meal. Exhibits introduce newcomers to local attractions, and gold cards offering discounts at area businesses are distributed. The Winter Visitors Crafts Fair kicks off in February, giving participants a chance to sell arts and crafts without the usual booth expense associated with such shows. In mid-March, Del Rio throws its big Winter Visitors Appreciation Party.

The chamber publishes a calendar of special events planned for winter visitors, including dessert cook-offs, Mexican shopping trips, museum tours, and more. For a copy, call the Del Rio chamber at (800) 889-8149 or (830) 775-3551.

CIUDAD ACUÑA, MEXICO

To reach the international border and Ciudad Acuña, take Spur 239 off Highway 90. Most travelers drive to the Texas side of the International Bridge and pay a small fee for secured parking. From there, you can take a cab across the river, a bus (every 30 minutes), or walk across the toll bridge.

A bus carries shoppers from Del Rio across the border to Acuña's (pronounced "a-COON-ya") shopping district. This place is filled with tourist shops, especially along Hidalgo Street. There is no central market here, but the shops are continuous for several blocks as you enter town. For a round-trip trolley and bus schedule, call (830) 774-0580.

To place telephone calls to Mexico, first dial the international code (011), then the country code (52), followed by the phone number.

WHERE TO SHOP

El Caballo Blanco. Hidalgo 110. This leather shop is filled, floor to ceiling, with handbags, billfolds, *huaraches*, boots, saddles, and even gun holsters. Look for traditional Mexican purses, hand tooled with cactus, Aztec, and eagle designs. Open daily. (No phone.)

Nick's Warehouse. Hidalgo 185. Nick's calls itself the largest handmade dress shop in Acuña, and it is. Beautifully embroidered items in festive colors fill the racks, from infant clothes to one-size-fits-all women's dresses. Open daily. (877) 2-1631.

Casa Uxmal (Artesanías Mexicanas). Hidalgo 125. This shop has a little of everything, from abalone inlay jewelry and Mexican dresses to hand-blown glass. Open daily. (877) 2-0925.

WHERE TO EAT

Crosbys. Hidalgo 195. Both Americans and Mexicans frequent this lively restaurant for a good meal and a good time. From the etched glass and oak doors to the white columns separating the dining rooms, the look says "elegant" but the atmosphere definitely shouts "party." The menu features Tex-Mex food, steaks, seafood, and *de la presa la Amistad*—fish from nearby Lake Amistad. Try the *Camarón Relleno Estilo Crosbys* (shrimp stuffed with cheese and wrapped in bacon) or share a sampler platter, a massive tray of breaded quail, frog legs, stuffed shrimp, and beef strips. The margaritas are king-sized and served in glasses resembling goldfish bowls.

Service on Friday and Saturday nights can be slow by American standards. Open daily for lunch and dinner. $$; ☐. (877) 2-2020.

SEMINOLE CANYON STATE HISTORICAL PARK

To reach the entrance of Seminole Canyon State Historical Park, drive west on US 90 from Del Rio, 9 miles past the town of Comstock. This is a stop archaeology buffs shouldn't miss. During the warmer months, make this an early morning trip because the canyon can be very hot during the afternoon hours.

Seminole Canyon was occupied by early humans about 8,500 years ago. Little is known of that early culture, but archaeologists believe these people were hunter-gatherers, living on plants and small animals. The former residents left paintings on the caves and canyon walls that represent animals, Indians, and supernatural shamans, but their meaning is still unknown. Sadly, these artifacts are fading, and it is unknown how much longer the images will last. Scientists currently are studying ways to slow the deterioration.

Visitors can see the pictographs on a ninety-minute guided tour conducted Wednesday through Sunday at 10:00 A.M. and 3:00 P.M. This is a somewhat strenuous 1-mile hike, so bring along a small canteen of water (there are no drinking facilities in the canyon). The trip also takes in Fate Bell Shelter, named for the archaeologist who discovered the pictographs.

In the park campground, both tent and trailer sites are available, along with electrical and water hookups. Open daily. Fee. For more information on camping, call (915) 292–4464, or write: Park Superintendent, Seminole Canyon State Historical Park, P.O. Box 820, Comstock, TX 78837.

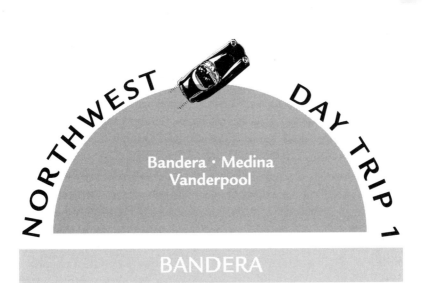

Bandera · Medina
Vanderpool

BANDERA

Follow TX 16 northwest for 50 miles to Bandera, "The Cowboy Capital of the World." This town is well known for its plentiful dude ranches, country-western music, rodeos, and horse racing.

Once part of the "Wild West," Bandera Pass, located 12 miles north of town on TX 173, was the site of many battles between Spanish *conquistadors* and both Apache and Comanche Indians. Legend has it that following a battle with the Apaches in 1732, a flag (or *bandera* in Spanish) was hung at the pass to mark the boundary between the two opposing forces.

Bandera has open rodeos weekly from Memorial Day to Labor Day. Typically rodeos are held Tuesday night at Mansfield Park and Saturday night at Twin Elm Guest Ranch, and, during the summer, several rodeos at Mansfield Park. For more schedule information, call the Bandera Convention and Visitors Bureau (800) 364-3833.

Today the wildest action in town occurs in the dance halls every night except Monday and Tuesday. Put on your boots, crease your best jeans, and get ready to two-step with locals and vacationers alike.

WHERE TO GO

Frontier Times Museum. 13th Street, 1 block north of the courthouse. Established in 1927, this museum is a good place to learn more about Bandera's early days. The stone building is filled with cowboy paraphernalia, Indian arrowheads, and prehistoric artifacts. Its most

Northwest Day Trip 1

unusual exhibit is a shrunken head from Ecuador, part of a private collection donated to the museum. Open daily. Fee. (830) 796-3864.

Historical Walking Tours. Have a look at the buildings that witnessed Bandera's evolution from a frontier town to a vacation destination with a self-guided tour. Thirty-two sites along the route lead visitors to the county courthouse, the Old Jail, Bandera's first theater, and many homes that date back to the community's earliest days. Pick up your walking tour brochure at the Bandera County Visitors Center, 1808 Highway 16 South. Free. (800) 364-3833.

Hill Country State Natural Area. South on TX 173 to FM 1077, then right for 12 miles. This rugged park preserves 5,400 acres of Hill Country land. Only primitive camping is available; you must bring your own water, and pick up and remove your own trash. This park was originally open primarily for equestrian use, but today it has become popular with hikers and bicyclists. There are 34 miles of quiet trails and camp areas for backpackers and equestrians. Cool off with a dip in West Verde Creek or fish for catfish, perch, or largemouth bass. Horse rentals are available offsite. Open Thursday through Monday. Fee. (830) 796-4413.

Medina River. TX 16, east of town. The cypress-lined Medina River is a popular spot during the summer months, when swimmers, canoeists, and inner-tubers enjoy the cool water. The Medina can be hazardous during high water, however, with rocky rapids and submerged trees. There is public access to the river from the TX 16 bridge in town. For rental or shuttle information or advice on the rapids, call (830) 796-3553.

Running-R Ranch Trail Rides. 11 miles from Bandera off FM 1077. Enjoy one-, two-, or three-hour rides with an experienced wrangler. The ranch also offers all-day rides with a picnic and cowboy cookout. Children six and up are accepted. Fee. (830) 796-3984.

The Silver Dollar Bar. 308 Main Street. Pick up a longneck, grab a partner, and start boot-scootin' at this Texas honky-tonk. Owner and singer Arkey Blue performs country-western hits here as crowds fill the sawdust-covered dance floor. (830) 796-8826.

WHERE TO SHOP

Bandera Forge. 803 Main Street. This shop includes a large stock of forged works, including windchimes and boot scrapers. The blacksmith will create a personalized branding iron for you to take back home as a souvenir. Open daily. (830) 796-7184.

WHERE TO STAY

The country around Bandera is dotted with dude ranches. Rates usually include three meals daily as well as family-style entertainment and supervised children's programs. Horseback riding is often part of the week-long package. A minimum stay of two or three days is required at most ranches during peak summer season.

For a complete listing of Bandera's dude ranches, as well as other accommodations and campgrounds, call the Bandera Convention and Visitors Bureau (800) 364-3833.

Mayan Ranch. TX 16, 2 miles west of Bandera. For over forty years this sixty-room ranch has entertained vacationers with cowboy breakfasts, cookouts, horseback riding, fishing, and hayrides. Summer also brings organized children's programs. Rooms are appointed with Western-style furniture. Call for rates; ⚓. (830) 796-3312.

Dixie Dude Ranch. South on TX 173 1½ miles to FM 1077, then southwest for 9 more miles. Five generations of the Whitley family have welcomed guests to this nineteen-room ranch since 1937. Rates include meals and two horseback rides daily. Call for rates; ☐. (800) 375-YALL.

Flying L Guest Ranch. From TX 16, turn south on TX 173 for 1.5 miles, then left on Wharton Dock Road. This 542-acre ranch has thirty-eight guest houses, each with two rooms, refrigerator, microwave, coffee pot, and TV. You can choose many different packages offering horseback riding, hayrides, and even golf at the ranch's eighteen-hole course. During the summer there's a supervised children's program, plus nightly entertainment ranges from Western shows to "branding" parties. Call for rates; ☐. (800) 292-5134.

The Silver Spur Dude Ranch. 10 miles south of Bandera on FM 1077. Pull on your boots and grab your Stetson before heading to this 275-acre ranch near the Hill Country State Natural Area. You'll stay busy out of the saddle with fishing, tubing, canoeing, and golf, plus swimming in the ranch pool. Call for rates; ☐. (830) 796-3037.

Twin Elm Guest Ranch. A half-mile off FM 470 from TX 16 (4 miles from Bandera). This 200-acre dude ranch is on the Medina River. All the usual cowboy activities are available, from fishing to horseback riding and horseshoe pitching. Call for rates; ☐. (830) 796-3628.

LH7 Ranch Resort. FM 3240 (5 miles from Bandera). This 1,200-acre ranch, which raises longhorn cattle, has cottages with kitchenettes plus RV hookups. There's plenty to keep any cowpoke busy, including fishing in a fifty-acre lake, hayrides, horseback riding, and nature walks. Call for rates; ☐. (830) 796-4314.

ESPECIALLY FOR WINTER TEXANS

Besides the dude ranches, Bandera has excellent RV parks. Many weekly activities are of special interest to the Winter Texans who call Bandera home. Country-western dances are held Wednesday through Saturday, and there's bingo on Fridays. For a complete listing, contact the Bandera Convention and Visitors Bureau at (800) 364-3833.

MEDINA

From Bandera, continue west on TX 16 to the tiny community of Medina, best known for its dwarf apple trees that produce full-sized fruit in varieties from Crispin to Jonagold.

WHERE TO GO

Love Creek Orchards. RR 337, west of Medina. From May through October, these beautiful orchards are open to the public by guided tour only; call to set up a tour time. Free. (830) 589-2588.

WHERE TO SHOP

The Cider Mill and Country Store. Main Street (TX 16), downtown. This shop offers Love Creek apples for sale from June through November. Butter, sauces, vinegars, jellies, syrups, pies, breads, and even apple ice cream are sold here year-round. If you're ready to start your own orchard but you're short on room, you can buy "the patio apple orchard," a dwarf tree grown on a trellis in a wooden planter. Open daily. (830) 589-2588.

VANDERPOOL

Vanderpool is a quiet getaway during all but the fall months. Tucked into the hills surrounding the Sabinal River, this small town is a center for sheep and goat ranching.

WHERE TO GO

Lost Maples State Natural Area. West on RR 337 to the intersection of RR 187; turn north and continue for 5 miles. This state park is very popular during the fall when the bigtooth maples provide some of the best color in Texas. Weekend visits during this time can be very crowded. For information on the autumn colors, call (800) 792-1112 after October 1.

There are 10 miles of hiking trails to enjoy all year along the Sabinal River Canyon. In the summer visitors can swim and fish in the river. Camping includes primitive areas on the hiking trails and a thirty-site campground with restrooms and showers as well as a trailer dump station. Open daily. Fee. (830) 966-3413.

KERRVILLE

To reach Kerrville from Vanderpool (NORTHWEST FROM SAN ANTONIO, DAY TRIP 1), retrace your steps east to Medina on FM 337 and head north on TX 16. You can also leave San Antonio on I-10, traveling through Boerne and Comfort before exiting at TX 27 for the final 19 miles. If you take this route, be sure to read NORTH-WEST FROM SAN ANTONIO, DAY TRIP 3 for attractions in these Hill Country towns.

Kerrville is popular with retirees, hunters, Winter Texans, and campers. The town of 19,000 residents is home to a 500-acre state park and many privately owned camps catering to youth and church groups. Started in the 1840s, the town was named for James Kerr, a supporter of Texas independence who died in the Civil War. With its unpolluted environment and low humidity, Kerrville later became known as a health center, attracting tuberculosis patients from around the country. The town is still considered one of the most healthful places to live in the nation because of its clean air and moderate climate.

Throughout Kerrville the Schreiner name appears on everything from Schreiner College to Schreiner's Department Store. Charles Schreiner, who became a Texas Ranger at the tender age of fifteen, came to Kerrville as a young man in the 1850s. Following the Civil War, he began a dry goods store and started acquiring land and raising sheep and goats. The Charles Schreiner Company soon expanded to include banking, ranching, and marketing wool and mohair. This was the first business in America to recognize the value of

0   10   20 miles

Northwest Day Trip 2

mohair, the product of Angora goats. Before long, Schreiner made Kerrville the mohair capital of the world.

In 1880 Schreiner acquired the Y. O. Ranch, which grew over the next twenty years to over 600,000 acres, covering a distance of 80 miles. Today the Schreiner family still owns this well-known ranch, located in nearby Mountain Home.

WHERE TO GO

Cowboy Artists of America Museum. 1550 Bandera Highway (TX 173). This hilltop museum features work by members of the Cowboy Artists of America. The building is constructed of eighteen *boveda* brick domes, an old construction method used in Mexico. Western-themed paintings and sculpture fill the museum. Visitors also can take in special programs on the folklore, music, and history of the Old West. Open daily. Fee. (830) 896-2553.

The Hill Country Museum. 226 Earl Garrett Street. This local history museum traces the development of Kerrville. Housed in Charles Schreiner's former mansion built in 1879, the building has

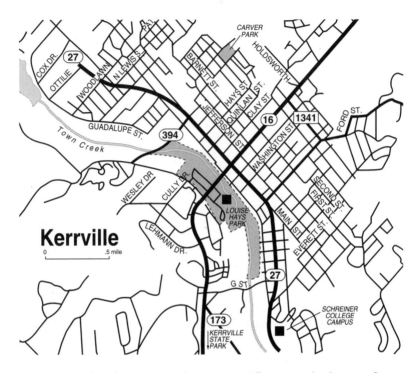

Kerrville

0   .5 mile

granite porch columns, wooden parquet floors, and a bronze fountain imported from France. Open Monday through Saturday. Fee. (830) 896-8633.

Kerrville State Park. 2385 Bandera Highway, 1 mile southwest on TX 173. This park offers 7 miles of hiking trails, as well as fishing and swimming in the Guadalupe River. Campsites include water, electricity, sewage hookups, and screened shelters. Fee. For park information, call (830) 257-5392.

Louise Hays City Park. Off TX 16 at Thompson Drive. Bring your picnic lunch to this beautiful spot on the Guadalupe River. Paddleboats are available for rent, and ducks and cypress trees abound. Days only. Free. (No phone.)

Mooney Aircraft Tours. TX 27 East. Take a one-hour plant tour to see single-engine aircraft on the manufacturing line. No cameras are allowed on the tour, and it is not recommended for children under eight. This tour passes through an unair-conditioned plant, so expect it to be warm during the summer months and bring comfortable walking shoes. Open Tuesday–Friday at 10:00 A.M. Free. (830) 896-6000.

Kerrville Camera Safari. 2301 Sidney Baker North, just north of I-10. Bring your camera or your binoculars to this game ranch and search for exotics such as addox, blackbuck, gazelle, elk, zebra, and gemsbok in the shade of tall live oaks. The drive is self-paced, with plenty of places to pull off the road to relax and view the wildlife. Open daily until sunset. Fee. (830) 792-3600.

WHERE TO SHOP

Pampell's. 701 Water Street. In its 1895 heyday, Pampell Opera House was a lavish venue for musical productions. Today the building is home to an antique store and an old-fashioned soda fountain. Many original furnishings remain, along with items from quilts to elaborate dollhouse miniatures. At the fountain, take a seat on one of the revolving stools and order up a thick malt or a dish of Brenham's Blue Bell ice cream. Open Monday through Saturday. (830) 257-8484.

James Avery, Craftsman. 3.5 miles north of Kerrville on Harper Road. Since 1954 James Avery has been one of Texas's premier silversmiths. He began crafting silver crosses and religious symbols, but today his work includes gold and silver renditions of many subjects, from prickly pears to dolphins. Retail shop open Monday through Saturday, visitors center open weekdays. (830) 895-1122.

WHERE TO STAY

Y. O. Ranch Holiday Inn. 2033 Sidney Baker, at TX 16 and I-10. This 200-room hotel salutes the famous Y. O. Ranch in Mountain Home, located 30 miles from Kerrville. The lobby is filled with reminders of the area's major industries—cattle and hunting. Twelve hotel suites include amenities such as fireplaces, furniture covered in longhorn hide, and wet bars. In keeping with the Wild West spirit, the hotel has a bar called the Elm Water Hole Saloon and a swim-up bar dubbed the Jersey Lilly. $$; ☐. (800) HOLIDAY or (830) 257-4440.

ESPECIALLY FOR WINTER TEXANS

Kerrville is home to over a dozen RV parks, some of which are designated "adults only." For a listing, contact the Kerrville Convention and Visitors Center at (800) 221-7958. The Kerrville Chamber of Commerce (830) 896–1155 can provide a listing of condominium and apartment properties with short-term leases. A welcoming committee greets Winter Texans as well as the many retirees who relocate to the area.

INGRAM

To reach Ingram, leave Kerrville on TX 27 and continue northwest for 7 miles. This small community on the banks of the Guadalupe River was started in 1879 by Reverend J. C. W. Ingram, who built a general store and post office in what is now called Old Ingram.

Old Ingram, located off TX 27 on Old Ingram Loop, is home to many art galleries and antique shops. Ingram proper lies along TX 27, and it features stores and outfitters catering to white-tailed deer, turkey, and quail hunters. The town is particularly busy during deer season, from November to early January. Hunting licenses are required and are sold at local sporting-good stores. For more information, call the Texas Parks and Wildlife Department at (800) 792-1112 in Texas or (512) 389-4800 elsewhere, or write: 4200 Smith School Road, Austin, TX 78744.

WHERE TO GO

Kerr County Historical Murals. At TX 27 and TX 39. Sixteen murals decorate the T. J. Moore Lumber Company building, the work of local artist Jack Feagan. The scenes portray historical events in Kerr County, starting with the establishment of shingle camps (where wooden roofing shingles were produced in 1846). Other paintings highlight cattle drives, the birth of the mohair industry, and the last Indian raid.

Hill Country Arts Foundation. TX 39, west of the Ingram Loop. Plays, art competitions and exhibitions, art shows, classes, and workshops are offered at this fifteen-acre facility. A gallery exhibits the work of many artists and is open daily. The Gazebo Gift Shop is a sales outlet for local artists, open Monday through Friday afternoons. Call for a schedule of play times or special events. (830) 367-5121.

WHERE TO SHOP

Guadalupe Forge. TX 27, just off TX 39. You can have your own brand made in this blacksmith shop, the walls of which are decorated with cattle brands ranging from simple initials to more elaborate renderings of stars or the rising sun. Open Monday through Saturday. (830) 367-4433.

Southwestern Elegance. Old Ingram Loop. This unique store specializes in Mexican collectibles and antiques (especially primitives), Mennonite furniture, and Tarahumara Indian collectibles. Open daily; call for hours. (830) 367-4749.

HUNT

Continue west on TX 39 for 7 miles to Hunt, a small community best known for its year-round outdoor recreational camps catering to Scouts as well as youth and church groups.

WHERE TO GO

Crider's Rodeo and Dance Hall. TX 39, 3 miles southwest of Hunt. Here's your chance to kick up your heels Texas-style on a wooden dance floor. This popular establishment opened in 1925 and continued on through Prohibition, when moonshine was sold in the parking lot. Today the dance hall and nearby rodeo are open May through September. Fee. (830) 238-4874.

Kerr Wildlife Management Area. RR 1340, 12 miles northwest of Hunt. Enjoy a driving tour over this 6,493-acre research ranch owned by the Texas Fish and Game Commission. Purchased to study the relationship between wildlife and livestock, the ranch is home to white-tailed deer, javelinas, wild turkeys, bobcats, gray foxes, and ringtails. Pick up a booklet at the entrance or write: Kerr Wildlife Management Area, Route 1, Box 180, Hunt, TX 78024. Open daily, but call during hunting season when the area may be closed for a hunt. Free. (830) 238-4483.

Stonehenge II. FM 1340, just out of Hunt. Located on private land, this replica of England's Stonehenge may be viewed from a roadside parking area. A sign provides information on the original Stonehenge and its smaller Texas cousin. Open daily. Free. (No phone.)

Y. O. RANCH

From Hunt, head west on FM 1340 to TX 41. Turn left and the Y. O. Ranch will soon appear on your right. This ranch dates back to 1880, a part of the 550,000 acres purchased by Captain Charles Schreiner, former Texas Ranger and longhorn cattle owner.

Presently the Y. O. spans 60 square miles and supports over 1,000 registered longhorns, the largest such herd in the nation. Charlie Schreiner III, the original owner's grandson, brought the breed back from near extinction in the late 1950s, founding the Texas Longhorn Breeders Association. The Y. O. hosts a longhorn trail drive at the ranch each spring.

After the devastating Texas drought in the 1950s, the Schreiners began to diversify the use of their ranch, stocking the land with the largest collection of natural roaming exotics in the country, including many rare and endangered species. Over 10,000 animals range the hills, including zebra, ostrich, giraffe, emu, and ibex.

You may visit the Y. O. Ranch by reservation only. Both day and overnight programs are offered. Day-trippers can enjoy the spread on a lunch tour or photo safari. The ranch also hosts an Outdoor Awareness Program, an environmental education camp that teaches horseback riding, rappelling, gun handling, and wildlife study. For general information, call (830) 640-3348; for information on a day visit or overnight stay, call (830) 640-3222.

Boerne · Comfort Sisterdale

This is an easy day trip from San Antonio, a journey through three small towns that share a strong German heritage. Although the excursion begins on sleek I-10, it includes some curving farm-to-market roads that are very susceptible to flooding. If it's raining heavily, save this trip for another day!

BOERNE

To reach Boerne (pronounced "Bernie"), take I-10 northwest for 22 miles to a spot filled with history, antiques, and natural attractions. Boerne is located on the banks of Cibolo Creek in the rolling Texas Hill Country. The community was founded in 1847 by German immigrants, members of the same group who settled nearby New Braunfels. They named the town for author Ludwig Börne, whose writings inspired many people to leave Germany for the New World.

During the 1880s, Boerne became known as a health spot, and vacationers came by railroad to soak in mineral water spas and enjoy the clean country air. Although no mineral spas remain today, Boerne still offers a quiet country atmosphere and dozens of antique shops in which to browse.

WHERE TO GO

Chamber of Commerce. One Main Plaza, beside Ye Kendall Inn. Stop here for brochures and maps to Boerne attractions and shopping areas. Open daily Monday through Friday, and Saturday morning. (830) 249-8000.

Northwest Day Trip 3

Agricultural Heritage Center. TX 46, 1 mile from Main Street. This museum features farm and ranch tools used by pioneers in the late nineteenth and early twentieth centuries, including a working steam-operated blacksmith shop. Six acres surrounding the museum are covered with hand-drawn plows, wagons, early tractors, and woodworking tools. Open Sunday and Wednesday afternoons. Free. (830) 249–8000.

Cascade Caverns. From I–10 take exit 543 and follow signs on Cascade Caverns Road. This family-owned cavern has a 100-foot waterfall, an unusual underground sight. Guided tours take forty-five minutes. For those who wish to stay longer, there's an RV park on-site as well. Open daily. Fee. (830) 755–8080.

Cibolo Wilderness Trail. Boerne City Park, TX 46 at Cibolo Creek. Enjoy grassland, marshland, and woodland in this park that offers a slice of the Hill Country. The wilderness area includes both reclaimed prairie and reclaimed marsh, with walking trails that range from .25 to 1 mile in length. Free. (830) 249–4616.

Kuhlmann-King Historical House and Graham Building and Museum Store. Main Street and Blanco Road. The Kuhlmann-King house was built by a local businessman for his German bride in 1885. Today the two-story stone home is staffed by volunteer docents. The Graham Building, located next door, is home to the Boerne Area Historical Preservation Society with exhibits on local history. Open Saturday and Sunday afternoons. Free. (830) 249-2030.

Guadalupe River State Park. 13 miles east of Boerne off TX 46 on Park Road 31. The star of this park is the clear, cold Guadalupe River. Camp, swim, hike, or just picnic on its scenic banks, or on Saturday mornings, take an interpretive tour of the Honey Creek State Natural Area to learn more about the plants and animals of the region. Fee. (830) 438-2656.

WHERE TO EAT

Ye Kendall Inn. 128 West Blanco Street, Main Plaza. In 1859 the owners of this two-story structure began renting rooms to stagecoach travelers, eventually developing the property into an inn. Over the years, its famous guests have included Confederate President Jefferson Davis and President Dwight D. Eisenhower. Along with seven bed-and-breakfast rooms furnished with period antiques, the inn includes a restaurant with adjoining bar that serves favorites such as burgers, salads, and soups along with specialties like lemon chicken *schnitzel,* chicken-fried steak, and Gulf shrimp. Open daily for lunch and dinner. $$; □. (830) 249-2138.

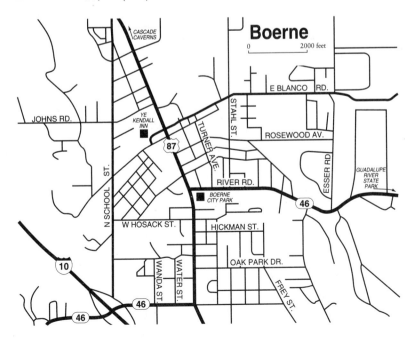

ESPECIALLY FOR WINTER TEXANS

Cascade Caverns Campgrounds. Campers visiting this beautiful 105-acre park surrounding Cascade Caverns find RV sites with hookups, barbecue pits, and picnic tables. Shower facilities, a dance hall, volleyball and badminton courts, and pool tables also are available. Fee. (830) 755-8080.

COMFORT

From Boerne, continue north on I-10 for 17 miles to road marker 524 and exit to the town of Comfort. This small community is big in history and attractions. The downtown area is a National Historic District, filled with homes and businesses built by early settlers.

Comfort was founded by German pioneers in 1854 who wanted to name the town "Gemütlichkeit," meaning peace, serenity, comfort, and happiness. After some deliberation, though, they decided on the easier to pronounce "Comfort" instead.

Today Comfort offers tourists numerous historic buildings to explore, filled with antique shops and restaurants. Visitors also find a historic inn and the oldest general store in Texas. Weekends are the busiest time to visit, but even then the atmosphere is relaxing, unhurried, and, well, comfortable.

WHERE TO GO

"Treue der Union" (True to the Union) Monument. High Street, between Third and Fourth Streets. During the Civil War, German residents of Comfort who did not approve of slavery and openly swore their loyalty to the Union were burned out of their farms. The Confederates responsible also lynched locals who refused to pledge their allegiance to the movement. Several German farmers decided to defect to Mexico but were caught by Confederate soldiers and killed on the banks of the Nueces River, their bodies left unburied.

Finally retrieved in 1865, the remains were returned to Comfort and buried in a mass grave. A white obelisk, the oldest monument in Texas and the only monument to the Union located south of the Mason-Dixon line, was dedicated here in 1866. One of only six such sites in the country, the shrine recently received Congressional approval to continually fly the flag at half mast. The flag that waves here has thirty-six stars, the same number it had when the marker was dedicated in 1866. Free. (830) 995-3131.

Ingenhuett Store. 830 High Street. Built in 1880 by Peter Ingenhuett, this general store is now operated by fourth- and fifth-generation family members. One of the oldest continually operated general stores in Texas, the shop includes an Ingenhuett history display, complete with photos of the Ingenhuett ancestors and Comfort's early days. Closed Sunday. Free. (830) 995-2149.

Bat Roost. FM 473, on private land. As you leave Comfort for Sisterdale, this historic structure sits 1 mile from town on the right side of the road behind private gates. While it's generally known now that bats feed on disease-spreading mosquitoes, the folks here have known about the importance of these furry mammals since 1918, when Albert Steves constructed hygieostatic bat roosts in an experimental attempt to control malaria. The roosts were intended to encourage the area's large bat population to remain in the region. Only sixteen such roosts were built in the country, and this is the oldest of three known still to exist. Free (at present visitors are not allowed to enter property). (830) 995-3131.

Bat Tunnel. 15 miles northeast of Comfort off TX 473 on old Highway 9. View the evening flight of 1.2 million Mexican free-tailed bats from this abandoned railroad tunnel now managed by the Texas Parks and Wildlife Department. Closed October to May. Free. (830) 995-3131.

WHERE TO SHOP

The Comfort Common. 818 High Street. This combination bed-and-breakfast inn and indoor shopping area is located within the historic Ingenhuett-Faust Hotel. Several buildings behind the hotel display antique primitives and furniture. Open daily. (830) 995-3030.

Bygone Days. High Street. This year-round Christmas store features handmade Santa Claus figures as well as numerous antiques, all in a historic building with original counters and fixtures. Open Tuesday through Saturday. (830) 995-3003.

Marketplatz. Seventh and Main Streets. This large antique store offers two floors of furniture, collectibles, quilts, and crafts, all housed in an 1883 building. Open Tuesday through Saturday, and Sunday afternoon. (830) 995-2000.

WHERE TO STAY

The Comfort Common. 818 High Street. This bed-and-breakfast operates within the 1880 Ingenhuett-Faust Hotel. The five suites are decorated in English country, American country, and Victorian decor. All rooms include private baths and period furnishings. The backyard cottage has a fireplace and complete kitchen. All rates include breakfast. As rooms book quickly for weekends, consider a mid-week stay. $$; ☐. (830) 995-3030.

    Brinkmann House Bed and Breakfast. 714 Main Street. Guests can stay in the Gardener's Cottage, decorated with twig furniture and country quilts, or the Heritage Cottage, where furnishings recall colonial America. Both include private bath and television; the Heritage Cottage also offers microwave, refrigerator, and dining area. A gourmet breakfast is included and can be served inside the cottage or on the porch. $$; no ☐. (830) 995-3141.

SISTERDALE

From Comfort, head out on FM 473 to nearby Sisterdale, best known as the home of a small winery. The burg was settled by a group of intellectuals like nearby Boerne. Today the population has dwindled to a handful of residents, and you have to look carefully to keep from passing right through town.

WHERE TO GO

Sister Creek Vineyards. FM 1376, off FM 473. These vineyards thrive in "downtown" Sisterdale, located between the East and West Sister Creeks. The winery, a restored cotton gin, produces traditional French wines. Weekday afternoon tours. Free. For information, call (830) 324-6704, or write: Route 2, P.O. Box 2481 C-1, Sisterdale, TX 78806.

    Sisterdale General Store. FM 473. This historic general store and adjoining bar have served generations of customers. The bar sells Sister Creek Wine. Closed Monday. (830) 324-6767.

Day Trips from Austin

Welcome to Austin, the state capital and gateway to attractions in Central Texas. With Austin as your base, you'll have a chance to visit both rugged hills to the west and miles of scenic roads and interesting small towns to the east. (For more information on Austin, see NORTHEAST FROM SAN ANTONIO, DAY TRIP 1.)

Austin is a high-tech city, with an economy based on computer-related industries and state government. The city of Austin takes in 485,000 residents, including a University of Texas population of over 50,000 students and faculty from around the world. This gives Austin an international feel, with many ethnic restaurants and specialty grocery stores. Many people have relocated here, attracted by the clean industry and beautiful weather.

Beyond the reach of Austin's bedroom communities, you'll find a Texas that's largely unchanged by the 1990s: bowling alleys still set pins by hand, businesses close on Friday nights during high school football season, and pickup trucks seem to outnumber every other form of transportation. Some of the best barbecue in the world comes from the small towns that nestle in the Hill Country, a region so-called because of its rugged terrain. The topographical change represents the 1,800-mile Balcones Fault, which has separated the western Hill Country from the flat eastern farmland ever since a 3.5-minute earthquake 30 million years ago.

This part of Texas gives you a chance to slow down, meet some local folks, and enjoy a good old-fashioned chicken-fried steak at the local diner.

For brochures and maps on Austin area attractions, call (800) 926-2282 or (512) 474-5171, or write: Austin Convention and Visitors Bureau, P.O. Box 2990, Austin, TX 78769.

ROUND ROCK

This Austin bedroom community located north on I-35 is named for the circular rock formation that lies in the middle of Brushy Creek.

Round Rock was the scene of a Wild West shoot-out a century ago. Sam Bass was a well-known outlaw in these parts back then, a stagecoach and train robber who boasted that he'd never killed a man. Bass planned to make his first bank robbery in Round Rock, but things went awry when the Texas Rangers learned his scheme. They were waiting as Bass and his gang rode into town on July 19, 1878, and they gravely wounded him during a gun battle in the 100 block of East Main Street. Bass fled from town and died two days later.

This colorful figure was buried in the old Round Rock cemetery, situated on what's now known as Sam Bass Road. The grave is near an interesting slave cemetery, a reminder of the cotton industry and plantation system that once dominated this area.

Round Rock was also once a part of the stagecoach route that stretched from Brownsville, Texas to Helena, Arkansas. Frontiersmen used the round rock to judge the depth of Brushy Creek before crossing. Today visitors still can see coach tracks in the Brushy Creek riverbed, just west of I-35.

Every July Round Rock hosts Frontier Days, recalling its Wild West heritage with a reenactment of the Sam Bass shoot-out.

WHERE TO GO

Palm House Museum. 212 East Main Street. Built in the 1860s, this historic home now contains a two-room museum and the local Chamber of Commerce. In the kitchen and parlor hang photos and artifacts from Round Rock's early days. Look for the silver bowl whose lid was blown off during the Sam Bass shootout. Open daily. Free. (800) 747-3479 or (512) 255-5805.

WHERE TO EAT

Brushy Creek Inn. I-35 South, Taylor exit. Originally an 1860s' home and now filled with antiques, this fine-dining establishment and special occasion restaurant features Continental cuisine. Open for dinner only; call for hours and reservations. $$-$$$; ☐. (512) 255-2555.

El Matador. 113 West Main Street. This is the way Tex-Mex should be served, with chips and salsa brought to your table as soon as you sit down. The menu offers combinations galore and plates piled high with rice and beans, all at very reasonable prices. $; ☐. (512) 244-3030.

North Day Trip 1

GEORGETOWN

Georgetown is an elegant community that rests on the border of farmland to the east and ranchland to the west. Located 10 miles north of Round Rock on I–35, this was once an active agricultural center. Today Georgetown is home to many Austin commuters and 1,200 students at Southwestern University, the oldest college in Texas.

Georgetown's first residents were the Tonkowa Indians, a resourceful group that drove buffalo off the bluffs of the San Gabriel River. Years later, the town of Georgetown was founded by a group of men that included George Washington Glasscock. After he donated the land for the town, it was named in his honor. Glasscock had come to Texas from the East after running a riverbarge business for a time in Illinois with Abraham Lincoln.

Georgetown became a cattle center after the Civil War and the starting point of many northern cattle drives. The community grew in size but remained a small town into the late 1900s. Austin's runaway growth during the 1980s eventually turned Georgetown into a bedroom community. Interstate 35 divides the city. To the west is "new" Georgetown, with many subdivisions along Williams Drive on the way to Lake Georgetown. "Old" Georgetown sits east of the highway, and among its main attractions are the winding North and South San Gabriel Rivers, which join together in shady San Gabriel Park.

Georgetown was recently selected as one of five national winners of the Great American Main Street awards. To view the award-winning revitalization project, take exit 261 off I–35 and continue right to Austin Avenue. Turn left at the light for a look at the restored courthouse square. With its stately oaks and shady lawn, it is so typical of Texas that it's been used as a set for several movies and TV shows.

WHERE TO GO

Georgetown History and Visitor Information Center. 101 West Seventh Street, on the square. Stop by for a copy of a Georgetown map, brochures on area attractions, and walking tour booklets and cassettes. The center also sells many Georgetown items, from posters to coffee cups. Open daily. (512) 863–5598.

Inner Space Cavern. West off I–35, exit 259. Discovered during the construction of the interstate, this cave is a cool getaway for summer travelers and was once a hideaway for animals as well. A skull of a peccary (a pig-like hoofed mammal) estimated to be a million years old has been found here, along with bones of a giant sloth and a mammoth. After reaching cave level aboard a small trolley, follow your guide for a tour of cave formations, a small lake, and evidence of those prehistoric visitors. Open daily. Fee. (512) 863–5545.

Lake Georgetown. FM 2338, 3.5 miles west of town. Built on the north fork of the San Gabriel River, this lake spans 1,310 surface acres. Three public parks offer swimming, fishing, boating, camping, and hiking opportunities. The 17-mile Good Water Trail follows the upper end of the lake. Fee. (512) 863–3016.

Firefighters' Museum. 103 West Ninth Street at Fire Station No. 1. This museum is home to an authentic 1922 Seagraves Fire Engine as well as antique fire extinguishers and old photos. Open daily. Free. (512) 930–3606.

WHERE TO SHOP

Georgetown presently has over a dozen antique shops. For a free map of the shops listing hours and specialties, call (512) 930–3545 or (800) GEO-TOWN for a copy, or stop by the visitors center on the square where other brochures are also available.

The Candle Factory. I-35 North, exit 259. This year-round factory produces thousands of varieties of handcrafted candles, from classic tapers to popular snowball creations. Open daily. (512) 863–6025.

Texas Sampler. I-35 South, exit 261A. Georgetown's largest antique shop is located in two connected homes that together offer fifteen rooms of antiques and collectibles. Open daily. (512) 863–7694.

Georgetown Emporium. 114 East Seventh Street. Over one hundred dealers in this antique mall sell everything from primitive furniture to estate jewelry. You'll also find the work of well-known Georgetown dollmaker Jan Hagara for sale here. Open daily. (512) 863–6845.

Jan Hagara Doll Collectibles. I-35, exit 264 on 40114 Industrial Park Circle. Jan Hagara Outlet features heirloom-quality Victorian children's products. From hand-sculpted dolls dressed in vintage clothing to collector plates and prints, Jan's collection is hard to resist. Open Monday through Friday; June, July, August open Saturday as well. (512) 863–9499.

The Windberg Gallery. 202 South Austin Avenue on the downtown square. Georgetown is home to the renowned Texas artist Dalhart Windberg. Known for his emotional portrayals of American landscapes and settings, the gallery offers a view of both original art and handsome prints. Open Monday through Saturday. (512) 819-9463.

WHERE TO EAT

Walburg Restaurant. North from Georgetown on I-35 to exit 268; right 4 miles to Walburg. This restaurant is housed in the 1882 Walburg Mercantile building and features authentic German food and music. Behind the restaurant, a converted cotton gin serves as a *biergarten.* The menu includes *weinerschnitzel,* bratwurst, *sauerbraten,* and some Texas favorites like chicken-fried steak and catfish. The restaurant hosts several annual celebrations, such as Harvestfest and Maifest. Closed Monday and Tuesday. Open for lunch and dinner Friday and Sunday; dinner on Wednesday, Thursday and Saturday. $$; ☐. (512) 863-8440.

WHERE TO STAY

Page House. 1000 Leander Road. This grand three-story Queen Anne–style structure dates back to 1903. The stables out back were once the training center for horses used as polo ponies, ridden by folks in Western wear in a game called "Cowboy Polo." Today the stables are a bed-and-breakfast accommodation, along with several upstairs rooms in the home. $$; ☐. (800) 828-7700 or (512) 863-8979.

Claibourne House. 912 Forest Street. Walk to the courthouse square from this Victorian home, built in 1896. The four bedrooms are elegantly furnished. $$; ☐. (512) 930-3934.

SALADO

Continuing north on I-35, Salado presents a shopping stop for interstate travelers. Antique stores, artists' galleries, and specialty shops fill the historic downtown buildings. Salado (pronounced "sa-LAY-dough") is a Spanish word meaning either "salty" or "amusing," although residents prefer the latter interpretation.

This retirement community is located where Salado Creek flows beneath I-35. The site once was a stagecoach stop on the old

Chisholm Trail and served the line that stretched from San Antonio to Little Rock.

Today the old rest stop has been converted to the modern Stagecoach Inn, located on the east side of I–35. Visitors' accommodations are found in a new addition, and the original building, where Sam Houston once delivered an antisecession speech, has become an elegant restaurant.

The former stagecoach route, now called Main Street, is lined with historic structures housing antique shops and specialty stores. In all, eighteen of these buildings are listed in the National Register of Historic Places, and twenty-three boast Texas historical markers.

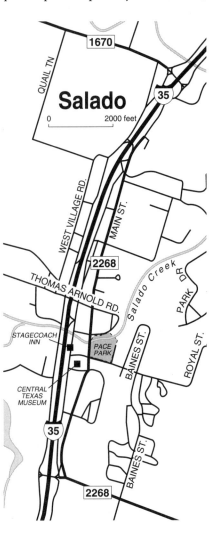

WHERE TO GO

Central Texas Museum. Main Street, across from Stagecoach Inn. This museum traces the history of the Salado area and all of the Brazos Trail—the rich farming area near the Brazos River. Open by appointment and during festivals. Fee. (254) 947–5232.

Pace Park. Downtown, off Main Street. This beautiful area filled with tall oaks is an excellent spot to bring a picnic lunch and wade in the creek. Don't miss the statue of Sirena, located in the middle of the creek just behind the Grace Jones Shop (1 Royal Street). Local artist Troy Kelley sculpted the statue cast in bronze of the legendary Indian maiden who was transformed into a mermaid by a magical fish. Mornings you can see steam rising from the chilly waters of the pure springs near the statue. Free. (254) 947–5040.

Driving Tape Tour. Prepared by the Bell County Historical Commission, this cassette tour directs you past twenty-two historic Salado sites. You'll see "driving tape tour" signs throughout town that correspond to an explanation on the cassette. Budget about two hours for the excursion, which explains the history and background behind each location. The tapes are available for rent at the Stagecoach Inn, Salado Galleries, and the Inn at Salado. Fee. (254) 947–5040.

WHERE TO SHOP

Shopping is the main drawing card of Salado, and many stores are open daily. Most are expensive and sell one-of-a-kind, handmade items.

Salado Galleries. Main Street, across from Stagecoach Inn. Fine art, including many paintings of central Texas bluebonnet fields, fill this gallery. Closed Monday. (254) 947–5110.

Royal Emporium of Salado. Main and Royal Streets. This store has a little bit of everything, from cowboy statues and teddy bears to Hoosier cabinets and delicate glassware. (254) 947–5718.

Salado Pottery. Beside the Stagecoach Inn. Here you'll find beautiful Salado-made pottery, from water pitchers to bird feeders. (254) 947–5935.

Shady Villa. Main Street, across from Stagecoach Inn. This open-air mini-mall sells everything from unique kaleidoscopes and collectibles to Victorian jewelry and gifts from around the world. Most shops are open daily.

The Women's Exchange. North Main Street at Salado Creek. Built in 1860, this structure has served as a drugstore, a law office, a stagecoach shop, and Salado's only saloon. Today it's filled with antiques and collectibles. (254) 947–5552.

Grace Jones. 1 Royal Street. You wouldn't expect to find the latest New York fashions in a Texas town of little more than 1,000 residents, but here it is. The store's owner, Grace Jones (not the singer/actress), was once a fashion model. Open Monday through Saturday. (254) 947–5555.

Sir Wigglesworth. Rock Creek at Main Street. Glass and ceramics, antique linens, baskets of every shape, and concrete animals from pigs to ducks are just a few of the items for sale in this crowded store. (254) 947-8846.

Fletcher's Books and Antiques. Main Street at Old Mill Road. If you're looking for a Texas-related book, this is the place to go. Fletcher's has been in business for sixty years, thirty of those in Salado. The family-owned bookstore specializes in new, used, and rare Texana books and also carries a selection of antiques. Open daily. (254) 947-5414.

WHERE TO EAT

Stagecoach Inn. I-35, east side. This tony restaurant features waitresses who come to your table and recite the day's offerings by heart. Entrees include chicken-fried steak, baked ham, whole catfish, roast prime rib of beef, and T-bone steak. Don't miss the hush puppies or the banana fritters. Open daily for lunch and dinner. $$-$$$; ☐. (254) 947-5111.

Robertson's Hams and Choppin' Block. 1-35, exit 285. Enjoy a deli sandwich of sugar-cured ham then shop for kitchen collectibles in the extensive gift shop. $; ☐. (800) 458-HAMS or (254) 947-5562.

WHERE TO STAY

Stagecoach Inn. I-35, east side. This reminder of Salado's early days started out as the Shady Villa Inn, an important rest stop on the Chisholm Trail. Today guests stay in a modern addition, and the original building, where Sam Houston once delivered an antisecession speech, is now an elegant restaurant. Notable guests have included George Armstrong Custer, Robert E. Lee, and outlaw Jesse James. $$; ☐. (254) 947-5111.

The Inn at Salado. North Main Street at Pace Park. This lovely white two-story bed-and-breakfast is located in the main shopping district. Room rates include a full breakfast. $$; ☐. (254) 947-8200.

Inn on the Creek. On Center Circle. Seven rooms greet guests with 1892 Victorian elegance. Some rooms boast brass beds; all have private baths. A block away the **Reue House** has four bedrooms, mid-1800s style. All guests receive a full breakfast. $$; ☐. (254) 947-5554.

Beyond Georgetown and Salado (see NORTH FROM AUSTIN, DAY TRIP 1 for attractions in those towns), I-35 continues its northward journey to two larger central Texas communities. If you're a military buff, take a short detour to Killeen, home of the largest military base in the free world. Vacationers interested in taking a step back in time will enjoy The Grove, a privately owned community frozen in the late 1800s.

BELTON

Built on the Leon River and Nolan Creek, this community was once named Nolanville, a place where merchants sold goods from wagons and tin cups full of whiskey from a barrel. Today Belton is a small town of 14,000 residents, best known as home of the University of Mary-Hardin Baylor. The Baptist college began here over a century ago and was once the women's school for Waco's Baylor University.

Two lakes, Stillhouse Hollow and the larger Belton Lake, lie outside the city limits. Both provide fishing, boating, camping, and a quiet retreat only a few minutes from busy I-35.

WHERE TO GO

Bell County Museum. 201 North Main. This National Register property was first a Carnegie library. Today the Beaux Arts-style building houses exhibits on Bell County's first century, 1850-1950. Special displays remember Miriam "Ma" Ferguson, Texas's first

woman governor. Open Tuesday through Saturday afternoons. Free. (254) 939-6110.

Summer Fun USA. 1410 Waco Road. This 6.5-acre water theme park offers over 900 feet of water slides to help you cool off in the Texas heat. Hop in an inner tube and enjoy the 750-foot-long Lazy River ride or slide into the water from a 40-foot tower. There's a picnic area and concession area as well. Open seasonally. Fee. (254) 939-0366.

Stillhouse Hollow. US 190, 4 miles southwest of Belton. Six public parks envelope this lake. You'll find the most facilities at Stillhouse Park, the first you'll come to on US 190. Free. (254) 939-2461.

Belton Lake. TX 317, 5 miles northwest of Belton. Built on the Leon River, this winding 7,400-acre lake features thirteen public parks within its 110 miles of shoreline. Trailer sites, camping, nature trails, and boat ramps are available. For information, call (254) 939-1829 or 939-0441, or write: Reservoir Manager, 99 FM 2271, Belton, TX 76513.

KILLEEN

Military buffs should take a detour at this point in the journey and head west on US 190 to the city of Killeen. Twenty-five miles west of Belton, this small town is dwarfed by Fort Hood, the largest military base in the free world.

WHERE TO GO

Fort Hood. US 190. Established in 1942, Fort Hood spans 339 miles, encompassing more people and machines than any other post in the free world. The base is home to more than 47,000 soldiers. Access to the base is not restricted, and the public is welcome at two museums: The 1st Cavalry and the 4th Infantry Division Museums.

The 1st Cavalry Museum. Building 2218, Headquarters Avenue (west of Hood Road from main gate). Fort Hood is also home to the 1st Cavalry Division Horse Detachment. Wearing authentic nineteenth-century uniforms, this group performs at exhibitions throughout Texas. This museum traces the history of that division from its days on the western frontier through its berm-busting attacks during Desert Storm. An outdoor area displays more than three dozen pieces of military equipment, including aircraft and tanks. Open Monday–Friday 9:00 A.M.–4:00 P.M., Saturday 10:00 A.M.–4:00 P.M., and Sunday noon–4:00 P.M. Free. (254) 287-3626.

The 4th Infantry Division Museum. Building 418, Battalion Avenue at 27th. Activated in response to the United States' Declaration of War against Germany in 1917, the 4th Infantry Division participated in four major campaigns during World War I. This museum allows the visitor to explore the history of the 4th Infantry Division through a series of self-guided exhibits which use artifacts, texts, and photographs showing the soldiers in service through three wars. Open Monday–Friday 9:00 A.M.–4:00 P.M., Saturday 10:00 A.M.–4:00 P.M., and Sunday noon–4:00 P.M. Free. (254) 287-8811.

Belton Lake Outdoor Recreation Area. Sparta Road northeast of Fort Hood. This 890-acre park offers woodland hiking and lakeside recreation. Fishing, boating, paddleboating, and swimming are available at the lake. Landlubbers can enjoy a nature path and equestrian trails. Open daily. Fee. (254) 287-4907.

THE GROVE

Once a colony founded by Wendish settlers in the mid-1800s, today The Grove is a community frozen in time. This agricultural center was once home to many businesses and almost 400 residents but eventually the community became a ghost town. Today The Grove Country Life Museum is privately owned and open on weekends for visitors to tour.

To reach The Grove, turn west from Temple on TX 36. The community is open to travelers on Saturday and Sunday for a small admission fee. You're welcome to have a look at the W. J. Dube General Store. With its coffee grinders and tin boxes still in place, it looks like the storekeeper has just temporarily walked out for a few minutes. Nearby, the Planters State Bank, which was in business from 1917 through 1932, also looks like it's open for business. A United States post office, doctor's office, and blacksmith's shop also interest visitors.

For more information, call (512) 282-1215.

TEMPLE

From Killeen and Fort Hood, return to I-35 and continue north to Temple. With over 45,000 residents, this city is the medical center for central Texas and an important industrial producer. Temple was established by the Gulf, Colorado and Santa Fe Railroad and named for its chief construction engineer, B. B. M. Temple.

WHERE TO GO

Czech Heritage Museum. 520 North Main Street. The Czech people played an important role in settling central Texas, and their contribution is remembered in this museum housed in the SPJST (Slovanska Podporujici Jednota Statu Texas, or Slavonic Benevolent Order State of Texas) Insurance Company. The museum contains Czech costumes, a circa A.D. 1530 bible, quilts, a handmade dulcimer, and household items. Open weekdays during working hours. Free. (254) 773-1575.

Railroad and Pioneer Museum. South 31st Street at Avenue H. The old railroad depot once located in nearby Moody was transported here, boards, floor, and all. It's now a museum and library. Open afternoons, Tuesday through Saturday. Fee. (254) 298-5172.

ESPECIALLY FOR WINTER TEXANS

Outdoor America. East side of I-35 in Temple. If you're headed south, take exit 297, cross under I-35, and head north on the frontage road. If you're traveling north on I-35, take exit 298. This shopping mall is dedicated to RVs, travel trailers, and fifth wheels. Although this is an authorized Winnebago center, it services all brands six days a week. With a scheduled appointment, you'll receive a free night of camping at the mall.

The retail stores carry parts and supplies for your vehicle as well as camping equipment, fitness items, and outdoor accessories.

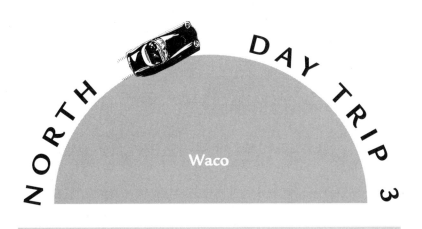
WACO

Located 106 miles north of Austin on I-35, this city of over 100,000 is named for the Hueco Indians who resided here before the days of recorded history. The Hueco were attracted to this rich, fertile land at the confluence of the Brazos and Bosque Rivers.

Although Spanish explorers named this site "Waco Village" in 1542, over 300 years elapsed before permanent settlement began. At that time, Waco was part of the Wild West, with cattle drives, cowboys, and so many gunslingers that stagecoach drivers called the town "Six-Shooter Junction." (Drivers commonly asked passengers to strap on their guns before the stagecoach reached the rowdy community!)

In the 1870s Waco became a center of trade with the completion of a 474-foot suspension bridge across the Brazos, the longest inland river in Texas. The bridge still stands today, designed by the same engineers that constructed New York's Brooklyn Bridge years later.

Today Waco's Wild West heritage is tempered by a strong religious influence. The city is home to Baylor University, a Baptist liberal arts college of 12,000 students. The university has several excellent museums open free to the public.

Some of the most scenic areas in Waco fall along the Brazos River. This waterway slices the city in half and provides miles of shoreline parks, shady walks, and downtown camping areas. The city recently completed a winding river walk to connect the suspension bridge at University Parks Drive with Fort Fisher on I-35.

North Day Trip 3

Waco

0   10   20 miles

Killeen

Belton

Temple

190

Salado

Lake Buchanan

Buchanan Dam

Burnet

Bertram

nd

281

1431

Leander

Cedar Park

Marble Falls

1431

Lake Travis

183

Lakeway

2222

Johnson City

620   71

290

Georgetown

Taylor

Thrall

Thorndale

Rockdal

190

Round Rock

Austin

Elgin

Manor

290

WHERE TO GO

Fort Fisher Park. I–35, exit 335B. This park was once the site of Fort Fisher, an outpost of the Texas Rangers built in 1837. The lawmen established a post here to protect the Brazos River crossing. Today the park contains the City of Waco Tourist Information Center, the Texas Rangers Hall of Fame, and a thirty-five-acre campground with screened shelters on the riverbanks. Free. Call (800) WACO–FUN for information.

   City of Waco Tourist Information Center. Fort Fisher. The visitors center provides helpful maps and brochures, and docents give advice on Waco attractions, accommodations, and restaurants. Open daily. Free. (800) WACO–FUN.

   Texas Ranger Hall of Fame and Museum. Fort Fisher. If you're interested in the taming of Texas, budget a couple of hours for this large museum. Visitors here can see guns of every description used by the Rangers, who had the reputation of lone lawmen who always got their man. Dioramas in the Hall of Fame recount the early days of the

Rangers, including their founding by Stephen F. Austin. A twenty-minute slide show runs on the hour. Open daily. Fee. (254) 750–8631.

Dr. Pepper Museum. 300 South Fifth Street. The famous Dr. Pepper soft drink was invented by pharmacist Dr. Charles Alderton at the Old Corner Drug Store in Waco, which once stood at Fourth Street and Austin Avenue. Today the drugstore is gone, but the original bottling plant remains open as a museum. Interesting exhibits and films offer a look at some early promotional materials as well as the manufacturing process of the unusual soft drink. (Also of note: the popular advertising slogan promoting Dr. Pepper as an energy booster to be consumed at "10-2-and-4.") After a look through the museum, visit the recreation of the Old Corner Drug Store fountain for an ice cream soda or (what else?) a Dr. Pepper. Open daily (afternoons only on Sunday). Fee. (254) 757–1024.

Armstrong-Browning Library. Eighth and Speight Streets, Baylor University campus. The works of Elizabeth Barrett Browning and husband Robert Browning fill this two-story library. The building also boasts the world's largest collection of secular stained-glass windows, which illustrate the works of both writers (including Robert Browning's *The Pied Piper of Hamlin*). Take a guided tour to see the up-

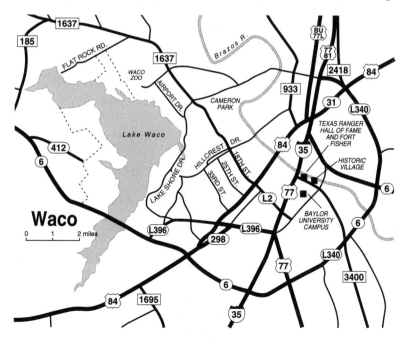

stairs rooms furnished with the couple's belongings. Open daily except Sunday and some university holidays. Free. (254) 755-3566.

Strecker Museum. Sid Richardson Building, Baylor University campus. The oldest continually operating museum in Texas, this natural history collection includes displays on the rocks, fossils, and wildlife of Texas. Closed Monday. Free. (254) 755-1110.

Governor Bill and Vara Daniel Historic Village. Behind Fort Fisher at University Parks Drive. For a taste of Waco's days as "Six-Shooter Junction," visit this recreation of a nineteenth-century cotton town. It holds a schoolhouse, a mercantile store, and, of course, a Wild West saloon. The buildings, once the property of Governor Daniel, were moved to this site from a plantation community in Liberty County, Texas, and restored by Baylor University. Open Tuesday through Friday 10:00 A.M. to 4:00 P.M.; weekends 1:00 P.M. to 5:00 P.M. Fee. (254) 755-1160.

Texas Sports Hall of Fame. University Parks Drive and I-35. Waco's newest attraction is a tribute to the athletes of the Lone Star State. Sports memorabilia highlight more than 350 sports heroes, including an autographed baseball by Texas Ranger Nolan Ryan, Earl Campbell's letter jacket, and one of Martina Navratilova's Wimbledon rackets, as well as displays featuring prominent Texas high school athletes. Open daily. Fee. (254) 756-1633.

Cameron Park. Brazos River at Herring Avenue. This 368-acre municipal park is one of the largest in the state and holds Miss Nellie's Pretty Place, a beautiful wildflower garden filled with Texas bluebonnets. Free. (800) WACO-FUN.

Cameron Park Zoo. North Fourth Street west of I-35. This zoo features natural habitats and displays including the African savanna, Gibbon Island, Sumatran tigers, and Treetop Village. Open daily. Fee. (254) 750-8400.

Suspension Bridge and Riverwalk. University Parks Drive, between Franklin and Washington Streets. Spanning the 800-mile-long Brazos River, this restored suspension bridge was once the longest in the world. Built in 1870, it eliminated the time-consuming process of having to cart cattle across the water by ferry. Today the structure is used as a pedestrian bridge bearing the motto "First across, still across." Open daily. Free. (800) WACO-FUN.

The Art Center. 1300 College Drive. This exhibit hall and teaching center is located in the Mediterranean-style home of the late lumber magnate William Waldo Cameron. Exhibits here focus on Texas artists in all media. Open daily except Monday. Free. (254) 752-4371.

Historic Home Tours. Historic Waco Foundation, 810 Fourth Street. Although a devastating tornado in 1953 destroyed many of Waco's historic structures, fortunately some still remain. Visitors see four historic homes as well as the McLennan County Courthouse on this tour, all in the downtown area. One of the most interesting stops is "East Terrace," an Italianate villa on the east bank of the Brazos. Here guests once slept in unheated dormitories to discourage them from overstaying their welcome! Call for hours. Fee. (254) 753-5166.

Taylor Museum of Waco History. 701 Jefferson. Learn more about the history of this city through displays that range from the city's earliest days through Mount Carmel, the Branch Dividian compound that put Waco on the news for many months. Open daily. Fee. (254) 752-4774.

WHERE TO EAT

Elite Cafe. On the circle at 2132 South Valley Mills Drive. For years this popular restaurant advertised itself as "the place where the elite meet to eat." Today it's known for its 1950s' decor and homemade hamburger buns. Open for breakfast, lunch, and dinner. $$; ☐. (254) 754-4941.

WHERE TO STAY

Clarion. 801 South Fourth Street, off I-35. The atrium in this two-story hotel encloses a swimming pool, a hot tub, and a restaurant. $-$$; ☐. (800) 275-9226 or (254) 757-2000.

ESPECIALLY FOR WINTER TEXANS

Fort Fisher Park. I-35, exit 335B. Behind the City of Waco Tourist Information Center and the Texas Rangers Hall of Fame, you'll find a very nice thirty-five-acre campground on the banks of the Brazos. This park makes a nice stopover for Winter Texans on the way south. Campground office open daily. Call (800) WACO-FUN for information.

NORTHEAST DAY TRIP 1

Taylor · Thrall
Thorndale · Rockdale
Calvert

TAYLOR

To reach Taylor, follow I-35 north into Round Rock (see NORTH FROM AUSTIN, DAY TRIP 1), then take the US 79 East exit and drive past the farming communities of Hutto and Frame Switch to Taylor. The route draws you through acres of cotton fields and blackland farms that stretch on for miles.

Taylor's claim to fame is its International Barbecue Cook-off in August and its controversial National Rattlesnake Sacking Championship and Roundup held every March. (See "Festivals and Celebrations" at the back of this book.)

Taylor was the hometown of former Texas governor Dan Moody as well as Bill Pickett, a black cowboy born in the area in 1860. Pickett originated the practice of "bulldogging"—throwing a bull by twisting his head until he falls. The well-known cowboy also had a habit of biting the steer's upper lip, a trick called "biting the bull" that he practiced on the rodeo circuit.

WHERE TO GO

Moody Museum. 114 West Ninth Street. Governor Dan Moody was born in this 1887 home, which today is filled with his furniture and personal belongings. He went to law school at the University of Texas, served in World War I, then returned to become governor at the age of thirty-three. The hometown hero was best known for prosecuting members of the Ku Klux Klan in Williamson County. Open Sunday afternoon. Free. (512) 352–8654 or 352–5134.

Northeast Day Trip 1

0   10   20 miles

Killeen
Belton
Temple
190
Calvert
Salado
6
Buchanan
Buchanan Dam
81
Burnet
79
Bertram
190
35
281
Georgetown
Rockdale
Leander
Taylor
Thorndale
Cedar Park
Thrall
le Falls
1431
Round Rock
LakeTravis
183
Austin
Lakeway
2222
Elgin
inson City
620 71
Manor

Taylor Bedding Company. 400 Second Street. This local success story began in 1903, when a local entrepreneur decided that he would rather sleep on home-grown cotton than corn-shuck mattresses. Taylor Bedding Company is now the home of Morning Glory Mattress. Call ahead to book a thirty- to forty-five-minute tour of the plant and watch mattresses and box springs being produced. Tours Monday through Friday during working hours. Free. (800) 725-2333.

WHERE TO EAT

Rudy Mikeska's Bar-B-Q. 300 West Second Street. This popular restaurant tempts diners with sausage, lamb ribs, pork ribs, ham, and baby back ribs. The Mikeskas are the most famous family in a state renowned for barbecue pitmasters. This restaurant has catered numerous governors' inaugurations and even served Prince Philip at a state event. Open for lunch and dinner, Monday through Saturday; lunch only on Sunday. $-$$; ☐. (American Express only.) (512) 352-5561.

Louis Mueller Barbecue. 206 West Second Street. One of the most authentic barbecue joints in Texas, this restaurant is cooled by ceiling fans and a breeze through the screen door. Diners eat off white butcher paper on simple tables, in a room decorated with free calendars and a corkboard filled with business cards (all imbued with enough smoke to give them the color of a grocery sack). But none of that matters. What matters is the barbecue: brisket, sausage, pork ribs, and steak. $-$$; no □. (512) 352-6206.

THRALL

When oil was discovered in 1915, Thrall's population skyrocketed as over 200 wells were drilled. As the saying goes, what goes up must come down, and Thrall was back on its way down as soon as oil production diminished. Today it's once again a quiet spot on US 79, composed of a few blocks of homes that run parallel to the railroad.

WHERE TO GO

Stiles Farm Foundation. US 79, east of Thrall. This 3,200-acre farm is administered by Texas A&M University. Here new techniques are demonstrated to area farmers and ranchers. Visitors can take guided tours to see everything from hog raising to cotton growing. This is a great chance to have a look at an operating Texas farm and ranch. Call for appointment. Free. (512) 898-2214.

THORNDALE

Tiny Thorndale lies northeast of Thrall on US 79. It's another farming community built alongside the railroad tracks. As you drive through town, you can't miss the enormous cottonseed processing mill on the right, another of the many industries that make up this agricultural part of central Texas.

ROCKDALE

Unlike most of the other towns on this day trip, Rockdale is not known so much for farming but for what lies beneath the soil. This region is rich in lignite, a soft brown coal used as a fuel to generate electricity. The resulting energy in turn fuels Alcoa, America's largest aluminum-producing facility.

WHERE TO GO

Alcoa (Aluminum Company of America). Between Thorndale and Rockdale on US 79, look for a roadside park sign that says TO ALCOA; turn and follow signs to the plant. Alcoa, the largest smelter in North America, is not open to the public because of open flames and molten metal. Visitors, however, can take a drive-by tour of the facility, which is lit up like Christmas at night. The twenty-four-hour operation has a 914-acre human-made lake and power plant on one side, and the smelter plant and mine on the other. (512) 446-8240.

CALVERT

To reach Calvert, continue northeast on US 79 to the intersection of US 190 in Hearne. Turn left and continue on US 190 (which becomes TX 6) to the town.

In 1868 Calvert was the end of the line for the Houston and Central Railway. With over 10,000 residents, it was the fourth largest city in the state. P. C. Gibson, a cotton trader, came to the area and built the world's largest cotton gin in the 1870s. A 1965 fire and a tornado a decade later all but demolished the once-grand business.

One of Calvert's most colorful figures was Myra Bell Shirley, better known as Belle Starr. Some say that Shirley was a Confederate spy; others say she befriended outlaws like Jesse James. Belle Starr's demise is the stuff of legend: She was shot in the back by her Indian lover, Sam Starr.

Calvert's boomtown status faded when the railroad was extended to Dallas. Things stayed quiet in Calvert for many years, but because of its many Victorian homes and refurbished downtown businesses, the town was declared a National Historic District in 1978. Today Calvert calls itself "The Antique Center of Texas," and several shops along Main Street offer buyers a nice selection of collectibles.

WHERE TO SHOP

Boll Weevil. 506 Main Street. This fine antique shop specializes in eighteenth- and nineteenth-century furniture and porcelain. Open Wednesday through Sunday. (409) 364-2835.

Milly's Antiques. 502 Main Street. This antique shop has a little of everything, including a wide selection of glassware. The owner has a special interest in marbles, and even the most cherished items in his collection are for sale. Open Thursday through Saturday. (817) 746-7890.

S & S Antiques. 517 Main Street. Primitives, Raggedy Ann dolls, lunch boxes, and antique linens are just a few of the offerings browsers find in this shop. Closed Tuesday and Wednesday. (409) 364-2634.

WHERE TO STAY

Our House Bed and Breakfast. 406 East Texas Street. This two-story, 5,000-square-foot home once was the residence of P. C. Gibson, the owner of the world's largest cotton gin. The home's five elegant guest rooms share two baths. Children are permitted, but smoking is not. Rates include a full breakfast. $$; no ☐. (409) 364-2909.

BRYAN-COLLEGE STATION

To reach the combined cities of Bryan-College Station, follow US 79 east of Round Rock to the town of Hearne on TX6. Turn south on TX 6 and continue for 18 miles to Bryan-College Station, one of the largest educational centers in the state. Home of Texas A&M University, these adjoining communities are home to over 123,000 residents and several attractions to interest travelers.

Bryan was chartered in 1855, located in the area where early colonists led by Stephen F. Austin first settled. Agriculturally rich, the city still has an emphasis on farming thanks to Texas A&M University, the first public institution of higher learning in Texas. The college is well known for its agricultural, veterinary, and engineering programs as well as its military Cadet Corps.

WHERE TO GO

Messina Hof Wine Cellars and Vineyards. 4545 Old Reliance Road. One of Texas's most celebrated wineries offers free tours and tastings by reservation. Started in 1983, the winery includes forty-five acres of vineyards and demonstrates the wine-making skills of the Messina, Italy, and Hof, Germany, regions. Call for hours and tour times. Free. (409) 778-9463.

Brazos Valley Museum of Natural History. 3232 Briarcrest Drive. Bring the whole family to this collection of natural history with ex-

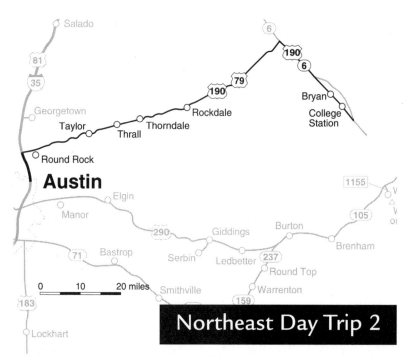

Northeast Day Trip 2

hibits on life in the Brazos Valley over 12,000 years ago. Open in summer months from Monday through Saturday; from September through May from Tuesday through Saturday. Fee. (409) 776-2195.

George Bush Presidential Library Center. West George Bush Drive, College Station. The nation's newest presidential library has opened with exhibits on the Bush presidency as well as research materials in the library center. (409) 862-2251.

Texas A&M University. Several sites at this large college are of special interest to visitors of this large college including the Floral Test Garden (Houston and Jersey Streets). Stroll among hundreds of varieties of flowers planted and studied by university students.

Sam Houston Sanders Corps of Cadets Center. Learn more about the Corps of Cadets through displays that trace the graduates service in both World Wars, Korea, Vietnam, Gulf War, and more recent conflicts. (409) 862-2862.

WHERE TO STAY

Vintor's Loft. 4545 Old Reliance Road. One of Texas's most unique bed-and-breakfast properties, the Vintor's Loft is located above the

Messina Hof Winery. Featuring a full-size bed, private bath, and television, couples can enjoy an evening alone in the vineyards at this romantic hideaway. Book early for this popular getaway on weekends and holidays. $$; □. (409) 778-9463.

Bed and Breakfast Texas Style, Inc. Call this reservation service for local bed-and-breakfast inns, guest cottages, and ranches. Prices vary with accommodation. (214) 298-5433 or 298-8586.

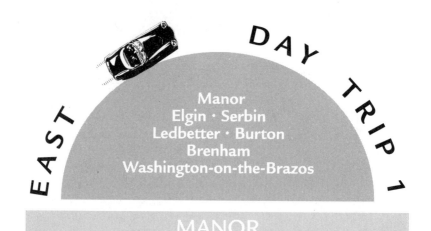

DAY TRIP 1

EAST

Manor
Elgin · Serbin
Ledbetter · Burton
Brenham
Washington-on-the-Brazos

MANOR

To reach Manor, drive east from Austin on US 290. This community was a quiet suburb until a few years ago, when Texas legalized pari-mutuel wagering. Today the town is home to Manor Downs, a quarterhorse track, with fall races from September through December and a spring season starting in February. Races are held on Friday, Saturday, and Sunday afternoons. Call for race times. Fee. (512) 272-4042.

ELGIN

Continue east from Manor on US 290 to Elgin. This small town enjoys star status because of Elgin sausage, a spicy concoction that's sold throughout this part of the state.

WHERE TO GO

Historic Tour. Pick up a copy of the free historic tour brochure at the Chamber of Commerce office at 15 North Main Street.

WHERE TO SHOP

Meyer's Elgin Sausage. 600 South Main Street. Stop here to buy a gift box or a freezer full of Elgin's most famous product: sausage. (800) 677-OINK.

Elgin Antique Mall. 100 US 290. This multidealer mall, spanning over 10,000 square feet, is filled with everything antique and collectible, from furniture to dolls to housewares. The merchandise changes continually, brought to the mall by over fifty dealers. Open daily. (512) 285-5655.

WHERE TO EAT

Southside Market and B-B-Q. 1212 US 290 West. This casual barbecue eatery has been the source of Elgin sausage since 1882. The back dining room is filled with Formica tables, the smell of smoke, and happy customers. Open for lunch, early dinner, and takeout. Closed Sunday. $; no ⌘. (512) 285-3407.

    City Cafe. 17 North Main Street. Stop by for the lunch buffet at this downtown diner that serves up traditional small-town cookin' at its best. $; ⌘. (512) 281-3663.

WHERE TO STAY

Ragtime Ranch Inn. Country Road 98. This bed-and-breakfast inn is a great getaway for those looking for a ranch atmosphere. Relax on

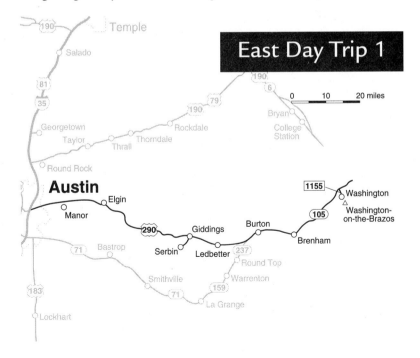

the wide porch, ride a horse, or float in the pool. Rooms include two queen beds and private baths and complimentary continental breakfast. $$; ☐. (800) 800-9743.

SERBIN

From Elgin, continue east on US 290 for 29 miles to Giddings. Turn south on US 77, then south again on FM 448, continuing on for 5 miles. At the intersection of FM 2239, turn right and continue 2 miles to the hamlet of Serbin.

This town was settled by the Wends, Germans of Slavic descent, who came to Texas in the 1850s and brought with them the Gothic architecture of their homeland. From 1865 to 1890 this was a thriving town, boasting dry goods, jewelry, drug, and music stores, three doctors, and two dentists. When Serbin was bypassed by the railroad, it quickly declined.

WHERE TO GO

St. Paul Lutheran Church. Off FM 2239. The historic St. Paul Lutheran Church, a smaller version of the elaborate German cathedrals of the eighteenth and nineteenth centuries, was built in 1859 of native sandstone. To replicate marble, the parishioners painted the plaster walls with turkey feather brushes. This church once had a very unusual seating arrangement: Men sat in the balcony across from the pulpit, women and children took the pews on the floor. Open daily. Free. (409) 366-2219.

Texas Wendish Heritage Museum. Off FM 2239, near St. Paul Lutheran Church. You'll find antique furniture and household items as well as photos of the early days in this local history museum. Open afternoons weekdays and Sunday; closed Saturday. Fee (students free). (409) 366-2441.

LEDBETTER

To continue on this day trip, retrace your steps back to Giddings and US 290. Drive east on US 290 for 9 miles to the tiny community of Ledbetter. Once the first town in the county to boast a railroad, its importance declined when nearby La Grange became a freight center.

WHERE TO GO

Stuermer Store. South side of US 290. This metal building has served as a general store since 1870. At one time, the current owner's grandfather ran a saloon next door. Now the businesses are joined, creating a general store, museum, and soda shop all in one. A working museum exhibits the tools of the early grocery, from cheese cutters to coffee grinders. Today the wildest drink in the old saloon is an old-fashioned malt. You can order up some local Blue Bell ice cream or fresh sandwiches at the fountain, and listen to a free tune on a jukebox packed with oldies. Open Monday through Saturday. Free. (409) 249-3330.

BURTON

Follow US 290 east past the tiny town of Carmine, which is full of antique shops (open Saturday only), to the tiny agricultural community of Burton, located just off US 290 on FM 390. With a population of slightly more than 300, this town has a surprising number of shops and businesses, many open only on weekends.

Take some time to walk around the historic buildings and drop in to the Burton Cafe. Here you can make arrangements for a guide to take you on a tour of the restored gin, railroad depot, and old caboose.

WHERE TO GO

Burton Cotton Gin. Main Street, across from the Burton Cafe. Stop in the Burton Cafe to arrange for a forty-five-minute tour of this restored gin, a National Historic Landmark. You'll see the engine room, the mechanical floor, the ginning floor, and an old cobbler shop where harnesses were made for the horses that pulled the cotton wagons. Tours also can be conducted in German. Open on a walk-in basis. Fee. (409) 289-5209 for groups of ten or more or 289-3849 for individuals.

BRENHAM

Return to US 290 and continue east to Brenham. In this state, Brenham means the Blue Bell Creamery. This is one of the biggest independent manufacturers of ice cream in the country, selling over 25 million half-gallon containers a year. It's as Texan as bluebonnets and two-stepping, and expatriates have been known to carry back picnic freezers full of Brenham's product.

Brenham has a host of other, less-fattening attractions as well, including a historic downtown that's filled with antique and specialty shops, and residential streets that showcase splendid antebellum and Victorian homes.

A free visitors' guide of historic sites is available from the Washington County Chamber of Commerce, 314 South Austin Street in Brenham, or by calling (888) BRENHAM or (409) 836-3695.

WHERE TO GO

Blue Bell Creamery. FM 566 off US 290 West. Blue Bell has been making ice cream since 1911, when they packaged their product in wooden tubs and delivered it by horse-drawn wagon. The "tasting room" here is a turn-of-the-century-style soda shop, where visitors can choose from among twenty-five flavors. After a free dish of your personal favorite, you can have a look around the Country Store, which sells everything from strawberry-ice-cream-scented pencils to piggy banks in the shape of the company's early delivery trucks. Open daily. Tours conducted Monday through Friday only; call for times. Fee. (800) 327-8135.

Monastery of St. Clare Miniature Horse Ranch. TX 105, 9 miles northeast of Brenham. This monastery is occupied by a group of Catholic nuns who raise miniature horses to support themselves. The tiny horses, some less than 34 inches tall, sell for anywhere from $3,000 to $30,000. On self-guided tours visitors see the barn and grooming facilities (with miniature carriages and harnesses) and the Mini Mansion where the horses are reared. The Art Barn brims with thousands of ceramics made by the nuns, including tiny reproductions of the horses. Open daily 2:00 to 4:00 P.M. Free. (409) 836-9652.

Ellison's Greenhouses. Horton and Stone Streets, south of Blue Bell Creamery on Loop 577. Ellison's produces African vio-

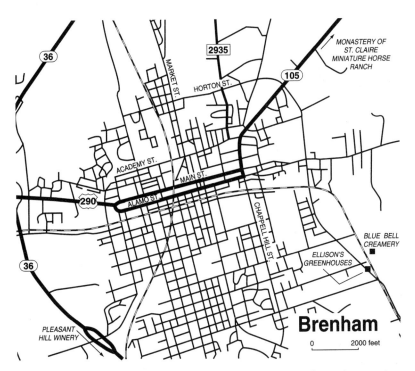

lets, Easter lilies, mums, tulips, and many other decorative flowers. Every year they grow 250,000 poinsettia cuttings and 80,000 finished poinsettias, some of which find their way to the State Capitol and Governor's Mansion. Open Monday through Saturday; guided tours daily (call for information). Free. (409) 836-0084.

Pleasant Hill Winery. 1441 Salem Road, just south of US 290 and TX 36 intersection. Travel just a few hundred yards west and a hillside vineyard will appear. Free tours and tastings are offered inside the carefully reconstructed old barn at the top of the hill. Enjoy the spectacular view of the vineyard below. Spend some time studying the corkscrew collection and winery artifacts, or just enjoy the warmth and beauty of the barn's interior. The tour will take you through the path of the grape as it makes its wondrous transformation from vine to fruit to wine. Gift shop with Texas wines and souvenirs for sale. Open Saturdays from 11:00 A.M. to 6:00 P.M. and Sundays from noon to 5:00 P.M. Groups may request other tour times by appointment. Free (409) 830-VINE.

WHERE TO STAY

The Brenham area is home to over thirty bed-and-breakfasts, many located in historic homes or on local farms. The city also provides lodging in several motels. For more information on accommodations, call (888) BRENHAM or write Brenham-Washington County Convention and Visitor Bureau, 314 South Austin Street, Brenham, TX 77833.

James Walker Homestead. Old Chappell Hill Road, a few miles east of Brenham. This structure was built in 1826 as the home of James Walker, one of the first 300 colonists who came to Texas with Stephen F. Austin. Today the original log construction is still visible inside the home, which is furnished with Texas antiques. The bed-and-breakfast does not accommodate children, and no smoking is permitted in the house. Lodging includes one bedroom with sleeper bed for extra guests. $$$; no ☐. (409) 836–6717.

WASHINGTON-ON-THE-BRAZOS

To reach this community, alternately called Washington and Washington-on-the-Brazos, take TX 105 northeast of Brenham for 14 miles, then turn right on FM 912.

The town dates back to the days of a ferry landing on the Brazos River that operated at the site from 1822. Washington has become best known, however, as the birthplace of Texas. On a cold March day in 1836, founders gathered here and signed the Declaration of Independence, establishing Texas as a sovereign nation.

From 1842 to 1845, Washington served as the capital of the republic, also gradually becoming a commerce center on the busy Brazos. Thus, when the seat of government was moved to Austin, the town hung on, kept alive by its position on the river. Eventually, though, in the 1850s, Washington was bypassed by the railroads, and the community dwindled to a tiny dot on the map.

WHERE TO GO

Washington-on-the-Brazos State Historical Park. Located on the banks of the Brazos, this quiet park is shaded by acres of walnut and pecan trees. This is a day-use park only, with picnic tables along the

Southeast Day Trip 1

trop." The Chamber of Commerce also rents bicycles so you can pedal through these historic neighborhoods. If you'd rather see the town from the seat of a boat, give the chamber a call for details on guided canoe trips. (512) 321-2419.

Lock's Drug. 1003 Main Street. This turn-of-the-century drugstore features an antique mirrored fountain where you can belly up for a thick, creamy malt. Built-in cabinets are still labeled with the names of their original contents, and old apothecary tools sit in the front windows. Open daily except Sunday. (512) 321-2551.

Bastrop County Historical Society Museum. 702 Main Street. This 1850 frame cabin contains Indian relics and pioneer exhibits. Open afternoons daily. Fee. (512) 321-6177.

Bastrop State Park. TX 21, 1.5 miles east of Bastrop. Beautiful piney woods are the main draw at this 3,500-acre park, the fourth busiest state park in Texas. Facilities include a nine-hole golf course, campsites, and a ten-acre fishing lake. The 1930s-built stone and cedar cabins are very popular and should be booked well in advance. They feature fireplaces, bathrooms, and kitchen facilities. Guided bus tours every other Saturday during summer months introduce visitors to the park's unique ecology and to an endangered resident:

the Houston toad. Fee. (512) 321-2101 for park information or
(512) 389-8900 for reservations.

Bastrop Opera House. 711 Spring Street. Built in 1889, this
building was once the entertainment center of town. After a major
renovation in 1978, it's again the cultural center of Bastrop, the site
for live theater ranging from mysteries to vaudeville. Call for show
schedule. (512) 321-6283.

Classic Carriages of Bastrop. Downtown. Take a tour past many
of Bastrop's 131 historic buildings on this half-hour evening tour.
Fee. (512) 321-6351.

Central Texas Museum of Automotive History. South on FM
304 to FM 535; left 1 mile to Rosanky. This private museum is dedicated to the collection and preservation of old cars and accessories.
The vehicles on display include a 1935 Rolls Royce Phantom, a La
France fire engine, and a 1922 Franklin. Open Friday through
Sunday October–March; Wednesday through Sunday April–September. Fee. (512) 237-2635.

WHERE TO SHOP

Park your car and enjoy an afternoon of browsing through the many
antique and specialty stores along Main Street.

Pine Cottage. 913 Main Street. This store features the works of
many area artists, including some beautiful clay hummingbird
feeders. Open Tuesday through Saturday. (512) 321-4121.

1010 Gallery. 1010 Main Street. Stop by this gallery for a look at
artwork by talented Texas and Southwestern painters. (512)
303-1010.

Old Town Emporium. 815 Main Street. You'll find all kinds of
crafts and specialty gifts in this large store. (512) 321-3635.

WHERE TO EAT

Bastrop BBQ and Meat Market. 919 Main Street. This old-fashioned Texas barbecue joint has a meat market up front and a
dining room in the back. Sausage, beef brisket, and chicken are the
order of the day, served with sides of beans and potato salad. Open
daily except Sunday for lunch and dinner. $; no ☐. (512) 321-7719.

WHERE TO STAY

The Colony Bed and Breakfast. 703 Main Street. This bed-and-breakfast treats guests to champagne and a full breakfast served in antique-filled rooms. The two-story home features four guest rooms and welcomes children. $; no ☐. (512) 303-1234.

Historic Pfeiffer House, 1802 Main Street. Built in 1901, this Texas Medallion home is listed in the National Register of Historic Places. The Victorian structure has three upstairs bedrooms decorated with antique furnishings. A full breakfast served in the dining room is included. Deposit required. $$; no ☐. (512) 321-2100.

ALUM CREEK

Continue east from Bastrop on TX 71 and soon you'll reach the crossing of Alum Creek. In 1828, this was the site of a fort used by several families during the area's most active Indian days. Years later this spot was used as a stagecoach stop. Today all that's left of the community of Alum Creek is a collection of over a dozen antique and junk shops. It's a fun stop for avid collectors. The shops are located on the left side of the road as you head east; many are open weekends only.

SMITHVILLE

Continue east from Bastrop on TX 71 to Smithville, a small town that's built alongside the railroad tracks at the edge of the piney woods and home of Buescher State Park. Smithville was once a riverboat ferry stop on the Colorado River. In the 1880s, the railroad replaced the ferries as the main mode of transportation, and tracks were laid across town. Today the railroad still plays an important part in Smithville's economy.

WHERE TO GO

Smithville Railroad Historical Park. 100 West First Street. Built beside the tracks, this park has two cabooses and a depot relocated here from West Point, a community east of town. The Chamber of Commerce office is housed in the depot as well. Open weekdays. Free. (512) 237-2313.

Buescher State Park. 3 miles north of town, via TX 71 and FM 2104, or access from Park Road 1. Buescher (pronounced "BISH-er") neighbors Bastrop State Park, but the two boast different environments. Oaks dominate this park, along with a few pines. The park is especially popular for its thirty-acre lake. Visitors can enjoy ample campsites and screened shelters, as well as a playground and picnic area. Fee. (512) 237-2241.

Smithville Heritage Society Museum. 602 Main Street. This 1908 home contains the Smithville archives and a museum of local memorabilia. Open Tuesday (call for other times). Free. (512) 237-4545.

Rocky Hill Ranch Mountain Bike Resort. FM 153, 2 miles northeast of Buescher State Park. Beginner, intermediate, advanced, and expert trails tempt mountain bikers with over 1,200 acres that include gentle slopes and challenging grades as well as stream crossings. Over 30 miles of trails are available for use by helmeted riders. The ranch includes a casual restaurant with horseshoes, shuffleboard, and beach volleyball; campsites are available along small creeks and spring-fed waterholes. Fee. (512) 237-3112.

LA GRANGE

Just 4 miles southeast of Smithville on the left side of TX 71 is a scenic overlook, an excellent place to pull over for a picnic. While you're here you can gaze at the miles of rolling hills and farmland that attracted many German and Czech immigrants a century ago.

Continue on TX 71 to the infamous community of La Grange. For generations this was a quiet town in the center of a farming region. In the 1970s, however, La Grange caught the attention of the public with the unveiling of the Chicken Ranch, a brothel that became the subject of the Broadway musical and movie, *The Best Little Whorehouse in Texas*. Today the Chicken Ranch is gone, but La Grange still has other sights to see.

WHERE TO GO

Monument Hill/Kreische Brewery State Historic Site. US 77, 1 mile south of La Grange. Located on a bluff high above town, this site is the home to two combined parks.

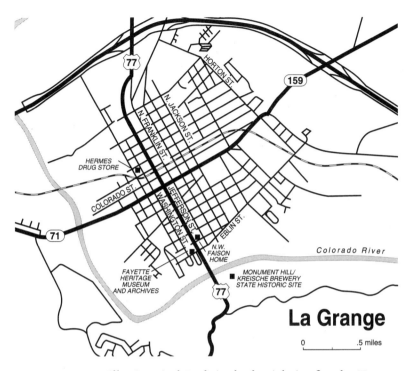

La Grange

0   .5 miles

Monument Hill Historical Park is the burial site for the Texans who died in the Dawson Massacre and the Mier Expedition, two historic Mexican conflicts that occurred in 1842, six years after the Texas Revolution. The Dawson Massacre took place near San Antonio when La Grange citizen Nicholas Dawson gathered Texans to halt the continual Mexican attacks. Dawson's men were met by hundreds of Mexican troops and thirty-five Texans were killed.

The Mexican village of Mier was attacked in a retaliatory move, resulting in the capture of Texas soldiers and citizens by Mexican General Santa Anna, who ordered every tenth man to be killed. The Texans were blindfolded and forced to draw beans: 159 of them white and 17 black. Men who drew white beans were imprisoned; those who drew black ones were executed.

The Kreische Brewery State Historical Site recalls a far more cheerful time in Texas history. Heinreich Kreische was a German who immigrated here from Europe. In 1849 he purchased the hilltop and the adjoining land, including the burial ground of those Texas heroes, for his brewery site. Eventually he became the third largest beer producer in the state, opening one of the first breweries in

Texas. Open daily until 5:00 P.M.; guided tours of the brewery ruins run on weekend afternoons. Fee (one admission covers both adjacent sites). (409) 968-5658.

Hermes Drug Store. 148 North Washington Street. Established in 1856, this is the oldest drugstore in continuous operation in Texas. Visitors can see authentic old-time structures, beveled mirrors, and more. Open Monday through Saturday. (409) 968-5835.

N. W. Faison Home. 822 South Jefferson Street. N. W. Faison was a survivor of both the Dawson Massacre and the Mier Expedition in 1842. The Faison family resided in this home for over twenty years, and today it contains the family's furniture as well as exhibits from the Mexican War. Open by appointment. Fee. (409) 968-5756.

Fayette Heritage Museum and Archives. 855 South Jefferson Street. Housed with the public library, this museum contains displays on the area's rich history. Open daily except Monday. Free. (409) 968-6418.

WHERE TO EAT

Bon Ton Restaurant. TX 71, west of town. This combination restaurant and bakery is always busy with locals and travelers who've heard of the Bon Ton's reputation for good home cooking. This is the best of Texas foods—chicken-fried steak, fried chicken, mashed potatoes, fried okra, and fresh rolls. There are daily specials, plus a popular buffet. Don't miss the homemade *kolaches* and bread. Open daily for breakfast, lunch, and dinner. $; □. (409) 968-5863.

Warrenton · Round Top

This day trip continues the journey through Bastrop and La Grange. Follow TX 71 through these communities, then join up with this day trip for a look at historic and cultural attractions plus some excellent shopping.

WARRENTON

From La Grange, head northwest on TX 159 to TX 237. Continue on TX 237 through Oldenburg to this tiny community. Warrenton is best known as the home of the smallest Catholic church in the world. St. Martin's, on the left side of the road as you head north, is a simple white frame building. Inside the Lilliputian house of worship, plain wooden benches serve as pews before an ornate altar. Step inside for a look; visitors are welcome.

ROUND TOP

St. Martin's is a preview of another pint-sized attraction along this day trip: the smallest incorporated town in Texas. Continue north on TX 237 to Round Top. Officially founded in 1835 by settlers from Stephen F. Austin's second colony, this town is filled with restored homes, log cabins, and country stores.

Round Top is also home to a world-class music facility. Festival Hill, located just outside of town, offers visiting symphony orchestras performances under the summer stars.

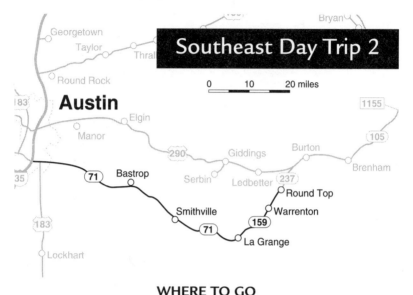

WHERE TO GO

Henkel Square. TX 237, on the town square. This is one of the finest restorations of pioneer buildings in the state. This collection of forty historic homes and businesses, dating from 1824 to 1915, was assembled from around Fayette County. The apothecary shop now serves as a visitors center, where tours of the schoolhouse-church, log house, and the Henkel house originate. Open Thursday through Sunday noon to 5:00 P.M. Fee. (713) 249-3308.

Festival Hill. TX 237, 5 blocks north of Henkel Square. This music and theater center was founded by noted pianist James Dick. During the school year, Festival Hill presents monthly concerts. In the summer, the center hosts students from around the world who entertain guests with musical performances. The center is housed in historic buildings, including an 1870 farmhouse and a former black school.

Even if you don't have the opportunity to attend a concert, call to schedule a tour of the center. Your look at Festival Hill can include the David Guion Museum Room, housing a collection of belongings and music of this Texas composer, and the Oxehufwud Room, a collection of Swedish decorative arts that recall the life of a Swedish noble family whose final member retired in La Grange. Bring a picnic lunch and enjoy the one hundred-acre grounds, planted with thousands of trees and including walking trails and a recently completed stonework bridge, constructed to resemble a Roman footbridge. Fee. (409) 249-3129.

Winedale Historical Center. 4 miles east of Round Top via FM 1457; north on FM 2714. Operated by the University of Texas at Austin, this center hosts annual Shakespeare productions. A cast of students from assorted disciplines have come to Winedale every summer for the past two decades to perform the works of the Bard in an old hay barn. For fifteen to eighteen hours a day, the students make costumes, prepare lighting, and practice for the performances that draw visitors from Austin and Houston. Public performances are held Thursday through Sunday evenings in late July and early August.

Although Shakespeare at Winedale is a summer-only activity, the center is a year-around attraction. The 215-acre complex is home to a collection of historic structures, a research center, a nature trail, and a picnic area. Weekend tours take visitors through homes furnished with period antiques and boasting features such as stenciled ceilings that recall the German culture of the area. Fee. (409) 278-3530.

WHERE TO SHOP

Round Top General Store. TX 237. Since 1848 this general store has been serving the community in many ways. Besides its role as general store and hardware store, it has operated as a barber shop, funeral home, and hotel. Today it offers an impressive array of gift items and antiques, and a confectionery up front serves homemade fudge (try the jalapeño!) prepared in the store. (409) 249-3600.

Herb Haus. TX 237, on the grounds of the Round Top Inn. This herb shop operates in an 1860s stone house. It's filled with the heady scents of dried flowers and herbs, sold with home accessories. (409) 249-5294.

Round Top Relics. White and Wandke Streets. Eight rooms of this former home now house a variety of antiques, everything from wardrobes to washstands and dressers to dishes. Owners Jim and Caroline Kline restore furniture and also create original pieces. (409) 249-5504.

WHERE TO EAT

Royers' Round Top Cafe. On the square. You wouldn't expect to find shrimp scampi, fresh fettuccine, or pasta with fresh marinara sauce at a small-town diner, but here it is. This lively joint serves up some of the best cooking in Central Texas, in a fun atmosphere that's popular with locals and visitors. It's all topped off with home-made pies that include butterscotch tollhouse, buttermilk, and that Texas favorite, pecan. Royers' operates a mail order and wholesale sauce business, featuring pepper sauce, citrus vinegar, mint vinegar, and marinades. Open Thursday through Sunday. $-$$; no ☐. (409) 249-3611 or (800) 624-PIES for mail order.

Klump's Restaurant. TX 237. Klump's started out as a grocery store serving barbecue on the weekends. Folks started asking for that 'que, though, and the Klump family decided to start a restaurant. Today barbecue is the special every Saturday, with Tex-Mex night on Wednesday, catfish on Friday, and fried chicken on Sunday. $; no ☐. (409) 249-5696.

WHERE TO STAY

Round Top Inn. TX 237. Stay in historic structures that have been painstakingly restored to the days of Round Top's earliest pioneers. The inn spans a city block, formerly the property of Johann Traugott Wandke, an herbalist and organ maker known to have handcrafted seven pipe organs from local cedar during his residence here. His home is part of the inn, with a living room and modern-day bath-room downstairs and a picturesque bedroom tucked under the eaves upstairs. Rockers invite guests to sit out on the porch and enjoy small-town life. Other structures at the inn date back from 1840 to 1879, and all are filled with period antiques and accessories that re-call the area's early days. $$; ☐. (409) 249-5294.

Heart of My Heart Ranch. County Road 217, 2 miles from Round Top. This Victorian home is tucked into the countryside sur-rounding Round Top and offers a quiet weekend getaway for city dwellers. Sit in the porch rockers for a spell, or go fishing at the pond just in front of the home. Bicycles, a small, flat-bottom fishing boat, paddleboats, and inner tubes are provided for guests looking for recreation. Accommodations are furnished with antique furniture, and guests share the downstairs living room with hosts Frances and Bill Harris. $$; ☐. (800) 327-1242.

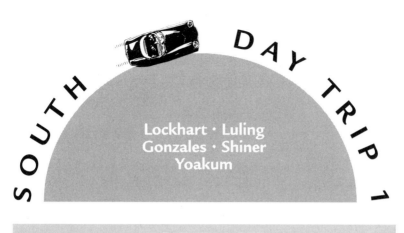

LOCKHART

Lockhart is a conglomeration of the stuff of Texas legends: Indian battles, cattle drives, cotton, and oil. This small town, located 23 miles south of Austin on US 183, contains a state park and lots of history.

The biggest event in Lockhart's past was the Battle of Plum Creek in 1840. Over 600 Comanches raided the community of Linnville and were on their way home when they passed through this area. A group of settlers joined forces with the Tonkowa Indians to attack the Comanches, driving the Indians further west and ending the Indian attacks in the region. This battle is reenacted every May at the Chisholm Trail Roundup.

Lockhart is also well known as the home of Mebane cotton. Developed by A. D. Mebane, this strain is resistant to the boll weevil, an insect that can demolish not only whole fields but entire economies as well.

WHERE TO GO

Lockhart State Park. FM 20, west of town. This 263-acre park has a nine-hole golf course, fishing on Plum Creek, picnic areas, a swimming pool, and campsites for both tents and trailers. Many of the facilities were built by the Civilian Conservation Corps in the 1930s. Open daily. Fee. (512) 398-3479.

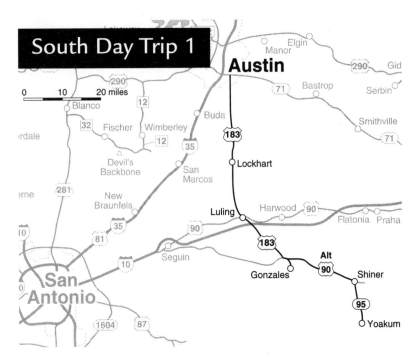

South Day Trip 1

0   10   20 miles

290 · Blanco · 12 · 32 · Fischer · Wimberley · 12 · Buda · Devil's Backbone · San Marcos · New Braunfels · 281 · 35 · 81 · 10 · Seguin · 35 · 90 · rdale · rne · San Antonio · 10 · 1604 · 87

Elgin · Manor · **Austin** · 290 · Gid · 71 · Bastrop · Serbin · 290 · Smithville · 71 · 183 · Lockhart · Luling · Harwood · 90 · Flatonia · Praha · 183 · Alt · 90 · Gonzales · Shiner · 95 · Yoakum

Dr. Eugene Clark Library. 217 South Main Street. Built in 1889, this is the oldest continually operating library in Texas. Modeled after the Villa Rotunda in Vicenza, Italy, it has stained-glass windows, ornate fixtures, and a stage where President William Taft once spoke. Open Monday through Saturday. Free. (512) 398–3223.

WHERE TO EAT

Kreuz Market. 208 South Commerce Street. Vegetarians, head elsewhere. This barbecue restaurant is a meat-only kind of place, offering spicy sausage, pork loin, prime rib, and pork ribs, all served in an atmosphere that's little changed since the present owner took over in 1948. The meat market's up front for take-out orders; the dining area sits in the back. The two are connected by a smoke-filled hallway and dinner counter. Open daily, early morning to evening. $-$$; no ⅃. (512) 398–2361.

Black's Barbecue. 215 North Main Street. This cafeteria-style restaurant is reputedly the oldest barbecue joint in Texas under the same continual ownership. Beef brisket is the specialty of the house, along with sausage, ribs, chicken, and ham. There's also a fully stocked salad bar. Open daily for lunch and dinner. $-$$; no ☐. (512) 398-2712.

LULING

Continue south on US 183 for 17 miles to Luling, an oil center that's still alive with pumping wells. Many of the pumpjacks are decorated as cartoon characters. (For more about Luling, read EAST FROM SAN ANTONIO, DAY TRIP 1.)

GONZALES

Continue south on US 183 for 13 miles to Gonzales, one of Texas's most historic cities. This is the "Come and Take It" town where the Texas Revolution began in 1835. (Read about this skirmish and the many attractions in Gonzales in EAST FROM SAN ANTONIO, DAY TRIP 2.)

SHINER

Take US 90A east of Gonzales for 32 miles to the tiny town of Shiner, best known as the home of Shiner beer. If you make the trip during the week, stop by for a free tour and a sample of the hometown product. (For information on the brewery and other Shiner attractions, see EAST FROM SAN ANTONIO, DAY TRIP 2.)

YOAKUM

From Shiner, drive south on TX 95 for 8 miles to US 77A. Turn right and continue for 2 more miles. Yoakum is home to eleven leather companies and thus is nicknamed "The Leather Capital of the World." Guided tours of these factories can be arranged. (See EAST FROM SAN ANTONIO, DAY TRIP 2.)

SOUTH DAY TRIP 2

Buda
San Marcos

BUDA

Head south from Austin on I-35 to the small town of Buda, located on Loop 4 to the west of the highway. This sleepy railroad town is a busy spot on weekends, when shoppers come to hunt antiques. (See NORTHEAST FROM SAN ANTONIO, DAY TRIP 2.)

SAN MARCOS

Head south on I-35 to San Marcos, the home of Southwest Texas State University, two amusement parks, and the crystal-clear San Marcos River. (See NORTHEAST FROM SAN ANTONIO, DAY TRIP 2).

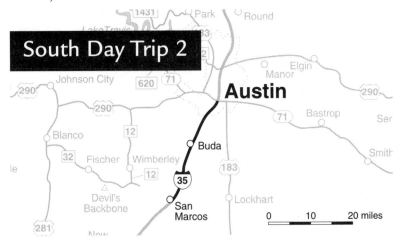

South Day Trip 2

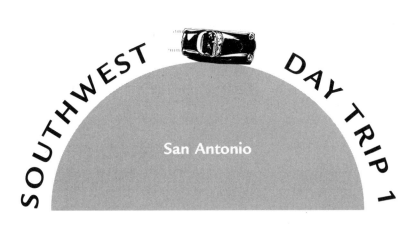

SAN ANTONIO

As Texas's third largest city, San Antonio has the reputation of a fun-loving town. Located 80 miles south of Austin on I-35, the city always has something going on to attract visitors. No matter when you choose to visit, you can bet that somebody, somewhere, is hosting a festival. Perhaps it has something to do with the sunshine or the fresh air. Whatever it is, you can feel it. It sizzles up like *fajitas* out of the city's Hispanic heritage, which abounds with colorful tradition and vivid memories.

San Antonio's rich cultural past dates back to the early Indians who settled the area. They were followed by the seventeenth-century Spaniards, who came here in search of wealth. Later a group of Franciscan friars established a chain of missions designed to convert the Indians of the Southwest to Christianity. In 1718 Mission San Antonio de Valero (better known as the Alamo) became the first of five such structures in the city.

Except for the Alamo, the missions are found in the San Antonio Missions National Historic Park, located within the city limits. The National Park Service has assigned interpretive themes to each of the four—the active parish churches of Mission Concepción, Mission San Juan Capistrano, Mission San Francisco de la Espada, and Mission San Jose. The latter, established in 1720, hosts a colorful "Mariachi Mass" each Sunday at noon.

San Antonio is also a foodie's paradise. This is the city that heralded the birth of *fajitas*—strips of marinated charcoal-grilled skirt steak. Here

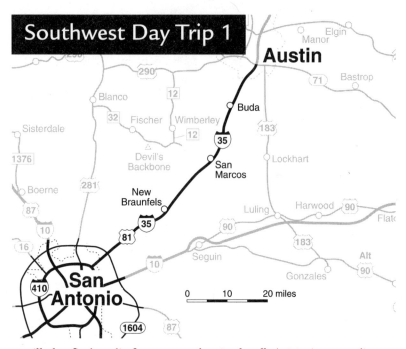

Southwest Day Trip 1

you'll also find to-die-for guacamole, *pico de gallo* (a Mexican condiment of onions, tomatoes, and chiles), and fresh flour tortillas.

With two excellent theme parks, a world-class zoo, and wonderful museums, San Antonio offers much more to see and do than this book can possibly list. For a complete rundown of possibilities, contact the San Antonio Convention and Visitors Bureau (call 800- 447-3372 or 210-270-8700; or write: P.O. Box 2277, San Antonio, TX 78298) or stop in the visitors center at Alamo Plaza (across from the Alamo), where you also can pick up information on the VIA streetcars that connect major tourist sites. The center is open daily.

DOWNTOWN: RIVER WALK AREA

The River Walk stretches for several miles from South St. Mary's Street to Alamo Street, and along Crockett and Market Streets. The Paseo del Rio, as it's also called, is a European-style river walk that lies below street level. Part of an urban renovation project five decades ago, the River Walk is now a top San Antonio attraction. Its winding sidewalks, which follow an arm of the San Antonio River, are lined with two-story specialty shops, sidewalk cafes, luxury hotels, art galleries, and bars. Like New Orleans's Bourbon Street, this area of San Antonio has an atmosphere all its own. Arched bridges connect the two sides of the walk, so visitors never have to venture up to street level.

One of the busiest sections of the Paseo del Rio extends from the Hyatt Regency San Antonio at Crockett Street to the Hilton Hotel at Market Street. This stretch of walk boasts most of the sidewalk restaurants and shops. From Commerce Street you can head up to the Convention Center and the Rivercenter Mall.

WHERE TO GO

The Alamo. Alamo Plaza, between Houston and Crockett Streets. Located in the very heart of San Antonio, the Alamo was once surrounded on all sides by the forces of Mexican General Santa Anna. Now it's enveloped by high-rise office structures and a central plaza.

This "Cradle of Texas Liberty," situated on the east side of Alamo Plaza, is probably the most famous spot in Texas. Established in 1718 as the Mission San Antonio de Valero, it plunged into history on March 6, 1836, when 188 men died after being attacked by the Mexican forces of General Santa Anna. Among the most famous defenders were Jim Bowie, William B. Travis, and Davy Crockett.

Symbol of the state's independence and courage, the Alamo draws continuous crowds throughout the year. Visitors entering the main building, the Shrine, can see exhibits such as Bowie's famous knife and Davy Crockett's rifle, "Old Betsy." Those interested also can take a self-guided tour of the museum, the Long Barracks, and the beautiful courtyard. Open daily. Free. (210) 225-1391.

River Taxis. River Walk at Commerce Street, across from Hilton Hotel and Rivercenter Mall. One of the most pleasurable and least expensive attractions in town, these open barges take passengers on forty-minute narrated cruises through the heart of San Antonio from morning until late evening. Special dinner cruises afford a romantic look at the city and are arranged by River Walk restaurants. Open daily. Fee. (210) 222-1701.

Tower of the Americas. HemisFair Park. This 750-foot tower is topped by a rotating restaurant that serves lunch and dinner. An ob-

servation deck offers an unbeatable view of the city. Open daily. Fee. (210) 299–8617.

Institute of Texan Cultures. HemisFair Park. This fascinating museum features exhibits and a multimedia presentation showcasing the twenty-six different ethnic groups who came here from around the world to settle the new frontier called Texas. Open Tuesday through Sunday. Free. (210) 226–7651.

IMAX Theater. Rivercenter Mall. This theater features *The Price of Freedom*, a forty-five-minute movie about the battle of the Alamo. The six-story screen and six-channel sound immerses you in the glory of the struggle, and it's a good thing to see before visiting the historic site. The theater alternates this movie with other IMAX features, so call for show times. Open daily. Fee. (210) 225–IMAX.

Hertzberg Circus Collection and Museum. 210 Market Street. One of the largest circusiana collections in the world, this unusual museum contains more than 20,000 items of big top memorabilia, including antique circus posters, Tom Thumb's miniature carriage, and a scale model of a three-ring circus. Open Monday through Saturday. Fee. (210) 207–7810.

Steves Homestead. 509 King William Street. This grand home was built in 1876 and is currently the only one in the elegant King William Historic District that is open to the public. The Victorian mansion's interior is filled with original furniture, and the grounds include several antique carriages and the gardener's quarters, now a visitors center. Open daily. Fee. (210) 225-5924.

Plaza Theatre of Wax. 301 Alamo Plaza. This attraction has wax figure displays of movie and TV celebrities as well as a theater of horrors. The "Heroes of the Lone Star" section is interesting, with realistic scenes depicting the fall of the Alamo. **Ripley's Believe It or Not!** is located in the same building, and you can buy separate or combination tickets to the two attractions. Open daily. Fee. (210) 224-9299.

The Texas Adventure. 307 Alamo Plaza. This state-of-the-art attraction calls itself the world's first Encountarium F-X Theater. The six-minute preshow does a good job of telling the story of the events that led up to the battle of the Alamo, then guests are ushered into a bench-lined room where holographic versions of Davy Crockett, William B. Travis, and Jim Bowie tell their story. It's interesting for all but the youngest of children, who may be frightened by "figures" materializing and disappearing throughout the presentation. Fee. (210) 227-8224.

WHERE TO SHOP

La Villita. Exit through Hilton Hotel, then 1 block right on South Alamo Street. This area on the east bank of the San Antonio River was developed in the mid-to-late eighteenth century by Mexican settlers who lived, without land title, on the outskirts of the Alamo mission. Today La Villita is San Antonio's finest crafts area, filled with weavers, glassblowers, sculptors, and even boot makers. Within the restored buildings, shops sell everything from woven wall hangings to silver jewelry, and the historic Little Church is often the site of weddings. Most shops open daily. Free.

Rivercenter Mall. Bounded by Commerce, Bowie, Crockett, and Alamo Streets. This three-story mall is home to several anchor stores as well as specialty shops and restaurants. On the enclosed bridge over the river vendors sell crafts and specialty items. The River Walk makes a U-turn in an outdoor dining area. Two hours free parking. Open daily.

WHERE TO EAT

Schilo's Delicatessen. 428 East Commerce Street. This deli is located on the street, not on the River Walk, but what it lacks in atmosphere it definitely makes up for history. Founded by Papa Fritz Schilo, the German immigrant opened a saloon in 1917, but when Prohibition came along he converted the operation to a deli. It was a lucky break for diners; mere suds could never match the subs and sandwiches that keep this spot packed with locals. Try a Reuben or a ham and cheese, or for dinner go all out with entrees like *wiener-schnitzel* or bratwurst. $; ☐. (210) 223–6692.

Boudro's. 421 River Walk. Ask many San Antonians for their favorite River Walk eatery and you'll hear this name. This steak and seafood restaurant offers the finest in Southwestern cuisine, usually with a twist that makes it unique even among San Antonio's plethora of excellent eateries. Start with a cactus margarita, a frozen concoction with a jolt of red cactus liqueur. Follow that eyeopener with an appetizer of smoked chicken or crab quesadillas, or crab and shrimp tamales. Save room, though, for Boudro's specialties—coconut shrimp, pecan-grilled fish fillet, or the specialty of the house, blackened prime rib. Seating is available on the River Walk or in the dining room. $$; ☐. (210) 224–8484.

Little Rhein Steakhouse. 231 South Alamo. Located on the River Walk near the Arneson River Theater, this restaurant offers an excellent selection of fine steaks served on terraces overlooking the river. On less pleasant days, you may choose to dine inside the historic steakhouse, built in 1847, which witnessed the development of San Antonio under six flags. The stone building also survived the battle of the Alamo, only a few blocks away. From the extensive menu, you can choose anything from T-bones to rib eye to Porterhouse steak, all served with Texas caviar (a mixture of black-eyed peas and chopped onion). Reservations are recommended. $$–$$$; ☐. (210) 225–2111.

WHERE TO STAY

Hyatt Regency San Antonio. 123 Losoya Street. This beautiful hotel, with its open atrium and glass elevators, is located directly on the River Walk. A stream flows through the hotel outside to the

River Walk, where an open-air jazz bar provides nightly entertainment. $$$; □. (800) 233-1234 or (210) 222-1234.

Ramada Emily Morgan Hotel. 705 East Houston Street, next to the Alamo. General Santa Anna was enamored with a mulatto slave named Emily Morgan, who acted as a spy for the Texas army. Thanks in part to her efforts, Sam Houston's troops defeated Santa Anna's men at San Jacinto on April 21, 1836, winning the Texas Revolution. Emily Morgan came to be known as "The Yellow Rose of Texas," the namesake of a famous song as well as this 177-room hotel. The rooms overlook the Alamo courtyard or Alamo Plaza, and all have Jacuzzis. $$; □. (800) 824-6674.

Plaza San Antonio. 555 South Alamo Street. This elegant establishment has the most beautiful grounds of any downtown hotel: six acres dotted with gardens, Chinese pheasants, and historic buildings. All 252 rooms have a private balcony. The hotel received international attention in 1992 by hosting the initializing ceremony of the North American Free Trade Agreement on the grounds. $$$; □. (800) 421-1172 or (210) 229-1000.

St. Anthony Hotel. 300 East Travis Street. This historic hotel a few blocks off the River Walk offers 350 rooms and access to a restaurant, health club, and swimming pool. $$$; □. (800) 338-1338 or (210) 227-4392.

DOWNTOWN: MARKET SQUARE

Colorful Market Square, bounded by San Saba, Santa Rosa, West Commerce, and Dolorosa Streets, is a busy shopping and dining area from early morning to late evening, as well as the scene of many San Antonio festivals.

To reach Market Square from the River Walk, follow Commerce Street west across the river to just east of I-10. Or, leave your car and take an inexpensive ride on the VIA streetcars, the open-air trolleys that stop at many downtown San Antonio attractions. (For information on VIA routes, stop by the San Antonio Visitors Center mentioned earlier.)

The history of Market Square goes back to the early 1800s, to a time when Mexico ruled the settlement of San Antonio de Bejar. Fresh produce and meats filled the farmer's market, and pharmaceutical items were available at Botica Guadalupana, today the oldest continually operating pharmacy in town (and a very interesting place to browse, even if you're feeling healthy).

Chili con carne, the state dish of Texas, was invented here over a century ago. Back then, young girls known as "chili queens" sold the spicy meat-and-bean concoction from kiosks.

Today Market Square includes the renovated Farmers' Market (now rife with Mexican imports and crafts rather than produce), an open-air restaurant and shopping area, and El Mercado, the largest enclosed Mexican-style marketplace in the country. Also located nearby are two historic structures: the Spanish Governor's Palace and Navarro House, home of a Texas patriot.

WHERE TO GO

El Mercado. Market Square. Styled after a typical Mexican market, El Mercado's fifty shops sell a rich profusion of goods, from silver jewelry, Mexican dresses, and *piñatas* to onyx chess sets, leather goods, and much more. Prices are slightly higher than in the Mexican markets, and you can't bargain with the vendors like you can south of the border. Open daily. Free. (210) 299–8600.

Spanish Governor's Palace. 105 Military Plaza. Part of an old Spanish fort that was built at the site in 1722, this structure was converted to a military commander's residence in 1749. San Antonio was once the capital of the Spanish province of Texas, and the Spanish governors occasionally resided here. The walls are 3 feet thick, and the home is filled with Spanish colonial antiques. Open daily. Fee. (210) 224–0601.

Jose Antonio Navarro State Historical Park. 228 South Laredo Street. This was the former residence of a signer of the Texas Declaration of Independence. The adobe and limestone structure includes an office used by Navarro, who was a lawyer and legislator. Open Wednesday through Saturday. Fee. (210) 226–4801.

WHERE TO EAT

Mi Tierra. 218 Produce Row. This is the place to head for an unbeatable Tex-Mex meal that includes homemade tortillas, enchiladas, and *chiliquiles*, a spicy egg and corn tortilla breakfast dish served with refried beans. Decorated year-around with Christmas ornaments, this San Antonio institution is open 24 hours a day, 365 days a year. $-$$; ☐. (210) 225-1262.

La Margarita. 102 Produce Row. This establishment also is owned by Mi Tierra and is best known for its excellent *fajitas*, which are brought to your table in cast-iron skillets. Open for lunch and dinner. $-$$; ☐. (210) 227-7140.

WITHIN THE CITY

Although the downtown area has plenty of attractions, other stops lie on the outskirts of the city, including a zoo, missions, and botanical gardens.

WHERE TO GO

San Antonio Missions National Historical Park. This national park stretches for 9 miles along the San Antonio River and is comprised of four remaining missions (outside of the Alamo) constructed by the Franciscan friars in the eighteenth century. The missions are active parish churches today, and all are open to the public. Each of the four illustrates a different concept of mission life:

Mission San Jose (6539 San Jose Drive), the most complete structure in the tour, was built in 1720. It has beautiful carvings, eighty-four rooms that once housed Indians, a restored mill with waterwheel, and what may be the only complete mission fort in existence. (210) 229-4770.

Mission Concepción (807 Mission Road), built in 1731, holds the title as the oldest unrestored stone church in the country. (210) 229-5732.

Mission San Juan Capistrano (9102 Graff Road) was relocated here from East Texas in 1731 but never completed. (210) 229-5734.

Mission San Francisco de la Espada (10040 Espada) was established in 1731. Its original chapel was in ruins by 1778 and the building was reconstructed around 1868. (210) 627-2021.

San Antonio Zoo. 3903 North St. Mary's Street. This world-class zoo features barless "habitat cages" for many of its animals. The cliffs of an abandoned quarry house over 3,000 birds, fish, mammals, and other fauna, making the zoo the third largest animal collection in North America. There's a children's petting area, a reptile house, and an aquarium. Open daily year-round; call for seasonal hours. Fee. (210) 734–7183.

Japanese Tea Gardens. 3800 North St. Mary's Street, by the zoo. San Antonio's semitropical climate encourages the lush flowers, climbing vines, and tall palms found inside this quiet, serene place. The ponds, with beautiful rock bridges and walkways, are home to hundreds of koi (large goldfish). Open daily. Free. (210) 734–0816.

San Antonio Botanical Gardens and Halsell Conservatory. 555 Funston Place, near Fort Sam Houston. Roses, herbs, a garden for the blind, and native plants are found within the lovely setting of these thirty-eight-acre gardens.

The centerpiece here is the $6.9 million Halsell Conservatory. A futuristic-looking, 90,000-square-foot structure is composed of seven tall glass spires. A self-guided tour of these seven areas takes visitors through the plants and flowers found in different environments, from desert to tropics. The conservatory sits partially underground for a cooling effect in the hot Texas summers. Open Tuesday through Sunday. Fee. (210) 821–5115.

Fort Sam Houston Self-Guided Tour. North New Braunfels Avenue and Stanley Road. This National Historic Landmark, an army base dating back to 1870, has nine times as many historic buildings as Colonial Williamsburg. These include the residence where General John J. Pershing lived in 1917; the Chinese Camp, once occupied by Chinese who fled Mexico to escape Pancho Villa; and the home where Lieutenant and Mrs. Dwight Eisenhower lived in 1916. Visitors can stroll past the structures (they are not open to the public). Call for hours. Free. (210) 221–6117.

The post also includes two museums. The **Fort Sam Houston Museum** is filled with exhibits on the site's early days. Open Wednesday through Sunday. Free. (210) 221–1886. The **U.S. Army Medical Department Museum** houses exhibits on military medical practices dating back to the Revolutionary War. Open Wednesday through Saturday. Free. (210) 221–6358.

Lone Star Brewery and Buckhorn Hall of Horns. 600 Lone Star Boulevard. There's nothing more Texan than Lone Star beer, and you can sample the product at the Buckhorn Saloon. This historic bar once was frequented by short-story writer William Sydney Porter (O. Henry), whose home has been relocated to the brewery grounds.

The Buckhorn Saloon building also contains the Buckhorn Hall of Horns and the Buckhorn Hall of Feathers, each containing their respective mounted specimens of animal horns and Texas birds. Separate buildings house the Hall of Texas History Wax Museum, with figures that recreate Texas's early historic events, and the Buckhorn Hall of Fins, which includes specimens from the Gulf and Texas rivers. Open daily. Fee. (210) 270-9467.

Witte Memorial Museum. 3801 Broadway. This excellent museum focuses on natural history, especially as it relates to the state's Indian, Spanish, and Mexican heritage. Open daily. Fee. (210) 820-2111.

McNay Art Museum. 6000 North New Braunfels Avenue. Located in a Spanish Mediterranean mansion that was once the home of art lover Marion Koogler McNay, the museum houses a nationally known collection of modern art as well as medieval and Gothic works. It also holds the largest collection of European and American graphic art in the Southwest. In the Tobin wing, visitors find one of the country's best theater arts research centers. Open Tuesday through Sunday. Free. (210) 824-5368.

FAR NORTHWEST

Beyond Loop 410, the city begins to give way to the Hill Country, the rolling, oak-covered land that's still largely rural. This is also the home of San Antonio's two theme parks.

WHERE TO GO

Sea World of Texas. Ellison Drive and Westover Hills Boulevard, off TX 151; 18 miles northwest of downtown, between Loop 410 and Loop 1604. This 250-acre, $170 million Texas-sized park is the largest marine-life park in the world. It's the home of Shamu the killer whale, plus dolphins, penguins, sea otters, and more. Visitors can enjoy two fast-moving water rides as well as acres of quiet gardens dotted with statues of famous Texans. Entertainment includes twenty-five shows, featuring a water-skiing extravaganza and breathtaking cycling performances.

Other attractions include a beautiful coral reef, a petting pool with people-friendly dolphins, and a Garden of Flags overlooking a map of the United States. Painted on concrete, the map is the size of a parking lot, and children are encouraged to race from "coast to coast." Open daily March through November; weekends only during cooler months. Call for hours. Fee. (210) 523-3611.

Fiesta Texas. I-10 and Loop 1604, 15 miles northwest of downtown. This $100-plus million theme park focuses on the history, culture, and music of San Antonio and the Southwest. Like its sister park, Nashville's Opryland, the main draw of this 200-acre spread is live entertainment. Seven theaters delight visitors with over sixty performances daily, including the award-winning and always packed "Rockin' at Rockville High" *Grease*-style musical production. For thrill seekers, there are thirteen rides that range from whitewater rafting to The Rattler, the tallest wooden roller coaster in the world and a real white knuckle ride.

The park is divided into four "villages," each featuring a different style of music and entertainment: Hispanic (Los Festivales), German (Spassburg), country-western (Crackaxle Canyon), and rock-'n'-roll (Rockville). The newest addition to the park is the Boardwalk, a 1950s-themed area complete with a roller-skating rink, paddleboats, a sand "beach," and a 90-foot Ferris wheel that provides an unbeatable view of the park and, just at the edge of the horizon, the city.

Open seasonally March through November; call for hours. Fee. (800) 473-4378.

WHERE TO STAY

Hyatt Hill Country Resort. 9800 Hyatt Resort Drive. This full-service resort offers the area's most luxurious getaway with an eighteen-hole golf course and a four-acre water park with a cascading waterfall and human-made Ramblin' River for inner-tube floaters. This 500-room resort nestles on 200 acres of a former cattle ranch, rolling land sprinkled with prickly pear cacti and live oaks. With its limestone architecture and Western decor, the four-story hotel has captured the atmosphere of the Hill Country, from windmills to gingerbread trim featuring the Lone Star (which often decorated homes of the German pioneers who settled the area). For meetings, the resort built a traditional Sunday house, modeled after the small, two-story homes that distant farmers often owned in town so that they could spend Saturday afternoon at market, Saturday night in town, and Sunday morning at church. $$$; ☐. (800) 233–1234 or (210) 647–1234.

ESPECIALLY FOR WINTER TEXANS

Admiralty Park. 1485 North Ellison Drive, off Loop 1604. This 240-pad RV park is located only minutes from Sea World and Loop 1604. It includes a heated pool, brick patios at each site, free clubhouse movies, cable TV hookups, and organized get-togethers during the winter (potluck dinners, card games, and dominoes). Winter residents can take advantage of special monthly and three-month rates. (800) 999–RVSA.

SOUTHWEST DAY TRIP 2

Gruene · New Braunfels

GRUENE

Once a separate community but now part of New Braunfels, Gruene is a popular destination for shoppers and water recreation lovers. Head south on I-35 for 30 miles to San Marcos (see NORTHEAST FROM SAN ANTONIO, DAY TRIP 2 for attractions in that city).

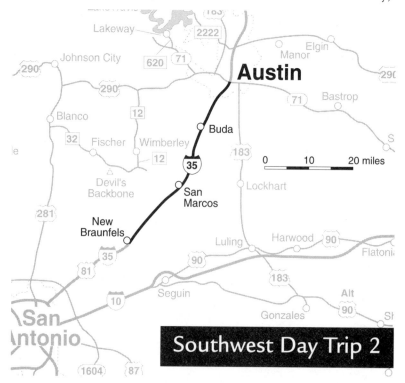

Southwest Day Trip 2

Continue south for 17 miles to exit 191. Turn west and continue to the intersection with Hunter Road, then turn left and continue to this historic area.

Once a ghost town, Gruene has been transformed into a very popular shopping destination. A historic inn, river rafting, lots of good food, and Texas's oldest dance hall draw visitors from around the state. (See NORTHEAST FROM SAN ANTONIO, DAY TRIP 3.)

NEW BRAUNFELS

Continue south on Gruene Road into New Braunfels. This city has just about everything to offer travelers, including historic buildings, German food, an enormous water theme park, and enough antique shops to merit the title "The Antique Capital of Texas." Learn more about New Braunfels's numerous attractions in NORTHEAST FROM SAN ANTONIO, DAY TRIP 3.

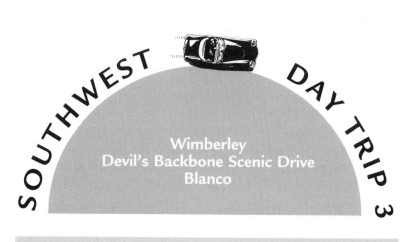

WIMBERLEY

From Austin, follow US 290 west to the small community of Dripping Springs. Turn south on RR 12 and continue 15 miles to Wimberley, a favorite shopping destination from Thursday through Monday. Wimberley's also a great summer destination because of its location on the Blanco River and Cypress Creek. (For the town's attractions, including one of Texas's prettiest swimming holes, see NORTH FROM SAN ANTONIO, DAY TRIP 1.)

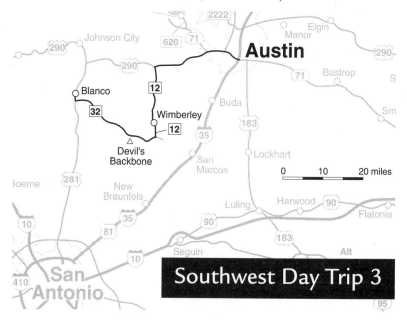

Southwest Day Trip 3

DEVIL'S BACKBONE SCENIC DRIVE

From Wimberley, continue south on RR 12 to RR 32. Turn west and sit back for this slow, scenic drive. (Read about these places in NORTH FROM SAN ANTONIO, DAY TRIP 1.)

BLANCO

After passing through Devil's Backbone, continue on RR 32 to US 281. Turn right and head north to Blanco, the home of a beautiful state park and a unique monastery. (See NORTH FROM SAN ANTONIO, DAY TRIP 1.)

To get back home, continue north on US 281. You can turn right on US 290 to go directly to Austin or continue north on US 281 to Johnson City. (For Johnson City attractions, read NORTH FROM SAN ANTONIO, DAY TRIP 2.) At the intersection of TX 71, 18 miles north of Johnson City on US 281, turn east and continue to Austin.

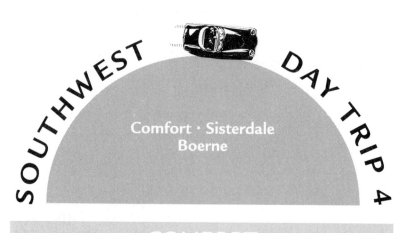

Comfort · Sisterdale
Boerne

COMFORT

To reach Comfort, follow US 290 west through Johnson City and Stonewall to US 87. Turn south on US 87 and continue for 23 miles. (As you take this drive, read NORTH FROM SAN ANTONIO, DAY TRIP 2 for attractions along the way.)

Downtown Comfort is a national historic district, filled with the homes and businesses constructed by the town's German pioneers. It's very popular as a weekend antique shopping spot or as a weekday getaway at the historic inn. (For a description of Comfort, see NORTHWEST FROM SAN ANTONIO, DAY TRIP 3.)

SISTERDALE

If you're a wine lover, take a detour on FM 473 to Sisterdale, home of the Sister Creek Vineyards. See NORTHWEST FROM SAN ANTONIO, DAY TRIP 3 for information on weekday tours.

BOERNE

From Sisterdale, take the 13-mile drive south on FM 1376 to Boerne. If you are traveling directly from Comfort, head south on I-10 for 17 miles. Boerne was also a German community, now home to many antique shops, two caves, and a beautiful park on the Guadalupe River. (Read more about Boerne in NORTHWEST FROM SAN ANTONIO, DAY TRIP 3.)

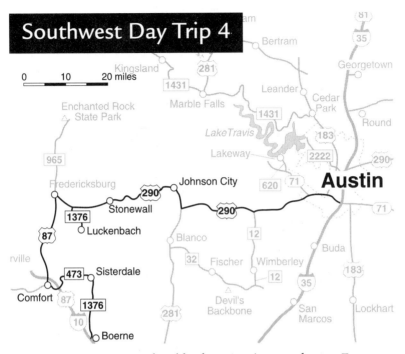

From Boerne, you can head back to Austin several ways. For more German atmosphere, drive 42 miles east to New Braunfels on TX 46 (see NORTHEAST FROM SAN ANTONIO, DAY TRIP 3), then hook into I–35 north to Austin. If you're not in a hurry, head east on TX 46 to US 281, then turn north and take the Devil's Backbone drive. You'll wind up in San Marcos by turning right on FM 306, left on FM 484, then right on FM 32. (See NORTH FROM SAN ANTONIO, DAY TRIP 1 and NORTHEAST FROM SAN ANTONIO, DAY TRIP 2.)

JOHNSON CITY

Head west of Austin on US 290 for 42 miles to the intersection of US 281. Turn north and continue for six miles to LBJ country. President Johnson's boyhood home is open to visitors, along with the Johnson Settlement where LBJ's grandfather organized cattle drives over a century ago. (Read about these attractions in NORTH FROM SAN ANTONIO, DAY TRIP 2.)

STONEWALL

Continue west on US 290 to Stonewall, the capital of the peach industry and home of the LBJ National and State Historic Parks, where you can tour the late president's spread. This is a great opportunity to visit a working cattle ranch. (For information on these free attractions, see NORTH FROM SAN ANTONIO, DAY TRIP 2.)

LUCKENBACH

To see this tiny community made famous by a country-western song, turn south on FM 1376. Don't rely on signs to get to this hamlet; they're often stolen by souvenir seekers. (See NORTH FROM SAN ANTONIO, DAY TRIP 2.)

FREDERICKSBURG

Retrace your steps from Luckenbach and return to US 290. Continue west to Fredericksburg, a German town that's best known for

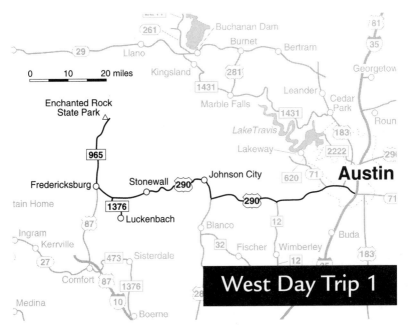

its shopping and its many historical sites. Weekends are always busy in this charming burg. (See NORTH FROM SAN ANTONIO, DAY TRIP 2.)

ENCHANTED ROCK STATE PARK

If you've saved some energy, head for a look at Enchanted Rock State Park on FM 965. This is the second largest stone formation in the country. (See NORTH FROM SAN ANTONIO, DAY TRIP 2.)

**Mount Bonnell · Lake Travis
Lakeway**

This is a popular hot weather day trip. Bring your swimsuit from April through October, along with an old pair of sneakers to navigate the rocky Lake Travis beaches.

MOUNT BONNELL

A beautiful lookout is located within the Austin city limits. Turn left off RR 2222 onto Mount Bonnell Road, which will take you to the highest point in town with a panoramic view of the city and the surrounding hills. Visitors must park and walk up some steep steps to the lookout, but the view is well worth the climb. Free.

WHERE TO EAT

County Line on the Lake. 5204 RR 2222. This is one of the few barbecue restaurants in Texas where you could wear a coat and tie and not look like a "city slicker." Enjoy full table service at this excellent restaurant on Lake Austin, ordering from a menu that features brisket, sausage, and ribs. Open for lunch every day but Saturday; dinner daily. $$–$$$; □. (512) 346-3664.

LAKE TRAVIS

Continue northwest on RR 2222. This winding road is filled with treacherous curves, so take it *slow*. At the intersection of RR 620, you have two choices: turn west onto RR 620 and continue to Mansfield

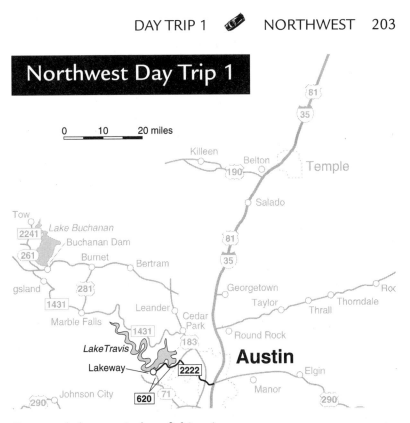

Northwest Day Trip 1

0   10   20 miles

Killeen

Belton   Temple

190

Salado

Tow

Lake Buchanan

2241

Buchanan Dam

261

Burnet

Bertram

81

35

gsland   281

Georgetown   Roc

Taylor   Thorndale

Leander   Thrall

1431

Cedar
Park

Marble Falls

1431

183

Lake Travis   Round Rock

Lakeway   **Austin**

2222

Elgin

290   Johnson City   620   71   Manor

290

Dam and the remainder of this trip, or turn east to some county parks and Austin's best known outdoor dining spot. This side excursion affords a beautiful drive by some of Austin's most expensive homes.

WHERE TO GO

McGregor/Hippie Hollow Park. From RR 620, turn right onto Comanche Trail. This is a clothing-optional park, the only one in the Austin area. On summer weekends, it is packed with nudists, curious onlookers, and swimmers who want to enjoy a beautiful swimming hole. The parking area is located away from the bathing area. (Nudity is not permitted in the parking lot.)

Onlookers outnumber nudists many weekends, but to see the beach (and the swimmers) you must leave your car and walk down the trail to the water's edge. The swimming area is protected from curious boaters, who are kept at a distance by patrolling Parks Department boats. No children allowed. Fee. Day use only. (512) 266–1644.

Bob Wentz at Windy Point. Comanche Trail, 1 mile past Hippie Hollow. This park is very popular with windsurfers and scuba divers. Open for camping. Fee. (512) 266-3875.

Slaughter-Leftwich Winery. A mile past the dam, take a right on Eck Lane and follow the signs. This winery overlooks Lake Travis from an elevation of 3,300 feet above sea level (that's *high* for this state). The elevation helps the vineyards enjoy cool evenings, and, according to the winery, produces a more intense character in the wines. The tasting room is open daily except Mondays. From Friday through Sunday (and also on Thursdays during peak season), enjoy a tour of facilities. Free. (512) 266-3331.

WHERE TO EAT

Oasis Cantina Del Lago. 6550 Comanche Trail. Known as "The Sunset Capital of Texas," this restaurant is famous for its open decks overlooking Lake Travis. On weekends this becomes a popular stop after a day of boating or swimming. The lake views and the surrounding hills provide a lovely backdrop for a sunset meal, the highlight of the day at this unusual restaurant. Open for lunch and dinner daily. $-$$; □. (512) 266-2441.

WHERE TO STAY

Lake Austin Spa Resort. 1705 Quinlan Park Road. Located on the shores of Lake Austin, this well-known resort caters to guests with special menus, dietary consultations, and European spa services. $$$; □. (800) 847-5637 or (512) 266-2444.

LAKEWAY

Continue west on RR 620 across Mansfield Dam to the village of Lakeway and the Lakeway Resort and Conference Center. This 1,200-person resort community boasts recreational facilities and accommodations for golf and tennis buffs. You can't miss it; just look for the water tower shaped and painted like a golf ball.

Lakeway offers thirty-two tennis courts, three championship golf courses, a golf academy, a full-service marina, party boats, horseback riding, hayrides, two swimming pools, a fitness center, and a conference center. The World of Tennis, one of the finest tennis facilities in the country, is also located here. Guests can stay at the Lakeway Inn, purchasing various packages that include the use of these facilities.

WHAT TO DO

Golf. The Live Oak and the Yaupon eighteen-hole courses are open to the public. Golf packages in conjunction with the Lakeway Inn also are available. For fees and reservations, call the pro shop at (512) 261-7572 or 261-7573.

Students of the Academy of Golf hone their skills on three full-length holes, a driving range, and a putting green. The academy is located in The Hills of Lakeway, a private eighteen-hole course designed by Jack Nicklaus. Call for class information; reservations required. Closed Monday. (800) 879-2008.

Tennis. 1 World of Tennis Square. The World of Tennis has twenty-six world-class indoor courts, including a stadium court. Tennis packages in conjunction with the Lakeway Inn are available. Open daily. (512) 261-7222 or 261-7257.

WHERE TO STAY

Lakeway Inn. 101 Lakeway Drive. Adjacent to the marina, this large hotel has 170 rooms featuring Southwest decor and a lake view. Some accommodations include fireplaces and kitchens. A lobby bar serves evening cocktails, and an attractive restaurant offers breakfast, lunch, and dinner. $$$; ☐. (800) LAKEWAY or (512) 261-6600.

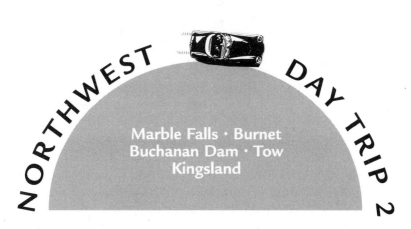

The Highland Lakes region is comprised of a series of seven lakes that form back-to-back "stair steps" along the Colorado River. Built in the 1930s by the Lower Colorado River Authority (LCRA) to bring electricity to rural Texas and to control flooding along the river, the lakes now provide 150 miles of water recreation.

MARBLE FALLS

To reach Marble Falls, take US 183 north of Austin to Cedar Park. (For attractions in this community, see NORTHWEST FROM AUSTIN, DAY TRIP 3.) Turn west on FM 1431 and sit back for a forty-minute ride dotted with cattle ranches, small creeks, magnificent fields of wildflowers, and some incredibly beautiful Hill Country vistas.

Drive south on US 281 to the overlook at the edge of town for a terrific view of the 780-acre Lake Marble Falls. It's said that this sight inspired local songwriter Oscar J. Fox (who also penned "Home on the Range" and "Get Along Little Dogie") to write his popular tune "Hills of Home." Today a marker commemorates this local hero.

Normally the falls that gave this town its name are beneath the lake, but occasionally the falls are visible when the LCRA does repair work on the dam.

While the town may be named for marble, granite is king here. Granite Mountain at the edge of town is the home of a huge quarry that sells pink granite around the country. This quarry supplied the granite used in building the State Capitol and also many of the jetties along the Texas coast. Visitors are not allowed in the quarry but can observe the operation from the rest stop on the side of FM 1431.

WHERE TO GO

Marble Falls/Lake LBJ Chamber of Commerce. US 281. Stop by this one hundred-year old railroad depot station to get brochures and maps on area shopping, dining, and park recreation. Open Monday–Friday 8:00 A.M.–5:00 P.M. (800 759-8178 or (830) 693-4449.

　Highland Arts Guild Gallery. 318 Main Street. Have a look here at the work of over fifty local artists who call the Highland Lakes their home. The gallery sells original arts and crafts, including many bluebonnet paintings. Open daily. (830) 693-7324.

WHERE TO SHOP

Wildlife Sportsman. Located on FM 1431, west of the intersection of US 281. This store stocks plenty of hunting and fishing gadgets

Northwest Day Trip 2

and gizmos. It specializes in game calls made to attract everything from deer to wild turkey. Live rattlesnakes are on display as well. Open daily. (830) 693-7072.

WHERE TO EAT

Inman's Ranch House Barbecue and Turkey Sausage. US 281 and Sixth Street. This little restaurant uses Texas's favorite cooking method—barbecue—on turkey to produce a spicy sausage that's mighty tasty and not as greasy as its pork cousin. Beef brisket and sides of coleslaw and beans also appear on the menu. $; no ☐. (830) 693-2711.

Blue Bonnet Cafe. US 281 near the bridge. This is an example of a good old-fashioned Texas diner at its best. For over sixty years, the Blue Bonnet Cafe has served locals and visitors plenty of country cooking, including chicken-fried steak, fried chicken, and burgers. $-$$; no ☐. (830) 693-2344.

WHERE TO STAY

Horseshoe Bay Resort and Conference Club. RR 2147, west of Marble Falls. Horseshoe Bay, located on Lake LBJ, is one of the premier resorts in Central Texas. Golfers have their choice of three courses, including Robert Trent Jones' Applerock. Other features include Oriental gardens, a yacht club, horseback trails, and tennis courts. $$$; ☐. (800) 252-9363 in Texas or (800) 531-5105 outside of Texas.

Liberty Hall. 119 Avenue G. This historic guest house was originally the home of General Adam Rankin Johnson, founder of Marble Falls. In later years, the two-story home was the residence of "Birdie" Harwood, a woman elected mayor—by an all-male voting population. Today the B&B includes cozy bedrooms with brass beds, antique furnishings, and a homey atmosphere. (830) 693-4518.

BURNET

From Marble Falls, go north to Burnet on US 281, a road lined with fragrant bluebonnet fields in April. Burnet is the closest town of any size to Lake Buchanan (pronounced "BUCK-an-an"). It's a good place to stop for picnic supplies and sunscreen products during summer visits (there are few facilities once you leave the city limits). Outdoor activities including spelunking and bird-watching are popular throughout the year here.

WHERE TO GO

Fort Croghan Museum. From US 281, turn left onto TX 29 and continue to the western edge of town. Fort Croghan was constructed here in the 1840s, one of eight forts built from the Rio Grande to the Trinity Rivers to protect the region from Indian attack. The museum and the adjacent fort sit on the left side of the road. Exhibits include household items used by residents over one hundred years ago. You can take a walking tour of the fort, the blacksmith shop, the powder house, and a two-room cabin where one family raised ten children. Open Thursday through Saturday during peak season; by appointment only during winter months. Free. (512) 756-8281.

Vanishing Texas River Cruise. A few miles past Fort Croghan on TX 29, turn right on FM 2341 and follow the signs. This excellent bird-watching cruise is popular with travelers who come to see American bald eagles from November through March. The rest of the year, you might see javelinas, wild goats, and white-tailed deer. The route takes in 50-foot Fall Creek Falls and a narrow, cliff-lined passage on the Colorado River. Cruises also travel past Fall Creek Vineyards on the lake's shore. Dinner cruises May through October; reservations required. Closed Tuesday. $$; ☐. Fee. (512) 756-6986.

Inks Lake State Park. From TX 29, turn left onto Park Road 4. This 1,200-acre park offers camping, lakeside picnicking, swimming, and even a golf course. White-tailed deer are a common sight during evening hours. Open daily. Fee. (512) 793-2223 for park information; (512) 389-8900 for reservations.

Confederate Air Force Museum. At the Burnet Municipal Airport off US 281, 1.5 miles south of Burnet. Here you can have a look at World War II airplanes as well as memorabilia from the men who fought the battles. Open weekends. Fee. (512) 756-2226.

Longhorn Cavern State Park. From TX 29, turn left onto Park Road 4. This cavern has few formations but a long and interesting history. In one story, Comanches raided San Antonio, kidnapped a young woman named Mariel King, and brought her back to the cavern, unknowingly followed by three Texas Rangers. A hand-to-hand battle ensued, and Mariel King was rescued. Ending the story with a fairy-tale flourish, Miss King later married one of her rescuers, and the couple lived on in Burnet. The guided tour is nonstrenuous, with wide, well-lit trails through the huge limestone rooms. Open daily. Fee. (512) 756-4680.

From the cavern, return to Burnet by retracing your steps on Park Road 4.

BUCHANAN DAM

Continue driving west on TX 29 to the village of Buchanan Dam, a fishing and retirement community. Lake Buchanan, the jewel of the Highland Lakes with over 23,000 surface acres of water, is formed by Buchanan Dam, the largest multiarch dam in the world.

Lake Buchanan's own gem is the freshwater pearl. Created by freshwater mussels in the Colorado River, some pearls found here have been valued at several thousand dollars.

WHERE TO GO

Buchanan Dam Visitors Center. TX 29, at the dam. Here you can find brochures on area campgrounds and activities as well as maps of the Highland Lakes. A museum adjacent to the center provides a look at how the mighty Colorado was tamed. Photographs recount the backbreaking labor involved in the massive project. During spring and summer months, tours of the dam leave on Saturday and Sunday afternoons; call for times. Open daily. Free. (512) 793-2803.

Buchanan Dam Art Gallery. TX 29, 1 mile past the dam. This is the oldest continually operating artists' cooperative in the country, and it's a great place to buy a bluebonnet painting at a reasonable price. The April arts and crafts show is held here, with booths set up outdoors. During the show local artists sell bluebonnets painted on everything from saw blades to mussel shells. Open daily. Free. (512) 793-2858.

WHERE TO EAT

Big John's Bar-B-Q. TX 29 and FM 1431, 2 miles west of Buchanan Dam. There's nothing fancy about this old-fashioned barbecue joint, serving sliced beef, ribs, and sausage. Dine indoors or out on big picnic tables. Open Thursday through Sunday for lunch and dinner. $$; no ☐. (512) 793-2261.

TOW

If you're interested in wine, take a drive up to the community of Tow (rhymes with "cow") on the edge of Lake Buchanan. From TX 29, head north 8 miles on TX 261, then 6 miles on FM 2241.

Fall Creek Vineyards. 2.2 miles northeast of the Tow Post Office on FM 2241. Since opening in 1975, Fall Creek has been known as one of the top wineries in Central Texas, winning numerous awards. Located right on the shores of Lake Buchanan, the vineyards here span sixty-five acres. You can take a tour of the entire operation and sample the wine made on the premises. Tours run Monday through Friday, 11:00 A.M. to 3:00 P.M.; Saturday, noon to 5:00 P.M. From March through October, tasting and sales (no tours) are also available on Sunday afternoons. Free. (512) 476-4477 (Austin sales office) or (915) 379-5361 (winery).

KINGSLAND

From Tow, you can return to Austin or take a little different route for a peek at another of the Highland Lakes: Lake LBJ. Return to TX 29 by retracing your steps from Tow. Continue west for 1 mile on TX 29, then turn south on FM 1431 and drive 6 miles to the retirement and fishing community of Kingsland.

Once named Granite Shoals, Lake LBJ was renamed for President Lyndon Baines Johnson who, as a young senator, brought the lakes project to Central Texas. Today the narrow, winding lake is popular with both fishers and skiers. Edged by steep hills, its clear and calm waters are protected from the winds that often buffet the larger lakes.

Kingsland is a sleepy community catering to those who come to enjoy a few days of bass fishing. Several lodges lie near the junction of the Llano and Colorado Rivers, where quiet coves afford a catch of black bass, white bass, crappie, catfish, and perch. Be sure to stop at the scenic overlook on FM 1431 just past the edge of town for a grand view of the lake and its shoreline homes.

WHERE TO GO

Kingsland Archaeological Center. East from Kingsland on FM 1431, then right at the Hidden Oaks sign or County Road 126; follow signs to the parking area. Discovered in 1988, this archaeological site has yielded artifacts dating from the Paleo-Indian (over 10,000 years ago) to the late prehistoric period (700 years ago). A small visitors center and museum house artifacts from the site. Open for tours on Sunday afternoons and by appointment. Free. (800) 776–5272, ext. 2753.

WHERE TO STAY

Longhorn Resort. RR 2900, at Llano River Bridge. This fishing resort has air-conditioned units with kitchenettes, a covered fishing marina, boat stalls, and launch ramp. It also provides camper hookups. $$; □. (915) 388–4343.

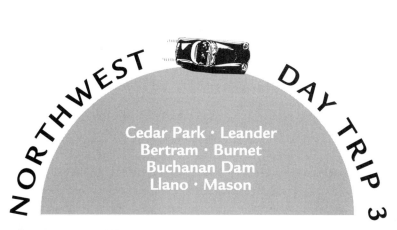

Cedar Park · Leander
Bertram · Burnet
Buchanan Dam
Llano · Mason

This day trip is filled with winding roads, historic attractions, and natural wonders. It also includes Llano and Mason, two of the best rock-hunting destinations in the country.

Visitors to this Hill Country vicinity must travel over some dirt and gravel roads, especially in rock-hunting areas. Near Mason are numerous low water crossings, and on some back roads you must drive across dry creek beds. Flash flooding is a very real hazard in the Hill Country, especially during the spring and fall months. Be aware of weather conditions when you make these trips, and never cross swiftly flowing water.

CEDAR PARK

Cedar Park is a thirty-minute drive north from Austin via US 183, a congested highway that leads to the Texas Hill Country. Now primarily a suburb, once this was called "cedar chopper" country. Cedar choppers were independent people who worked the hilly land to the west, cutting juniper trees to provide fence posts for area ranchers. This generations-old trade is still plied by some Hill Country families today. The town celebrates its heritage with an annual Cedar Chopper Festival in June.

WHERE TO GO

Austin Steam Train. US 183 and FM 1431. Take a ride on the *Hill Country Flyer*, running from Cedar Park to Burnet (where visitors stop for lunch and shopping). Each of the 1930s-era cars is restored to original splendor. The locomotive, donated to the city of Austin by the Southern Pacific Railroad in 1956, resided for many years in a

Northwest Day Trip 3

downtown park as playground equipment. After a complete restoration in 1991, she's once again whistling through Central Texas. Reservations required. Fee. (512) 477–8468.

Hill Country Cellars. US 183, north of FM 1431. This winery is noted for a 200-year-old native grapevine transplanted at the site. Acres of vineyards along US 183 produce a Chardonnay, a Hill Country Blush, and a Cabernet Sauvignon. Free. (512) 259–2000.

WHERE TO SHOP

Callahan's General Store. US 183 North, in Cedar Park. This classy general store stocks everything Texan, from Western wear to blue-speckled dinnerware to gourmet gift items, not to mention agricultural supplies. (512) 335–8585.

Lakeline Mall. US 183 and RR 620. Shop this Texas-sized mall, with a decor that's complete with a free-standing replica of the State Capitol dome and the Austin skyline. Open daily. (512) 257–7467.

WHERE TO EAT

La Fiesta. 200 Buttercup Boulevard. Bring a big appetite to this top Tex-Mex spot. Try the regular dinner, with a cheese enchilada and a tamale plus sides of rice and beans, or the La Fiesta Salad—a taco, guacamole salad, and a dollop of *chile con queso*. $-$$; ☐. (512) 331-0055.

LEANDER

Continue north on US 183 to neighboring Leander, a small town that boasts many historic markers. To the right as you approach town, you'll see a marker for the Blockhouse Creek subdivision, named for a blockhouse used as an interim prison by the Texas Rangers a century ago.

Another historic marker stands just east of US 183 on FM 2243. The Davis Cemetery, as the marker recounts, is the site of a mass grave, a reminder of an Indian attack that ended with the deaths of many pioneers.

WHERE TO GO

Dinosaur Tracks. South San Gabriel River, just north of town. Park your car at the bridge and walk upstream for a half mile to see these three-toed dinosaur tracks. Free. (512) 259-1907.

BERTRAM

From Leander, continue north on US 183 to the intersection of TX 29. Drive west then on TX 29 for 12 miles to Bertram. This is a sleepy little town most of the year, but on Labor Day weekend the streets throng with travelers from around the state who come for the annual Oatmeal Festival. Visitors flock here then for the chance to witness an oatmeal cook-off, take part in a fun run, or witness a parade. The festival is named for the hamlet of Oatmeal, located 6 miles south of Bertram on RR 243.

WHERE TO SHOP

Jimmy's Antiques. TX 29. If you're looking for Texas antiques, this is a good place to start. Jimmy's has the usual glassware, china, and jewelry found in most such stores, but it also handles many local treasures such as Texas Ranger saddlebags, Western saddles, Indian artifacts, and arrowheads. Open daily. (512) 355-2985.

BURNET

From Bertram, continue west on TX 29 for 10 miles to Burnet, the home of Longhorn Caverns and Fort Croghan. (For information on these and other Burnet attractions, see NORTHWEST FROM AUSTIN, DAY TRIP 2.)

BUCHANAN DAM

Buchanan Dam, located on the shores of Lake Buchanan, is a resort and retirement community located 13 miles west of Burnet on TX 29.

(For information on Buchanan Dam, see NORTHWEST FROM AUSTIN, DAY TRIP 2.)

LLANO

Continuing west on TX 29 from Buchanan Dam, you'll see more and more granite outcroppings—huge boulders protruding from the rugged land. This entire region is called the Llano Uplift, a geological formation caused by igneous rocks from 40 miles below ground being pushed up to the surface.

As a result of the formation, the rich minerals found here turned Llano into a boomtown in the 1880s. Huge deposits of iron ore were found in the area, and some industrialists had dreams on making Llano the "Pittsburgh of the West." Tent cities were erected, mining went full swing, and downtown Llano was spruced up with the money that came pouring into town. All too soon, though, one hard fact came to light: to make steel you have to have coal as well as iron, and there was no coal in the area. To bring coal in was far too costly. As quickly as it began, the iron ore business came to a swift halt.

But Llano was by then well known for another mineral: granite. During its heyday, the city boasted ten granite quarries and five finishing plants, shipping several varieties of granite around the country. When rail prices increased, Llano's granite business also came to a stop, although vast quantities of granite still remain.

Granite brought many prominent people to the area. Sculptor Frank Teich, a nationally famous German artist, owned a monument company (as well as the town of Teichville). His World War I monument still stands on the courthouse lawn here. Teich came to

Llano for its healthy climate when doctors told him that he had only six months to live. Either the doctors were wrong in their diagnosis or Llano's healthy atmosphere really worked, because Teich lived in the town for another thirty-eight years! Even today, Llano is listed by the U.S. Census as one of the healthiest places to live in the country.

Another prominent Llano citizen was Professor N. J. Badu, a mineralogist who came to town to operate a manganese mine and tried to focus the attention of the mineralogy world on Llano's many minerals. Today his elegant home is a busy bed-and-breakfast inn.

The Llano area is still a collector's paradise, with over 240 different rocks and minerals discovered in the region. The area's granite, feldspar, graphite, and talc have commercial value, while the more precious yields, such as garnet, amethyst, tourmaline, and quartz—even gold and silver—are sought by eager visiting rock hounds.

Public rock hunting is allowed on the Llano River in town. Stop by the park on the south bank of the river just across from the public library and try your luck. The riverbanks are dotted with rocks of all varieties and offer some pretty picnic spots as well. To have a look at Llano's rocks and minerals before you begin your search (or to buy some if your hunt was unsuccessful), stop by the Llano Uplift Rock Shop downtown and talk to owner Billy Hazlewood.

WHERE TO GO

Llano County Historical Museum. 310 Bessemer Avenue (TX 16). Visitors find this museum housed in the old Bruhl Drugstore, with displays on the area's early Indian history and Llano's boomtown days. An exhibit contains samples of Llano's many rocks and minerals. Open Tuesday through Sunday during the summer; Friday through Sunday after Labor Day. Free. (915) 247-4598.

Walking Tour of Llano. Stop by the Chamber of Commerce office (700 Bessemer Avenue) Monday through Friday for a brochure outlining twenty-six historic stops in town. Free. (915) 247-5354.

WHERE TO SHOP

Llano Uplift Rock Shop. 805 Berry Street, on the square. This is a store for serious rock hounds and for curious travelers who'd like to take home a sample of Llano's offerings without spending a day in the field. Here numerous rocks and minerals are sold, as well as jewelry, gold-panning equipment, and lapidary supplies. Open Wednesday through Sunday. (915) 247-3747.

WHERE TO EAT

Inman's Kitchen and Catering Service. 809 West Young (TX 29 West). Barbecue is king here, including beef brisket, chicken, pork, and the restaurant's specialty: turkey sausage. This spot is more elegant than many barbecue restaurants, with a carpeted, air-conditioned dining area. Lunch and dinner served Monday through Saturday; open Sundays during deer season. $; no ☐. (915) 247-5257.

Cooper's Old Time Pit Barbecue and Catering. 604 West Young (TX 29 West). Step up to the smoker and pick out your meat—brisket, sausage, pork ribs, beef ribs, chicken, sirloin steak, pork chops, or even goat. The pitmaster slices off the amount you want, then you go inside and help yourself to white bread, beans, and sauce in the cinder block dining room. $; no ☐. (915) 247-5713.

WHERE TO STAY

The Badu House. 601 Bessemer Avenue (TX 16). This two-story stone and brick inn, circa 1891, was the former home of mineralogist N. J. Badu, who put Llano on the map by discovering the mineral llanite here at the turn of the century. The building has been elegantly renovated, and all eight bedrooms feature private baths, ceiling fans, air conditioning, and period furnishings. Late afternoon cocktails are served in a club adjacent to the restaurant that offers everything from filet mignon to oven-roasted quail. $$-$$$; ☐ (915) 247-4304.

Dabbs Hotel. 112 East Burnet Street, behind the Llano Museum. At the turn of the century, this railroad hotel was the last outpost of civilization before heading west. Today's guests are treated to twelve quiet rooms with period furnishings, double beds, a breezy screened porch, and a peaceful atmosphere overlooking the Llano River. Saturday nights feature Western cookouts. Dinner reservations required. $; no ☐. (915) 247-7905.

MASON

From Llano, continue west on TX 29 for 34 miles to Mason, once the home of the late Fred Gipson, author of *Old Yeller*. Like neighboring

Llano, the land around Mason is rocky and dotted with granite.

Mason was settled by cattle ranchers and German families who came from nearby Fredericksburg. In 1851 Fort Mason was built on a hilltop to afford a better look at oncoming Comanches. (The post's best-known soldier was Lieutenant Colonel Robert E. Lee.) Constructed of sandstone, in 1869 the fort was dismantled and the salvaged stone was used to build local businesses and homes.

Even after the fort was no longer necessary, frontier justice was still a part of Mason. In 1875 the Mason County War, also known as the Hoodoo War, broke out. It all started when the sheriff arrested a group of men who were taking cattle to Llano, allegedly without the owner's permission. The men were set free on bond and ordered to remain in town, an order they promptly forgot. The sheriff rearrested as many of the rustlers as he could find. A few nights later, a group freed the prisoners, sparking a round of shootings and lynchings that left a dozen men dead. The feud continued until January 1877, when the Mason County Courthouse was set fire, destroying any evidence against the cattle rustlers.

Rock hounds come to Mason County today in search of topaz, the Texas state gem, which develops in colors ranging from clear to sky blue. Most local topaz turns up near the small communities of Streeter, Grit, and Katemcy, all north and northeast of Mason. Searchers usually find the stones in streambeds and ravines by using picks and shovels to loosen rocks and a wire screen to sift.

WHERE TO GO

Fort Mason. Follow Post Hill Street south from the courthouse to Post Hill. These reconstructed officers' quarters are furnished with typical 1850s' belongings as well as photographs from Mason's early days. The back porch has an unbeatable view of the town below and miles of Hill Country beyond. Open daily. Free. (915) 347-5758.

Gene Zesch Woodcarving Display at the Commercial Bank. 100 Moody Street, on the square. Gene Zesch is one of Mason's most famous citizens, known for his humorous woodcarvings of modern cowboys. His work was collected by President Johnson and is sold in galleries nationally. This exhibit features woodcarvings and bronzes made by the artist. Open Monday through Friday. Free. (915) 347-6324.

Mason County Museum. 300 Moody Street, south of the square. This local history museum is housed in an old elementary school built in 1887. The contents include typical items used by area ranchers and housewives a century ago, from toys to needlework to farm equipment. There is also a display of local rocks and minerals. Call for hours. Free. (915) 347-5758.

Seaquist House. 400 Broad Street. This sandstone mansion, with twenty-two rooms and fifteen fireplaces, was built in the 1880s for a local banker. Today visitors can tour the third-floor ballroom, billiards room, and formal parlor and dining room. Tours by appointment only. Fee. (915) 347-6659 or 347-6415.

Eckert James River Bat Cave. Write or call the Mason Chamber of Commerce (P.O. Box 156, Mason, TX 76856; (915) 347-5758) for directions and a map to this bat cave, located about 13 miles south of Mason. The cavern is home to about 6 million Mexican free-tail bats. This is a "maternity cave," used during the spring and summer months by female bats to bear and rear their young. You can view the evening flight out of the cave, a sight heralded by high-pitched sounds. Open Thursday–Sunday 6:00-9:00 P.M., May–October. Free.

White-tailed Deer Hunting. Mason County claims to have more white-tailed deer per acre than any other county in Texas. Hunters flock here from around the Southwest to stalk deer during the winter months. For information on hunting licenses, call the Mason Chamber of Commerce (915) 347-5758 well before deer season begins.

Topaz Hunting. Two private areas charge a daily fee of $10 per person for topaz hunting. Visitors must bring their own equipment (including water during warm summer months) and may keep whatever they find. The following ranches offer topaz hunting from mid-January through October:

Wayne Hofmann Ranch, c/o Wesley Loeffler, Menard Route, Mason, TX 76856; (915) 347-6415.

Garner Seaquist Ranch, P.O. Box 35, Mason, TX 76856; (915) 347-5713. (This ranch also offers camping facilities, both tent sites and camper hookups, with water, electricity, and showers.)

WHERE TO SHOP

Country Collectibles. US 87 North. If your search for topaz comes up empty, stop by this antique store, which sells topaz and other stones indigenous to the area plus arrowheads, willow furniture, and collectibles of every description. (915) 347–5249.

WHERE TO STAY

Mason County is filled with bed-and-breakfast accommodations, RV campsites, and guest ranches located outside of town. For a free copy of their "Bed and Breakfast and RV Sites" brochure, contact the Mason Chamber of Commerce at (915) 347–5758, or write: P.O. Box 156, Mason, TX 76856.

Regional Information

NORTH FROM SAN ANTONIO

Day Trip 1
Blanco Chamber of Commerce
P.O. Box 626
Blanco, TX 78606
(830) 833–5101

Wimberley Chamber of Commerce
P.O. Box 12
Wimberley, TX 78676
(512) 847–2201

Day Trip 2
Johnson City Chamber of Commerce
P.O. Box 485
Johnson City, TX 78636
(830) 868–7684

Fredericksburg Convention and Visitors Bureau
106 North Adams
Fredericksburg, TX 78624
(830) 997–6523

Stonewall Chamber of Commerce
P.O. Box 1
Stonewall, TX 78671
(830) 644-2735

NORTHEAST FROM SAN ANTONIO

Day Trip 1
Austin Convention and Visitors Bureau
201 East Second Street
Austin, TX 78701
(800) 926-2282 or (512) 478-0098

Day Trip 2
San Marcos Chamber of Commerce
P.O. Box 2310
San Marcos, TX 78667
(888) 200-5620 or (512) 396-2495

Buda City Hall
P.O. Box 1218
Buda, TX 78610
(512) 295-6331

Day Trip 3
New Braunfels Chamber of Commerce
390 South Seguin Street
New Braunfels, TX 78130
(800) 572-2626

Gruene Information Center
1601 Hunter Road
New Braunfels, TX 78130
(830) 629-5077

EAST FROM SAN ANTONIO

Day Trip 1
Luling Area Chamber of Commerce
421 East Davis Street
Luling, TX 78648
(830) 875-3214

Flatonia Chamber of Commerce
P.O. Box 651
Flatonia, TX 78941
(512) 865-3920

Schulenburg Chamber of Commerce
P.O. Box 65
Schulenburg, TX 78956
(409) 743-4514

Day Trip 2
Seguin-Guadalupe County Chamber of Commerce
427 North Austin Street
Seguin, TX 78155
(800) 580-7322 or (830) 379-6382

Gonzales Chamber of Commerce
P.O. Box 134
Gonzales, TX 78629
(830) 672-6532

Shiner Chamber of Commerce
810 North Avenue E
P.O. Box 221
Shiner, TX 77984
(512) 594-4180

Yoakum Chamber of Commerce
P.O. Box 591
Yoakum, TX 77995
(512) 293-2309

SOUTHEAST FROM SAN ANTONIO

Day Trip 1
Goliad Chamber of Commerce
P.O. Box 606
Goliad, TX 77963
(800) 848-8674 or (512) 645-3563

Day Trip 2
Victoria Convention and Visitors Bureau
P.O. Box 2456
Victoria, TX 77902
(512) 573-5277

SOUTH FROM SAN ANTONIO

Day Trip 1
Aransas Pass Chamber of Commerce
452 Cleveland Boulevard
Aransas Pass, TX 78336
(800) 633-3028 or (512) 758-2750

Port Aransas Tourist and Convention Bureau
P.O. Box 356
Port Aransas, TX 78373
(800) 45-COAST or (512) 749-5919

Rockport-Fulton Area Chamber of Commerce
404 Broadway
Rockport, TX 78382
(800) 242-0071

Day Trip 2
Corpus Christi Convention and Visitors Bureau
P.O. Box 2664
Corpus Christi, TX 78403
(800) 766-BEACH

King Ranch Visitor Center
P.O. Box 1090
Kingsville, TX 78364
(512) 592-8055

Kingsville Convention and Visitors Bureau
101 North 3rd
P.O. Box 1562
Kingsville, TX 78364
(800) 333-5032

SOUTHWEST FROM SAN ANTONIO

Day Trip 1
Laredo Area Chamber of Commerce
P.O. Box 790
Laredo, TX 78042
(800) 292-2122 or (956) 722-9895

WEST FROM SAN ANTONIO

Day Trip 1
Eagle Pass Chamber of Commerce
P.O. Box 1188
Eagle Pass, TX 78852
(830) 773-3224

Day Trip 2
Castroville Chamber of Commerce
P.O. Box 572
Castroville, TX 78009
(800) 778-6775 or (830) 538-3142

Uvalde Convention and Visitors Bureau
300 East Main Street
Uvalde, TX 78801
(800) 5-UVALDE or (830) 278-3363

Day Trip 3
Del Rio Area Chamber of Commerce
1915 Avenue F
Del Rio, TX 78840
(800) 889–8149 or (830) 775–3551

NORTHWEST FROM SAN ANTONIO

Day Trip 1
Bandera County Convention and Visitors Bureau
P.O. Box 171
Bandera, TX 78003
(800) 364–3833

Day Trip 2
Kerrville Chamber of Commerce
1700 Sidney Baker, Suite 100
Kerrville, TX 78028
(830) 896–1155

West Kerr County Chamber of Commerce
P.O. Box 1006
Ingram, TX 78025
(830) 367–4322

Day Trip 3
Greater Boerne Area Chamber of Commerce
One Main Plaza
Boerne, TX 78006
(830) 249–8000

Comfort Chamber of Commerce
P.O. Box 777
Comfort, TX 78013
(830) 995–3131

AUSTIN

NORTH FROM AUSTIN

Day Trip 1
Round Rock Chamber of Commerce
212 East Main Street
Round Rock, TX 78664
(800) 747-3479 or (512) 255-5805

Georgetown Convention and Visitors Bureau
P.O. Box 409
Georgetown, TX 78627
(800) GEO-TOWN or (512) 930-3545

Salado Chamber of Commerce
P.O. Box 81
Salado, TX 76571
(254) 947-5040

Day Trip 2
Belton Area Chamber of Commerce
412 East Central
P.O. Box 659
Belton, TX 76513
(254) 939-3551

Killeen Visitors and Convention Bureau
P.O. Box 548
Killeen, TX 76540
(800) 869-8265

City of Temple Tourism
2 North Main
Convention Center Box
Temple, TX 76501
(254) 298-5720

Day Trip 3
Waco Tourist Information Center
P.O. Box 2570
Waco, TX 76702
(800) WACO–FUN

NORTHEAST FROM AUSTIN

Day Trip 1
Taylor Chamber of Commerce
P.O. Box 231
Taylor, TX 76574
(512) 352–6364 or 365–8485

Calvert Chamber of Commerce
P.O. Box 506
Calvert, TX 77837
(409) 364–2559

Day Trip 2
Bryan-College Station Convention and Visitors Bureau
715 University Drive East
College Station, TX 77840
(800) 777–8292

EAST FROM AUSTIN

Day Trip 1
Elgin Chamber of Commerce
15 North Main Street
Elgin, TX 78621
(512) 285–4515

Burton Chamber of Commerce
P.O. Box 670
Burton, TX 77835
(409) 289–3402 (City Hall)

Brenham-Washington County Convention and Visitors Bureau
314 South Austin Street
Brenham, TX 77833
(888) BRENHAM or (409) 836-3695

SOUTHEAST FROM AUSTIN

Day Trip 1
Bastrop Chamber of Commerce
927 Main Street
Bastrop, TX 78602
(512) 321-2419

Smithville Chamber of Commerce
P.O. Box 716
Smithville, TX 78957
(512) 237-2313

La Grange Chamber of Commerce
171 South Main Street
La Grange, TX 78945
(800) LAGRANGE or (409) 968-5756

Day Trip 2
Round Top Chamber of Commerce
P.O. Box 216
Round Top, TX 78954
(409) 249-4042

SOUTH FROM AUSTIN

Day Trip 1
Lockhart Chamber of Commerce
P.O. Box 840
Lockhart, TX 78644
(512) 398-2818
See also EAST FROM SAN ANTONIO, Day Trips 1 and 2

Day Trip 2
See NORTHEAST FROM SAN ANTONIO, Day Trip 2

SOUTHWEST FROM AUSTIN

Day Trip 1
San Antonio Convention and Visitors Bureau
P.O. Box 2277
San Antonio, TX 78298
(800) 447-3372 or (210) 270-8700

Day Trip 2
See NORTHEAST FROM SAN ANTONIO, Day Trip 3

Day Trip 3
See NORTH FROM SAN ANTONIO, Day Trip 1

Day Trip 4
See NORTHWEST FROM SAN ANTONIO, Day Trip 3

WEST FROM AUSTIN

Day Trip 1
See NORTH FROM SAN ANTONIO, Day Trip 2

NORTHWEST FROM AUSTIN

Day Trip 1
Lakeway
One World of Tennis Square
Austin, TX 78738
(512) 261-6000

Day Trip 2
Marble Falls/Lake LBJ Chamber of Commerce
801 US 281
Marble Falls, TX 78654
(800) 759-8178 or (830) 693-4449

Burnet Chamber of Commerce
703 Buchanan
Burnet, TX 78611
(512) 756-4297

Lake Buchanan Chamber of Commerce
P.O. Box 282
Buchanan Dam, TX 78609
(512) 793-2803

Kingsland Chamber of Commerce
P.O. Box 465
Kingsland, TX 78639
(915) 388-6211

Day Trip 3
Cedar Park Chamber of Commerce
200 South Bell Boulevard
P.O. Box 1464
Cedar Park, TX 78613
(512) 258-8007

Leander Chamber of Commerce
200 West Willis
P.O. Box 556
Leander, TX 78641
(512) 259-1907

Llano Chamber of Commerce
700 Bessemer Avenue
Llano, TX 78643
(915) 247-5354

Mason Chamber of Commerce
P.O. Box 156
Mason, TX 76856
(915) 347-5758
See also NORTHWEST FROM AUSTIN, Day Trip 2

Festivals and Celebrations

Texas undoubtedly has more festivals than any other state. Regardless of the weekend, you'll find some town whooping it up with parades, music, and lots of food. There are festivals for every interest, whether yours is pioneer heritage, German food, or watermelons.

For a quarterly list of Texas's annual events, write the Texas Department of Transportation for the free Texas events calendar at P.O. Box 5064, Austin, TX 78763-5064, or call (800) 8888-TEX or 452-9292.

You can also receive a free annual events calendar from the Texas Festivals Association at 900 Congress, Suite 301, Austin, TX 78701; (512) 476-4472.

FEBRUARY

George Washington's Birthday Celebration, Laredo and Nuevo Laredo. Since 1898 the border towns of Laredo and Nuevo Laredo have celebrated this holiday. Festivities span from Tuesday through Saturday with a *charro* rodeo, games, and a general party atmosphere. (210) 722-9895.

Land of Leather Days, Yoakum. The last weekend in February celebrates the importance of leather in "The Leather Capital of the World." There are saddle-making demonstrations, plus a chili cook-off and plenty of leather products for sale. (512) 293-2309.

Williamson County Gem and Mineral Show, Georgetown. Dealers from around the United States showcase and sell the latest gems and minerals on the market. Demonstrations, exhibits, and lectures are given throughout the day. (512) 869-4711.

MARCH

Texas Independence Day Celebration, Washington-on-the-Brazos. Held the weekend nearest March 2, this celebration of the signing of the Texas Declaration of Independence in 1836 includes demonstrations of pioneer cooking, frontier crafts, and folk music. There's even a reenactment of the signing. (409) 878-2461 or 836-3695.

Fulton Oysterfest, Fulton. Spend the first weekend in March downing fried or raw oysters to celebrate the culmination of the oyster harvest. Besides oyster eating and shucking contests, there are games, entertainment, and dances. (800) 242-0071 or 826-6441.

National Rattlesnake Sacking Championship and Roundup, Taylor. This is one of the most unusual annual events in Texas, held on the first weekend of the month. Two-person teams compete in this national event to see who can sack ten rattlers in the shortest amount of time. (512) 352-6364 or 365-8485.

SXSW (South by Southwest), Austin. This music conference, held in mid-March, attracts over 3,500 people from the music industry to the capital city for music conferences and nighttime entertainment. During the four-day festival, over 400 acts perform at clubs throughout town. Wristbands permit music lovers to take in show after show, from rock to blues to Cajun music. (800) 888-8AUS.

APRIL

Buccaneer Days, Corpus Christi. Near the end of April Corpus Christi's swashbuckling days are relived with pioneer parades, a terrific fireworks display over the bay, and a huge carnival. (800) 678-OCEAN or (512) 882-3242.

Easter Fires, Fredericksburg. Relive the Easter fires of 1847, when Comanches sat in the hills over Fredericksburg while women and children awaited the results of a peace talk. Mothers calmed their children's fears by explaining that the campfires belonged to the Easter bunny. This story is recreated in a pageant on the Saturday eve before Easter. Advance tickets are suggested. Fredericksburg Easter Fires, P.O. Box 506, Fredericksburg, TX 78624; (830) 997-6523.

Eeyore's Birthday Party, Austin. Held the last Saturday of April, this is one of Austin's wackiest festivals, paying tribute to Eeyore of Winnie-the-Pooh fame. Outrageous costumes, live entertainment, food, drink, and games. A unique celebration of springtime. (800) 926-2282.

Fiesta, San Antonio. The granddaddy of San Antonio's festivals, this week-long celebration includes a water parade, a battle of flowers, art shows, lots of great food, and more. Find out about parking alternatives before heading into the congested River Walk area where the festival takes place. (800) 447-3372 or (210) 270-8700.

Highland Lakes Bluebonnet Trail, Burnet, Buchanan Dam, Llano, and area communities. The fragrant bluebonnet is the state flower of Texas. For two weekends in early April, a self-guided driving tour will take you past the area's prettiest bluebonnet fields. Each town on the trail, from Burnet to Llano, celebrates with art shows, and a festival atmosphere. (512) 793-2803.

Round Top Antiques Fair, Round Top. Held the first weekend of April, this show features dealers from across the nation. It has been called the best antiques show in the state. (281) 493-5501.

Viking Fest, Georgetown. Held in even years during the last weekend in April, this Texas-Scandinavian heritage festival boasts its authentic Vikings, arts and crafts, food, entertainment, and Viking ship. (800) 436-8696.

Yesterfest, Bastrop. Return to the pioneer days on the banks of the Colorado River and try your hand at quilting, corn shucking, candle dipping, and doll making. (512) 321-2419.

MAY

Chisholm Trail Roundup, Lockhart. Relive the Battle of Plum Creek, where the Texas militia joined forces with Tonkowa Indians to defeat a band of Comanches. You can also enjoy a dance, a parade, and a carnival. (512) 398-2818.

Cinco de Mayo and State Menudo Cook-off, San Marcos. This festival is held on the weekend closest to "Cinco de Mayo" (May Fifth), the celebration of the Mexican victory over the French. Besides a carnival and musical performances, there's plenty of Mexican food, including *menudo* (a dish made from tripe, hominy, and spices). (800) 782–7653.

Cinco de Mayo, Del Rio. This border city celebrates its "Best of the Border" binational heritage at historic Brown Plaza. (800) 889–8149 or (210) 775–3551.

Fiesta Laguna Gloria, Austin. This festival combines art with the spirit of a Mexican party, complete with mariachis and Mexican folk dancers. Over 200 artists and crafters bring their work to this mid-May celebration. (800) 926–2282 or (512) 474–5171.

Funteer Days, Bandera. If they had festivals back in the Wild West days, they must have looked like this one. Professional Rodeo Cowboys Association (PRCA) rodeo, arts and crafts, country-western dances, fiddlin' contests, and an Old West parade draw crowds for this weekend late in May. (800) 364–3833.

Kerrville Folk Festival, Kerrville. This is one of the biggest outdoor music festivals in the state. For 18 days, Quiet Valley Ranch is filled with music lovers who come to hear both local and nationally known performers. (800) 221–7958 or (830) 227–3600.

May Fair, Air Show, and Art Walk on the Square, Georgetown. The first weekend in May, hosts MayFair with over one hundred vendors on hand selling arts and craft items, antiques, jewelry, and furniture in San Gabriel Park under the shady oak trees. The Air Show located at the municipal airport is the largest acrobatic air show in Central Texas displaying war birds, fighter planes, and World War II planes. Art Walk on the Square showcases local artists' work, from sculptures to paintings; there is something for everyone. (800) 436–8696.

Texas State Arts and Crafts Fair, Kerrville. Every Memorial Day weekend this festival opens its gates on the grounds of Schreiner College. Originally founded by the state of Texas, this enormous show features the paintings, sculptures, jewelry, and other artwork of over 200 Texas artists, all available to answer questions about their work. A special children's area includes crafts instruction. Musical entertainment rounds out the day. (830) 896–5711.

JUNE

Cedar Chopper Festival, Cedar Park. This festival, always held the second Saturday of June, celebrates the "cedar chopper" heritage of the area. At one time, people here made their living cutting juniper trees into fence posts. Starting with a parade, the festival includes arts and crafts, rides, and a dance. (512) 258-8007.

Indian Hobbyists Meeting, Llano. Over 300 people come here in mid-June from around the state, setting up tepees and keeping alive Indian traditions. There's trading of Indian artifacts and products and a relaxed atmosphere. (915) 247-5354.

Peach Jamboree, Stonewall. The peach capital of Texas shows off its crop on the third Friday and Saturday of June. The local peach pit-spitting record is over 28 feet. (830) 644-2735.

Watermelon Thump, Luling. On the last Thursday, Friday, and Saturday of June, you can enjoy seed-spitting contests, watermelon-eating contests, and champion melon judging. There's also an arts and crafts show, carnivals, live entertainment, and street dances. A Guinness World Record was set here in 1989 for spitting a watermelon seed almost 69 feet. (830) 875-3214.

JULY

Deep Sea Roundup, Port Aransas. Fishers come from everywhere for a chance at the purse in the biggest fishing tournament on this part of the coast, held the weekend after July Fourth. Stay at the pier and watch the competitors weigh in their catch. (800) 45-COAST.

Fourth of July Celebration, Round Top. One of the oldest celebrations in the country of Independence Day winds through Round Top. Round Top Chamber of Commerce, Round Top, TX 78954. (409) 249-4042.

Half Moon Holidays, Shiner. On the first Sunday in July, Shiner celebrates summer with a brisket cook-off, barbecue dinner, fireworks, carnival, horseshoe-pitching tournament, dance, and lots of music. (512) 594-4180.

International Apple Festival, Medina. This celebration of the apple harvest is held in late July, with lots of apple pies, barbecue, and games. (830) 589-2588.

Frontier Days, Round Rock. Come to Round Rock on the Friday and Saturday after Fourth of July to watch a reenactment of the infamous shoot-out between outlaw Sam Bass and the Texas Rangers. There's also plenty of food, games, and the atmosphere of a summer festival. (800) 747-3479.

AUGUST

AquaFest, Austin. The Southwest's largest music festival stretches over three consecutive weekends, with multiple stages featuring from rock to country-western to zydeco. Several big names always perform, along with lots of local talent. There are also jet ski demonstrations, yacht races, a lighted water parade, and a midway for the kids. (800) 926-2282 or (512) 472-5664.

Grape Stomping Harvest Celebration, Tow. Jump in a bin of red grapes and start stomping during this late August festival. Other activities include Cork Toss, Grape Walk, hayrides, and music. (512) 476-4477.

International Barbecue Cook-off, Taylor. Barbecue beef, chicken, and sausage reign supreme at most Texas barbecue joints, but this mid-August cook-off also features seafood, lamb, goat, and even wild game. Over one hundred teams compete in categories ranging from theatrics to most elaborate cooking equipment. (512) 352-6364 or 365-8485.

St. Louis Day, Castroville. Since 1889, this Alsatian town has celebrated the feast day of St. Louis with a feast of its own on the Sunday closest to August 25. Local residents pitch in to prepare barbecue, Alsatian sausage, cabbage slaw, and potato salad, all served picnic-style in Koenig Park. The afternoon is filled with a country auction, arts and crafts, singers, and performances by the Alsatian Dancers of Texas. (210) 538-3142.

Salado Art Fair, Salado. Over 200 artists set up booths on the shady banks of Salado Creek in Pace Park. This weekend-long festival in early August is one of the most popular art shows in the state. (254) 947-5040.

Texas Folklife Festival, San Antonio. Texas's many cultures are represented in this four-day event in early August. Costumed crafters demonstrate how to make a horse-hair rope, pluck a goose, or shuck corn. Folk dancers perform everything from the polka to Indian dances. Plenty of traditional and ethnic cuisine is served. This festival is held at the Institute of Texan Cultures at HemisFair Park. (800) 447-3372 or (210) 226-7651.

SEPTEMBER

Annual Republic of Texas Chilympiad, San Marcos. Belly up to a bowl of red at this cook-off featuring more than 600 competitors. Arts and crafts, sporting events, a battle of the bands, and games are also featured. (800) 782-7653 ext. 177.

Deis y Seis de Septiembre, Del Rio. First named San Felipe, Del Rio celebrates its historic past with Mexican food, Mexican bingo, and plenty of music. (800) 889-8149 or (830) 775-3551.

Fiesta en la Playa, Rockport. This Labor Day weekend celebration with a south-of-the-border flair includes everything from tamale- and jalapeño-eating contests to a *piñata* contest to performances by Ballet Folklorico. (800) 242-0071.

Hummer/Bird Celebration, Rockport. Thousands of migrating hummingbirds stop to refuel in Rockport, which celebrates the event with four days of lectures by birding authorities, arts and crafts displays, boat tours, and Audubon-guided bus tours to sites swarming with as many as 150 hummingbirds. (800) 242-0071 or 826-6441.

Oatmeal Festival, Bertram. This Labor Day weekend festival is named for the nearby community of Oatmeal, and all the events from the street parade to the midway continue the theme. (512) 355-2197 or 355-2268.

Port A Days, Port Aransas. This three-day farewell-to-summer festival starts with an "anything that will float but a boat" parade, and includes a gumbo cook-off, a street dance, a horseshoe tournament, and lots of fine Gulf food. (800) 45-COAST.

OCTOBER

"Come and Take It" Days, Gonzales. This reenactment of the famous "Come and Take It" skirmish that started the Texas Revolution takes place the first weekend in October. Over 30,000 visitors come to enjoy the battle as well as the games, a carnival, a *biergarten,* helicopter rides, and a street dance. (830) 672-6532.

Czhilispiel, Flatonia. When tiny Flatonia needed a doctor years ago, local citizens decided to send a hometown girl to medical school. To fund her education, they began this chili cook-off (now the second largest in Texas) and festival held in late October. There's lots of music, a quilt show, "the world's largest tented *biergarten*," and a barbecue cook-off as well. (512) 865-3920.

Fiesta de Amistad, Del Rio and Ciudad Acuña. The friendship between Del Rio and Ciudad Acuña is celebrated with a chili cook-off, a battle of the bands, and an international parade—the only one that starts in one country and ends in another. (800) 889-8149 or (830) 775-3551.

Halloween on Sixth Street, Austin. In the capital city, October 31 is not just for kids. The treat is the sight of thousands of revelers in wild costumes parading through the Sixth Street entertainment district. After the late-night bacchanalian outing, the trick may be getting up the next morning. (800) 888-8AUS.

Heart O' Texas Fair and Rodeo, Waco. This ten-day fair draws over 200,000 visitors for a look at a championship rodeo, livestock shows, an art show, and nationally known entertainment. (800) WACO-FUN.

Llano Heritage Day, Llano. This Hill Country town remembers its historic roots with Wild West shoot-outs, living history exhibits, wagon rides, and antique shows on the third Saturday in October. (915) 247-5354.

Oktoberfest, Fredericksburg. On the first weekend in October, you can head to the "Old Country" by driving to this German Hill Country town. You'll find polka dancing and sausage galore, as well as arts and crafts, a street dance, and rides for the kids. Friday through Sunday. (830) 997-6523.

Oktoberfest, Round Top. Unlike other Oktoberfest celebrations, this one does it in the pioneer spirit, with demonstrations on everything from soap making to spinning. (409) 278-3530.

Old Leander Days, Leander. This fall festival includes a parade, a carnival, a domino tournament, a stock show, entertainment, and an auction on the third Saturday in October. (512) 259-1907.

Rockport Seafair, Rockport. For over two decades this coastal village has celebrated Columbus Day weekend with food and festivities. Crab races, a sailing regatta, and a gumbo cook-off keep the weekend busy. (800) 242-0071.

Round Top Antiques Fair, Round Top. Called by some the best such show in the state, this extravaganza features antiques dealers from across the United States. Held the first weekend of the month, it attracts shoppers from around the country. (281) 493-5501.

NOVEMBER

Fall Arts Trail, Buchanan Dam, Kingsland, Burnet, Llano, and Marble Falls. The Highland Lakes Arts Council sponsors this early November arts and crafts trail along the same route as the spring bluebonnet festival. Each community has an art show, including Buchanan Dam's Arts and Crafts Gallery, the oldest artists' cooperative in the United States. (512) 793-6666.

Gathering of the Scottish Clans, Salado. Put on your tartans and grab your bagpipes for the oldest Scottish gathering in the Southwest. If there are Gaels and Celts in your ancestry, you can learn more about your family genealogy. Even if you're not a lass or laddie, enjoy traditional folk dances, Highland games, lots of bagpipe music, and Scottish foods like meat pies and scones. (254) 947-5040.

O Tannenbaum, San Antonio. Start your Christmas shopping early at this old-fashioned German Christmas market, held at San Antonio's former German-English School. The market includes German artisans, a *biergarten*, and traditional German foods. (210) 229-1000.

Wurstfest, New Braunfels. Early in November, pull on your *lederhosen*, take out your beer stein, and join the fun at this celebration of sausage making. One of the largest German festivals in the country, Wurstfest features oompah bands and great German food. (800) 221-4369 or (210) 625-9167.

DECEMBER

Christmas Lighting Tour, Johnson City, Llano, Fredericksburg, Blanco, Burnet, and Marble Falls. The Hill Country joins together for this trail of Christmas lights and festivities. Blanco's historic courthouse square is lit with festive lights, and Marble Falls celebrates with a walkway of lights every evening. Fredericksburg puts on a Kinderfest, Kristkindl Market, and candlelight tours of homes. Llano features a Santa Land. Johnson City, the boyhood home of LBJ, is aglow with over a quarter-million lights.

On the first weekend, there's a special Pickup Truck Parade (only in Texas!), with decorated trucks to ring in the Christmas season. Finally, Stonewall celebrates with an annual tree lighting at the LBJ Park, a live nativity scene, and pioneer foods served by candlelight at the Sauer-Beckman Farm. (830) 868-7684 or 644-2252.

Christmas Stroll, Georgetown. The courthouse square lights up with thousands of miniature white lights followed by an evening of shopping, story-telling, and a children's village. The town also hosts a holiday homes tour through several historic structures. (800) 436-8696.

Fort Croghan Spirit of Christmas Past, Burnet. Held the first two Saturdays in December, this festival is a recreation of a pioneer Christmas. A holiday dinner is served in the Old Country Store, then the festivities move to Fort Croghan, lit by glowing lanterns. Visitors on the candlelight tour are met by carolers and costumed docents. (512) 756-8281.

Harbor Lights, Corpus Christi. The Christmas spirit starts in Corpus Christi with the Christmas Tree Forest at the Art Museum of South Texas, with all trees decorated on a special theme. Santa Claus arrives in this port city aboard (what else?) a boat, and the bayfront twinkles with thousands of tiny lights. (800) 678-OCEAN.

Las Posadas, San Antonio. This beautiful ceremony dramatizes Joseph and Mary's search for an inn with costumed children leading a procession down the River Walk. Holiday music selections are sung in English and Spanish. (800) 447-3372.

Main Street Bethlehem, Burnet. Held the first two weekends in December, this festival reenacts a biblical-era village, complete with live animals and Mary, Joseph, and infant Jesus. (512) 756-4481.

Appendix A
Entering Mexico

A trip across the border is easy, safe, and fun. The easiest way to enter Mexico is by walking across the International Bridge or *Puente Internacional* for a small toll. On your return, pay another small toll, walk across the bridge, then head through U.S. customs. (See Appendix B, "Shopping in Mexico," for details.)

Every border town has taxi service into and out of Mexico. The ride is only a few dollars each way. Call the local chamber of commerce for information on transportation to Mexican shopping areas or dining spots.

Driving into Mexico can be a somewhat frightening prospect because auto mishaps are a criminal rather than civil offense across the border. (If you are in a wreck, you might find yourself in a Mexican jail, a sure way to spoil a vacation.) Short-term Mexican insurance is required of every driver. Your car insurance is not valid in Mexico. Every Texas border town has several insurance companies that sell short-term Mexican insurance. Call the local chamber of commerce for information on these companies.

Once you are in Mexico, look for secured parking. The larger restaurants have pay parking lots, and these are preferable to parking on the streets.

Remember that Mexican speed signs are posted in kilometers. Also, Mexican traffic lights are slightly different than those in the United States. When you see a yellow light begin to blink, it means that yellow will soon change to red.

Mexican streets are very narrow, and often one way, especially in the main tourist areas.

Appendix B
Shopping in Mexico

No trip to the Mexican border is complete without some shopping. For many South Texans, this is a chance to purchase quality jewelry, blankets, and liquor at prices far below those in the United States.

All shopping in the border towns is done with American currency. The "Casa de Cambio" signs are seen on many streets, but you do not need to exchange currency before you go. Most shopkeepers speak fluent English, especially in Nuevo Laredo and Ciudad Acuña. In Piedras Negras, bring along a Spanish-English dictionary if you plan to venture beyond the market area.

Buying is usually done by *negociación*. Many stores do not label items with a price. The shopkeeper names a price, one higher than he knows is acceptable. The shopper asks for the "best price," and a friendly haggling ensues. Usually both the merchant and the shopper part company happy with their deal.

Making purchases from street vendors is also done through *negociación*. Street vendors have good prices on paper flowers, hammocks, lace tablecloths, inlaid earrings (not sterling silver), and wood carvings.

Currently silver jewelry is the hottest item in border shops. Look for the "921" stamp on the back of the piece to ensure silver quality. Many of the better stores sell jewelry by weight, with a fixed price per ounce. Even so, silver is very reasonably priced in comparison to U.S. stores. You can also get a good bargain on silver and black onyx jewelry.

Glass (especially pitchers, bowls, and blue-rimmed drinking glasses) and leather goods also make excellent purchases. Onyx chess sets, papier-mâché fruits and vegetables, elaborately embroidered Mexican dresses, and woven blankets are other good buys.

Heading home, you must cross through U.S. customs, located on the American side of the International Bridge. Certain items cannot be carried back into the United States. These include fruits, vegetables, animals and birds, and meats (including canned items). Fireworks, switchblade knives (sold by nearly every street vendor), firearms, liquor-filled candy, lottery tickets, and items made from endangered species will be confiscated. Although you can go to the *farmacia* and buy any item without a prescription, you cannot bring it back to the United States. This includes Mexican diet pills.

Be careful of counterfeit trademark items, such as $40 Rolex watches sold in many shops. These can be seized, and you must forfeit them if stopped by a customs official.

When you return to the United States, the customs official will ask if you are an American citizen. He may ask what you purchased, and he may also ask to see your purchases and other belongings.

You must also pass by a booth to pay tax on imported liquor and cigarettes. If you are over twenty-one years of age, you may bring back one liter of liquor and 200 cigarettes. Texas places a tax on both these items, but the savings is still substantial, especially on items like Mexican beer and tequila.

As far as other goods, you may return with $400 worth of merchandise without paying duty. Every person in your party, regardless of age, has this $400 exemption.

If you've made large purchases, save your receipts. You must pay a 10 percent duty on goods over $400 but less than $1,400.

For more information on customs, obtain Publication 512, "Know Before You Go," by writing: U.S. Customs Service, P.O. Box 7407, Washington, DC 20044.

Appendix C
Especially for
Winter Texans

If you're among the many lucky travelers who've adopted the Lone Star State as their winter home, welcome to Texas. You've chosen a destination where you can enjoy the excitement of the West, the zest of Old Mexico, the tranquility of the Gulf, and the history of a rambunctious republic, all in one journey. Some of the best seasons and reasons to see the state include the changing post oak leaves in fall, the glittering Christmas festivals, and the often sunny Texas winter days.

To introduce you to winter attractions throughout the state, there's a free publication available called *Winter Texan Magazine*. It includes information on campgrounds, motel discounts for Winter Texans, festivals, and attractions. Call the magazine at (800) 728-1287 or the Texas Department of Transportation at (800) 8888-TEX or 452-9292.

Texas has an excellent network of state parks, most of which provide campsites with hookups. Generally there is a fourteen-consecutive-days limit for camping at each park. The central reservation number for all Texas state parks is (512) 389-8900 during weekday business hours.

Winter Texans will be interested in the two different discount programs available at state parks. If you reached 65 years of age or more before September 1, 1995, or are a 60 percent VA-disabled veteran, you are eligible for the free State Parklands Passport. (If you reached 65 years since September 1, 1995, you pay a discounted rate if you are a Texas resident; nonresidents pay full price.) This sticker, which attaches to your windshield, exempts the holder from the entry fee at all state parks. It is good indefinitely, but you must obtain the passport yourself. Bring identification that shows your birthdate to any state park or to the Parks and Wildlife Headquarters at 4200 Smith School Road in Austin.

The newest discount program is the Gold Texas Conservation Passport. You pay an annual fee for the sticker, but it will waive all entry fees and give you discounts on camping. For more information on this program, see Appendix D, "Texas State Parks."

Appendix D
Texas State Parks

Texas has an excellent system of state parks offering camping, fishing, hiking, boating, and tours of historical sites. Facilities range from those with hiking trails, golf courses, and cabins to others that are largely undeveloped and exist as an example of how the region once looked.

Reservations are recommended for overnight facilities. Credit cards are not accepted. Pets are permitted if they are confined or on a leash shorter than 6 feet. The central reservation number for all Texas state parks is (512) 389-8900, Monday–Friday 9:00 A.M.–6:00 P.M. For TDD service, call (512) 389-8915 weekdays. To cancel a reservation, call (512) 389-8910.

For travelers 65 years or older (or those with at least a 60 per cent VA disability), there is the free State Parklands Passport. This windshield sticker permits free entry into any park.

If you visit state parks frequently, consider purchasing a Gold Texas Conservation Passport, which is renewable annually. It provides free entrance into all parks as well as discounts on all campsites and overnight facilities. With it, you receive a newsletter of upcoming events, a directory of access conditions to special wildlife management areas that require a Conservation Passport, and access to guided tours. The Conservation Passport can be purchased at any state park, at the Smith School Road headquarters in Austin, or by mail (4200 Smith School Road, Austin, TX 78744). For more information, call (512) 389-4901.

Admission to wildlife management areas (not state parks) is available with the Silver Texas Conservation Passport.

For more information on Texas state parks, call the Texas Parks and Wildlife Department at (800) 792-1112 Monday through Friday during working hours, or at (512) 389-8950 in the Austin area.

Appendix E
Guide to Tex Mex Food

You'll find Tex-Mex food everywhere you go in Central and South Texas. It's a staple with all true Texans, who enjoy stuffing themselves at least once a week with baskets of tostadas, the Mexican plate (an enchilada, taco, and rice and beans), and cold *cerveza*. Unlike true Mexican food, which is not unusually spicy and often features seafood, Tex-Mex is heavy, ranges from hot to inedible, and can't be beat.

CABRITO—young, tender goat, usually cooked over an open flame on a spit. In border towns, you'll see it hanging it many market windows.

CERVEZA—beer.

CHALUPA—a fried, flat corn tortilla spread with refried beans and topped with meat, lettuce, tomatoes, and cheese.

CHILE RELLENOS—stuffed poblano peppers, dipped in batter and deep fried.

ENCHILADA—corn or flour tortillas wrapped around a filling and covered with a hot or mild sauce. The most common varieties are beef, chicken, and cheese, and sometimes even sour cream and shrimp.

FAJITAS—grilled skirt steak strips, wrapped in flour tortillas. Usually served still sizzling on a metal platter, with condiments (*pico de gallo,* sour cream, cheese) on the side.

FLAUTAS—corn tortillas wrapped around shredded beef, chicken, or pork and fried until crispy; may be an appetizer or an entree.

FRIJOLES REFRITOS—refried beans.

GUACAMOLE—avocado dip spiced with chopped onions, peppers, and herbs.

MARGARITAS—popular tequila drink, served in a salted glass; may be served over ice or frozen.

MENUDO—a soup made from tripe, most popular as a hangover remedy.

MOLE ("MOLE-ay")—an unusual sauce made of nuts, spices, and chocolate that's served over chicken enchiladas.

PICANTE SAUCE—a Mexican staple found on most tables, this red sauce is made from peppers and onions and can be eaten as a dip for tortilla chips; ranges from mild to very hot.

PICO DE GALLO—hot sauce made of chopped onions, peppers, and cilantro; used to spice up tacos, *chalupas,* and fajitas.

QUESADILLAS—tortillas covered with cheese and baked; served as a main dish.

SOPAPILLAS—fried pastry dessert served with honey.

TAMALES—corn dough filled with chopped pork, rolled in a corn shuck, steamed and then served with or without chile sauce; a very popular Christmas dish.

TORTILLA—flat cooked rounds of flour or corn meal used to make many main dishes, and also eaten like bread along with the meal, with or without butter.

VERDE—green sauce used as a dip or on enchiladas.

About the Authors

John Bigley and Paris Permenter are a husband-wife team of travel writers. Longtime residents of central Texas, they make their home in the Hill Country west of Austin near Lake Travis.

John and Paris write frequently about Texas and other destinations for numerous magazines and newspapers. Their articles and photos have appeared in *Reader's Digest, Texas Highways, Austin American-Statesman, San Antonio Express-News, Caribbean Travel Life,* and many other publications. They also write a monthly column on daytrip travel for San Antonio's Fiesta magazine.

John and Paris's other books include *Caribbean for Lovers, Gourmet Getaways, Texas Getaways for Two, The Alamo City Guide,* and *Texas Barbecue,* named best regional book by the Mid-America Publishers Association.

Both Paris and John are members of the American Society of Journalists and Authors and the prestigious Society of American Travel Writers.